MIDNIGHT'S BORDERS

Suchitra Vijayan was born and raised in Madras, India. Her essays, photographs and interviews have appeared in *The Washington Post*, *GQ*, *The Nation*, *The Boston Review*, *Foreign Policy*, *Lit Hub*, *Rumpus*, *Electric Literature*, *NPR*, *NBC* and *BBC*.

A barrister by training, she previously worked for the United Nations war crimes tribunals in Yugoslavia and Rwanda before co-founding the Resettlement Legal Aid Project in Cairo, which gives legal aid to Iraqi refugees.

She is an award-winning photographer, and the founder and executive director of the Polis Project, a hybrid research and journalism organisation. She lives in New York.

Praise for *Midnight's Borders*

'A book that will enlighten every citizen of every nation. *Midnight's Borders* is part investigation, part meditation on the lines drawn on land or water that separate India from its neighbours. It offers brief historical notes on how the nation's current borders came into force alongside accounts of increasing militarisation, disputes, "little massacres" and forgotten pogroms, no-man's-lands, and the people through whom the border runs like barbed wire. As the author notes, here, beauty and violence coexist, but never as a binary.' – **Annie Zaidi, author of *Prelude to a Riot***

'Peeling away at the contrived image of a rising and shining India, Suchitra Vijayan tells the gripping untold story of those living in its borderlands devoid of elementary rights of citizenship and the boons of a much touted "secular democracy". A sensitive and impassioned portrayal of an unknown India, her 9,000-mile long journey traversing India's contested borders ably documents the struggles for existence by the marginalised and discriminated against. A lucid and accessible narrative, *Midnight's Borders* is a highly recommended read for anyone interested in South Asia's past, present, and future.' – **Ayesha Jalal, Mary Richardson Professor of History, Tufts University**

'An intervention like no other when it comes to thinking through not just the history of India but for reflections on borders, migration, the elusory nature of nations. With sharp political analyses, dense historical research and lyrical, image-rich prose, Vijayan's journalism displays an inspiring ethic, one that is invested in the micro-histories of the "small man", the one existing on the fringes of history and the one that most requires urgent representation.' – **Bhakti Shringapure, author of *Cold War Assemblages: Decolonization to Digital***

'Unique and ambitious, Vijayan's project gains urgency and significance from our moment of resurgent nationalisms, when borders are being aggressively reasserted, in India and across the globe.' – **Gaiutra Bahadur, author of *Coolie Woman***

'What experiences and lives unfold in these pages. Heartbreaking, and still, something we must all notice and understand.' – **Maaza Mengiste, author of *The Shadow King***

'An essential, beautifully written report from the hellish margins of a modern mega-state struggling to be a nation, of people whose lives continue to be shaped by violent political marches across age-old homes and habitats. A memorable, humane "museum of forgotten stories" that we must all read and remember.' – **Mirza Waheed, author of *The Collaborator***

'Suchitra's account of her journeys across the undefinable and ever-shifting borders between India and its neighbours is gripping, frightening, faithful and beautiful. In Afghanistan, Kashmir and India, from one dangerous conflict zone to another, she spoke with people, ate with them and listened to their stories. As a bedouin who grew up listening to beautiful stories from beautiful storytellers around a fire, I was transported by her storytelling. This is a serious, often funny and deeply revealing book.' – **Mohamedou Ould Salahi, author of *Guantánamo Diary***

Reviews of *Midnight's Borders*

An Electric Literature Favorite Nonfiction Book of 2021
A Booklist Best History Book of 2021

'*Midnight's Borders* is an important book, a journey of self-discovery by an Indian who, like many, grew up unaware of the complexities and sufferings at the edges of a nation whose glory was celebrated every morning at school assembly. It is, furthermore, a record of our times and a reminder, to those of us spoiled by the comforts of our self-exiled lives in the West, about those of our fellow beings who have become the debris of callous geopolitical shifts, whose hopes for even a safe, painless tomorrow are so precarious.' – ***The Los Angeles Review of Books***

'By looking beyond maps to create a "museum of forgotten stories", Vijayan has given voice to those who live on the fringes like Ali or Sari. The black and white pictures accompanying the chapters add a thousand words more.' – ***The Hindu***

'These stories are likely to haunt a reader long after the reading is done. Not many books manage to be evocative and provocative at the same time. This one does. It is written with passion, poignancy and anger.' – ***The Tribune* (India)**

'A candid and heartbreaking work of exposé journalism … Vijayan is adept at teasing out the fraught, complicated social, political, and spiritual dynamics at play in each region. Dozens of powerful, intimate stories of people affected traumatically by India's expedient geopolitical borders.' – ***Kirkus***

'*Midnight's Borders* is fascinating, eloquent in its insights, and unflinching in its depiction of the dark side of nation-building." – ***Booklist*, Starred Review**

'Suchitra Vijayan's debut book, *Midnight's Borders*, is a genre-bending book of nonfiction—made of stories, encounters, vignettes, and photographs—about home, belonging, and displacement.' – ***Electric Lit***

'The stories in the book are a testament to the bloody colonial legacy of the subcontinent and implore us to look at the nation which the author has found 'in the middle of an extraordinary crisis'. The book makes for a good read for people wanting to understand the lasting impact of the colonial cartographic disasters and for those wanting to understand India through its people.' – ***The Book Review* (India)**

'The stories in the book have been documented with precision and empathy and narrated with eloquence … A good read for people wanting to understand the lasting impact of the colonial cartographic disasters and for those wanting to understand India through its people.' – ***South Asia Books Review***

'A much-needed conversation on thinking about freedom beyond the idea of nation and its illusory lines.' – ***Southern Review of Books***

'*Midnight's Borders* is timely, first-rate journalism made human; it recounts the deep personal consequences of colonialism and forced national identity.' – ***Foreword Reviews*, Starred Review**

'A stunning work of narrative reportage … With profound empathy and a novelistic eye for detail, Vijayan shows us the forgotten people and places in the borderlands and brings us face-to-face with the legacy of colonialism and the stain of extreme violence and corruption. The result is the granular portrait of modern India we've been missing.' – ***British Muslim Magazine***

MIDNIGHT'S BORDERS

A PEOPLE'S HISTORY OF MODERN INDIA

SUCHITRA VIJAYAN

cntxt

First published in hardback by Context, an imprint of Westland Publications Private Limited, in 2021

First published in paperback by Context, an imprint of Westland Books, a division of Nasadiya Technologies Private Limited, in 2022

No. 269/2B, First Floor, 'Irai Arul', Vimalraj Street, Nethaji Nagar, Allappakkam Main Road, Maduravoyal, Chennai 600095

Westland, the Westland logo, Context and the Context logo are the trademarks of Nasadiya Technologies Private Limited, or its affiliates.

ISBN: 9789395767293

10 9 8 7 6 5 4 3 2 1

Typeset by SÜRYA, New Delhi

Printed at Parksons Graphics Pvt Ltd

For Meera, Amma and Appa

'It is the coloniser's map, and they had no respect for our land. Why should we respect their borders?'

– Commander Mahmud, Afghan Local Police,
Paktika province, Afghanistan

CONTENTS

Foreword by Romila Thapar xiii

Prologue: (My) Ishmael 1

Introduction 5

PART I: THE AFGHANISTAN–PAKISTAN BORDER

1. SAR HAWZA: Trapped in the Coloniser's Map 28

PART II: THE INDIA–BANGLADESH BORDER

2. PANITAR: Playing Cricket in No Man's Land 41
3. NEAR JALPAIGURI: 'They Stole My Dreams' 64

PART III: THE INDIA–CHINA BORDER

4. TAWANG: Cartographic Confusion 79

PART IV: THE INDIA–MYANMAR BORDER

5. NAGALAND: Unimagined by My Nation's Cartography 93
6. NELLIE: Stuck Between Remembering and Forgetting 110
7. GUWAHATI: Tales of Three Detentions 124

PART V: THE INDIA–PAKISTAN BORDER

8. KASHMIR: Records of Repression 155
9. KASHMIR TODAY: The Revocation of Article 370 188

10. RAJASTHAN: The Tyranny of Territory 193
11. FAZILKA: Bunkered Territory 200
12. SRI GANGANAGAR: The Tractor Brigade 206
13. AMRITSAR AND NEW YORK: Histories Partitioned 212

Acknowledgements 228
Glossary of Inhuman Words 230
Notes 232
A *Note on the Maps* 250
Index 251

FOREWORD

Romila Thapar

Borders as we know them today have taken shape in recent history. Some are already changing as they have done almost every century. Others continue but with no guarantee of permanence. The borders of kingdoms and states in their history of the last couple of centuries are an illustration of this impermanence. Borders in past times were not recognised by red lines on a map and a strict surveillance of the line on the ground. These later indicators of borders took shape when cartography was established and the territory controlled by a state as agreed upon was carefully demarcated on a map.

Such finely defined borders lend themselves to altercations over ownership of territory that can on occasion end in hostilities. The lines could either be recorded after some movement and activity in the area, such as the Durand and McMahon Lines, and like these need not have been absolutely precisely charted, or else it could be a hastily put together marker such as the Radcliffe Line that became the basis of the Partition in 1947. This should certainly have been done with much greater care over a longer period of time.

The territory so demarcated could be altered after campaigns, with victors making claims. Alternatively, if the border was dependent on other identities of settled communities along the proposed line, such as religious identities, the demographic arithmetic could come into play. This happened with the partition of the Indian subcontinent in 1947. Sometimes the border ran through an open space, at other times alongside a village settlement, or it could cut through the middle of the settlement if the demographic identities differed in two adjoining areas. But is the border simply just such a line?

In times when cartography was not the foundational record of borders, and there were no red lines, there was a more flexible understanding of what was meant by a border and this could involve a larger territory on both sides of what was technically a border or a boundary. States often lay on either side of a geographical or environmental feature. These features—rivers, mountains, forests, deserts, seas and such like—were the dividers.

Rivers were clear-cut separators, ancestral to the red line on the map. It was a case of 'we' on this bank and 'they' on the other bank. Mountains were arduous to cross, hence the centrality of passes. Yet, it is incredible how largescale migrations of herders and their animals crossed high mountains in many parts of the world. Deserts had their own hazards, and still more often than not, they provided the best direct routes for traversing distances. Forests tended to be avoided simply because they sheltered those who fell upon the travellers passing through them. Seas were borders only along the coastline since the mid-sea routes were entirely open. Ecology could also affect border areas. The land could shift somewhat, sometimes marginally with the shifting sands of dunes in the desert, or more dramatically as with the small islands in the Sunderbans that can disappear with the rise of sea levels.

The characteristics of these borders or boundaries was that they were not lines, but areas, viewed as a kind of no-man's land. The claim of possessing such territories and locations was a little unclear as it could change from one side to the other. They were more in the nature of frontier zones than linear borders. As frontier zones, such areas had multiple roles. There could be political conflict over their control. They could become, as they often did, areas of intensive exchange and trade between the people from the two or more sides that traversed them. They had economic advantages as is illustrated by the huge volume of trade that came through the northern mountains of the subcontinent—the Hindu Kush and the North Himalaya—or the routes that crossed the desert of Thar, or cut their way through the heavy forests bordering eastern India, not to mention the environmentally entirely different western coastline of the subcontinent that provided a different pattern of exchange and communication.

In the world of today, borders are barriers, in that their use as points of crossing over are under severe scrutiny. This was not so in the past. One has only to track the many migrations into north India, for example, to understand that borders were almost incidental. Pastoralists from Central Asia migrated into northern India in small and large numbers—the Aryas, for example, or the Gujjars in later times. They traversed the frontier zones and settled wherever they found water and good pastures. Many others came in diverse capacities: invasions brought the Shakas, Kshatrapas, Kushans, Hunas, Shahis and Turushkas. They virtually nullified the northern borders by bringing with them facets of different religions and cultures that modified in some cases, and changed in others, the life of the people in the frontier zone or even further inland. The pattern of life underwent changes on both sides. If goddesses from across the northern borders eventually became part of the pantheon of Indian deities, and Sufi sects became part of the Indian religious landscape, Buddhism travelled out from northern India and became the religion of people and places on the Central Asian side extending to China. What demarcated two states and two cultures was not a linear border but a frontier zone. We need to consider the impact this had on shaping each side.

Without going into endless historical detail, I would simply like to say that in pre-modern times, frontier zones played a significant role in fostering communication between people on both sides and in defining new cultures. This is not to say that there were no hostilities. But hostilities were subjected to the bigger needs of the states concerned, and were not necessarily pinpointed in precise locations. And despite the hostilities, there was much coming and going and the crossing of frontiers. Pilgrimages to distant places, festivals observed on both sides, and even kinship links across the frontier, were not discontinued, despite some degree of hostility in or near the frontier zone.

Border areas, therefore, were once zones of acculturation, meeting points, locations of cultural exchange. In modern times, they have become the territorially lean passages of terror and violence, following a linear demarcation. I visited the western end of Kaccha and entered a dead town—Lakhpat. It was once on a trade route and was a town of considerable wealth, as the name indicates. What caused the change? An environmental event was partly responsible—an earthquake—but the death knell came with the politics of Partition when trade ceased. The location of the border killed the town.

Borders have little permanence. They have changed from century to century, largely determined by conquests, even with the continuance of local activities. The buffer zone was largely left to fend for itself and did so. Now, all this is subjected to strict control from both sides, a strictness that is ensured by cultivating animosity.

The present situation is described with empathy and sensitivity in Suchitra Vijayan's account of her visits to points along the extensive borders of India—an innovative way of assessing the sense of borders. *Midnight's Borders* is a lively and perceptive description of what she experienced and the many conversations she had with people at these points along the borders. It provides a close view of how people living in these areas perceive the concept of a border. This may sound predictable in many ways, but the book provides a new perspective on these areas, different from how borders are vaguely and casually known in current times, as also from the general perceptions of governments.

I recall visiting a few of the places that she speaks of about forty years ago. In Kashmir, I drove to the Kishenganga valley in summer with high snow banks on each side of the jeep track. The Indian and Pakistani outposts faced each other at some distance, but with visibility on each side. We stopped for tea at one of the Indian outposts, and soon the telephone rang. The Pakistani outpost was ringing to exchange news and to enquire about who the visitors were. The chit-chat went on for a bit, with jokes thrown in from both sides, and they insisted on greeting us and then rang off. It was a comfortable conversation that also included news of the people living in the area. This was just a few months before hostilities broke out in 1965.

The Jawaharlal Nehru University had a daughter centre in Manipur—now a full-fledged university—and some of the faculty from JNU had to visit there regularly to discuss courses and administration. On one occasion, I took a trip to Tamu, the town on the border of Myanmar and India. It gave the appearance of being a sleepy town with a few bars located along the road, which were dark and unwelcoming. Burman Buddhist monks, in their ochre pongees, wandered around and we were told that some were monks in the monasteries on the Myanmar side and others on the Indian.

These border points are currently viewed in entirely different ways and the ambience is anything but friendly. It forces one to ask the more relevant questions about the nature and reality of borders and how these have changed from past times. Above all, the major question that surfaces is, one that I seem to hear being addressed by Suchitra Vijayan: that admittedly this change has to do with changes in the politics of our times, but would it not be more purposeful to consider whether we cannot perhaps return to reintroducing some at least of the positive features of borders? This might ensure that their function is not confined to maintaining hostility but would extend to their potential as sources of mutual benefit.

Delhi
October 2022

PROLOGUE
(MY) ISHMAEL

'When someone asks me for my name, I say I am someone who has lost my home many times over.'

– Field notes, India–Bangladesh border

He had nothing left of his home except an old map of his city. The maps no longer looked like the map he had memorised as a student. It looked like a tilted triangle, but he called it the broken half of a whole. His school and the local factory that produced jams and juices had been turned into a camp. His city was remade, and his country doesn't exist anymore. He was a refugee twice over, an exile once and an orphan always.

After he arrived in this country, he renamed himself Ishmael, after the son who was supposed to be sacrificed to god, but lived. He did everything he could to begin anew. But he could never entirely cleanse himself of the violence he had encountered. The war never left him, that pain of having lost his family and his home clung to him. Time no longer made any sense to him, it no longer anchored him. For him, it no longer moved. It simply stagnated.

When I met Ishmael, he had a set of notebooks with collected news clippings from the war years. He called the collection his museum of forgotten facts. Flipping through his many notebooks, you would learn about an internment camp that men went to voluntarily because they thought they would be safer there than on the street filled with men in uniform. You'd come across the cellist who performed at funerals for free during the height of the siege when every street corner had a sniper positioned to attack civilians. And you'd encounter the journalist, who now cleans toilets in Sarajevo, who kept a hundred notebooks with names of the dead, and of the men he saw kill during those twenty days of carnage. Then there was the woman who had been starved at the internment camp. She lived, but lost the sense of taste, except the taste of cold prison floors. Freedom, once stolen, crippled and starved, never managed to recover.

Ishmael had a simple question. Why did his home not exist anymore? Why was it unmade and erased? Looking for answers, he said he would become a modern-day Ibn Battuta, travelling the contours of apartheid and occupation; the fractured lines that refused to become nations, and the ugly walls and fences that divided people. His lines did not match the lines that proclaim nations sovereign.

But he never left the city of his last refuge. He stayed, he waited, and he rotted a little every day.

~

What does it feel like to be the last one?
I can no longer live knowing I am the last one.
Not when they claim we never existed.

They found this note next to Ishmael's limp body. He had lived as a refugee, an exile and an orphan for over twenty years.

He had no executor; no living will. He left nothing behind, for no one. Everything he owned fit into a cardboard box that his Armenian landlord had donated to a thrift store—including his museum of forgotten facts, his notebooks full of news clippings, names, dates and maps of his city and a country that no longer exists.

When Primo Levi, the chemist, writer and Holocaust survivor, died in 1987, Elie Wiesel made an infamous observation: 'Primo Levi died at Auschwitz forty years later.'[1] Like Levi, Ishmael died at his home that was destroyed, nearly twenty years later. I don't know why he chose to end his life; perhaps living had become a terrible price to pay. 'Exacting', was the word he had used when we first spoke almost a decade ago.

For all his eloquence about war, violence and pain, Ishmael appeared childlike. He was a boy when he had lost everyone and everything to the war. He had never reconciled with the violence, and the loss of his country never made sense to him.

'Where do I belong?' Ishmael asked once. This question of belonging, which he left without answering, haunts me the most. Did he belong to his land? To this time? Or did he belong to silence and forgetting?

When I worked for the War Crimes Tribunal for Yugoslavia, I spent months reading the witness summaries of victims and survivors. Many of the witnesses who came before the tribunal were those who had survived heinous crimes, had witnessed them, or had family who were victims of ethnic cleansing and genocide. They talked of starvation, of the destruction of their homes and community; separation and disappearances of family members; physical torture; sexual violence and rape; abuse, torture and the killing of others; perilous flight or escape and forced exile. What they often spoke of as justice was really a deep longing to make sense of their loss. When people came to testify at the tribunal, they brought tokens with them; anything that would convey their loss, make them human and not another witness number or statement. Above all, they wanted their personal purgatories to be recorded, remembered and acknowledged. Some brought photographs of the family they had lost and gave them to the lawyers and investigators. Justice, for many of them, was about not being forgotten.

Ishmael was no different. In his museum of forgotten facts, he obsessively collected maps and old photographs of his home—proof that his memories were true, that his city was not imagined but had existed, even if they were clippings from newspapers. But the maps did not speak his language; they speak the language of the state, the bureaucrats, politicians and the armies. Maps are objects of power, and they do not belong to the people. Maps are keepers of a state's knowledge: the distances, the miles, the nautical and where things begin and end.

They are not keepers of people's memories. So Ishmael tinkered with the maps and vandalised them, hoping one day he would make them speak his language. 'To redraw the world and its contours is my magnum opus,' he had said many times over. He would break up the borders—those lines that bring order—into unruly curls and curves. He drew the places he had lost, and sometimes he drew them as places they would have become if they were allowed to exist.

His maps committed treason; his memories were disloyal to the state.

The struggle over geography, the struggle to define the frontiers of our home, has existed throughout history. But when maps became the arsenal of imperialism and colonial conquest, people, in turn, became surveys and statistics. For the maps of this world to make sense, many fictions have been put in place, and we have been taught to treat these fictions as fact. We imagine nations out of non-existent lines—sometimes amputating communities or whole cultures to make way for a country—and reinforce the lines with violence lest they cease to exist altogether. Borders make unequal people.

I have met many Ishmaels now. In Kigali, Khartoum, Kashmir, London, The Hague, Berlin, Arusha, Cairo, Kabul, Karbala, Mardin and Ni'lin. These many Ishmaels are people who live as exiles, as refugees, and as prisoners. Some were forced to flee, and some were born in exile. Others have returned home to their city emptied by bombs. There are those who live in cities that have now been remade into camps, dotted with bunkers, checkpoints and guns. Their every move surveilled. Their humanity first questioned and then denied.

Like Ishmael, they are all part of the histories of occupation violence and multiple exiles, and they are also all remarkable bards, storytellers trying to make sense of their world's injustices, inequities and violence. Landlocked between disquiet and desperation, they are not in search of great truths about the world, just about themselves. Caught between history, time and territory, they are the people who get trapped beneath the collapsing lines that willed nations into existence. And they are the unacknowledged casualties when those arbitrary borders shift, even a little.

INTRODUCTION

In 2013, I embarked on a 9,000-mile journey along India's borders. I didn't yet know that I was foolishly attempting to follow the outlines on a shifting map.

The journey was, for me, a return home. But after being away for more than a decade, I was coming back to a place I no longer recognised. I wanted to understand 'my country', and I wanted to make sense of the ongoing violence at its borders, the debates over nationalism, citizenship and the unanswered questions about belonging. I travelled to the frayed edges of the republic to meet the people who inhabit the margins of the state and to study the human toll of decades of aggressive, territorial nationalism.

In my quest to understand India through her border, I found a nation in the middle of an extraordinary crisis. The once great promise of an emerging 'global power' had waned. History was being swiftly rewritten.

~

When I made the decision to travel India's borders, I had just returned from Afghanistan—a place I had known and wanted to study for a long time. Weeks after the 9/11 attack, I had left my home in Madras to pursue my undergraduate studies in law in England. On my layover in Dubai, everyone seemed nervous. CNN streamed on the walls of the departure lounge, and commentators called Kabul the 'terror hotbed'. I was stepping into adulthood in a dystopian age. A few weeks later, the US government launched Operation Enduring Freedom. In the years to come, the TSA (the Transportation Security Administration, a wing of the US's Department of Homeland Security) demanded disrobing at security checks, and for brown and black folks, travel became fraught. Terms like 'radicalisation',

'Islamophobia' and 'the war on terror' entered our everyday language, and entire communities became the objects of state surveillance.

America went to a war with no foreseeable end.

I watched US Black Hawks fly across Tora Bora, and 15,000-pound daisy-cutter bombs raining from the sky. Afghanistan's modern history of war, copious amounts of unaccounted-for international aid, the creation of a war economy and the complicity of the American empire found little or no place in the reporting. I saw photographs of American soldiers, their tattoos and their forward operating bases published and granted the Pulitzer. But where, I wondered, were the Afghans?

It took me another ten years to get to Afghanistan, and in the intervening decade I lived in occupied lands, war zones and places often described as 'contentious'. I lived in The Hague, working for the War Crimes Tribunal for Yugoslavia, and later in Arusha, Tanzania, with the International Criminal Tribunal for Rwanda. I travelled through Palestine and Sudan. I lived in Cairo the year leading up to the Arab Spring, all with an Indian passport. There, I ran the Resettlement Legal Aid Project in 2008 to provide resources for the more than 5,000 Iraqi families who fled the invasion of Iraq. Amidst the fear of being shut down and regular visits from the Mukhabarat, the Egyptian intelligence services, we served close to 600 Iraqi families. Even as I fought for my clients to be resettled to another country, my own stay in Cairo was precarious.

Unlike the Europeans and the Americans who easily acquired long-term visas to stay, as an Indian, I had to appear every month to renew my visa at the Mogamma—a grey, imposing building in Cairo's Tahrir Square that housed the Passports, Immigration and Nationality Administration offices.

Every renewal was a laborious process that began with lining up early in the morning and moving from one counter to another, collecting signatures, stamps and authorisations. Every time I went to the Mogamma, I would run into someone I knew. My refugee clients also had to renew their residency every few months. They would arrive before the building opened and line up for an audience with the bureaucratic gods. Once inside, they were at the mercy of the officers, who screamed at, yelled at and insulted them. At any point in this process, a residency permit can be arbitrarily denied renewal.

Once, after a particularly long day at the Mogamma, all my documents were rejected, and I was made to wait. A functionary walked up to me and suggested that I meet the officer in charge at a hotel off Talaat Harb Street in downtown Cairo, to 'sort things out'. When I started screaming in disbelief, I was told to leave by the guard and return the next day. When I returned, my visa was only extended for a week. I had to apply for the renewal again in another six days. Despite the humiliation, I told myself I was lucky: unlike my clients, I had a passport, I wasn't stateless and I still had a country I could return to. For now, I can choose the time, place and circumstances of my arrivals and departures, even if my passport limits them.

~

Where you are born, what passport you hold, can shrink your world, cripple you and sometimes kill you.

Whether it was the testimonies I have read from Rwanda and Bosnia, or the stories Iraqi, Somali, Sudanese and Eritrean clients told me as I prepared their legal petitions, what became clear was this—political borders were unravelling across the world. We were living in an age of a great crisis of citizenship and belonging. Had we reached an impasse about how to think about citizenship, borders and the nations enclosed by them?

What function does a nation still perform if it has consistently failed to offer the most basic of human dignities to its people?

Various democracies are crumbling within these nation states. Could we, I wondered, envision a new world radically remade by freedom and justice? While I struggled with these questions for years, it was in Afghanistan, while researching counter-insurgency practices along the Afghanistan–Pakistan border, that the ideas, stories, arguments and images I had gathered over the years came together as a plan to explore these questions back home in India.

The idea of travelling along India's border, all 9,000 miles of it, was audacious. No one had done it before. I didn't know what such a journey would entail. Having conceived of this undertaking, I became obsessed with it. The idea consumed me.

I spent the next six months reading everything I could. The bibliography I kept at that time lists 113 books and another 150 essays. But even those six months of research, saving money and plotting did not prepare me for the task ahead.

The project I thought would take mere months took me over seven years.

It would have been easier to pick ten places on the border, parachute in, describe them and leave. That would have been the most efficient, but not the most truthful. From the farthest outposts of India to her ungoverned spaces and forgotten regions, I travelled to places shaped by an array of competing histories. The physical journey opened strange doors, and the days spent waiting for permits at borders, rummaging through archives and speaking with people in their homes became an integral part of the story. Returning regularly for seven years, I amassed endless notebooks, over a thousand images and more than 300 hours of recorded conversations.

How does one assemble these fragments into a book?

The book changed in multiple ways as I travelled, wrote, rewrote, edited, added and discarded material. The guide I can offer to my readers is this: view it as a scrapbook assembled as an archive of the personal, the social, the political, told through images, texts, lists, other people's poetry and maps. Like Ishmael from the Prologue, I have created my own museum of forgotten stories and objects.

Here you will encounter my images as impressions, slices of my memory placed into the present. Some chapters are image-rich, and

in others you will find an absence of visuals. In some chapters, the characters are sturdily situated in their places, and in others, they are just fleeting glimpses.

The book traces my travel along India's borders through a series of stories, encounters and vignettes over a period of seven years. The travels follow a route not easily mapped—just like the meandering, shifting and difficult-to-trace borders of the subcontinent.

~

Much has been written, repeated and recycled about the making of modern India, her diversity, her poverty, her heaving masses, her millions of gods and her incomprehensible people. In India today, I see a young nation ambushed halfway to freedom. Yet what we call India—the modern nation state—is a geopolitical myth. Before the British arrived, India the nation did not exist.

As Professor Amartya Sen writes, 'In fact, the ambitious and energetic emperors of India from the third century B.C.E. onward—Chandragupta Maurya, Ashoka, the later Chandragupta of the Gupta dynasty, Alauddin Khilji, the Mughal emperor Akbar, and others—did not accept that their regimes were complete until the bulk of what they took to be one country was united under their rule. Indian history shows a sequential alternation of large domestic empires and clusters of fragmented kingdoms.'[1] The Mauryas in 250 BCE and later the Mughal empire under Aurangzeb came close, but it was only the British who united the subcontinent under colonial administrative rule.

Even after the British Crown assumed direct control of colonial administration over India in 1858, sovereignty remained fragmented, fuzzy and confusing. Alongside the British government, hundreds of Indian princely states remained largely autonomous in ruling their feudal territories.[2] British officials organised several surveys to mark the boundaries between Britain-controlled India and these princely states.[3]

While British rule unified the subcontinent politically under a single administrative power, it further divided its people on religious grounds. To govern India, the British introduced separate Hindu and Muslim electorates, which further stoked Hindu–Muslim violence.[4]

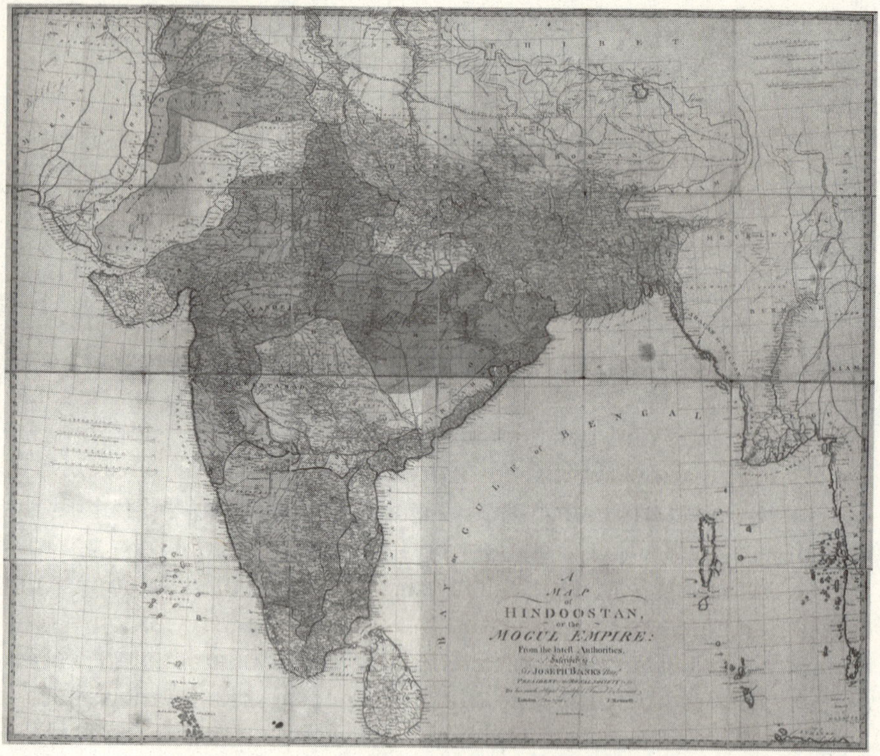

A colonised 'India'—the territory of which stretched across present-day Pakistan, India and Bangladesh—survived 190 years under the British rule, during which time fewer 'than 6,500 Englishmen [were] employed to rule over the 300 millions of India' and no more than 70,000 British soldiers, and colonised 'native staff' ruled over 300 million people.[5]

For most of that time, the British Parliament exclusively decided the fate of millions who lived within this territory, across caste, class and religion. 'Indians' never had the right to vote under the British. We were disposable colonial subjects, never citizens. The imperial argument in favour of this disenfranchisement was simple—the Indians were incapable of self-governance, incapable of finding 'a constitutional consensus among themselves'.

At the height of British constitutional generosity, a handful of Indians were elected to the Central Legislative Assembly based on a restricted franchise. Muslims could only vote for Muslim representatives and Hindus could only vote for their own representatives, cultivating a policy of political representation based on religious identities. British rule in India also witnessed the rise of Hindu and Islamic religious movements, and as the political struggle for Indian independence took shape, various factions rallied the masses using religion and religious symbols.

Gandhi understood how powerful symbols could be used to mobilise the country's diverse population. He actively employed Hindu symbols, phrases and icons towards nationalist ends by using the cartographic image of India as a Hindu goddess and invoking the mythology of Ram Rajya as the ideal form of governance. Gandhi equated the mythology of Ram to the foundation of an ideal Indian state. In India, where poverty and illiteracy are rampant, the use of religious symbols as the basis of political mobilisation had profound implications. While it galvanised the Hindu majority, this practice severely alienated Indian Muslims, who were unable to find themselves reflected in a nation defined by Hindu history, gods, symbols and the Gandhian ideals of Ram Rajya.

Despite these upheavals, as late as 1946, the idea of partitioning the subcontinent as a solution to the transfer of colonial power to self-rule was unthinkable. I spoke to many who survived the Partition, and to them the idea still seems unbelievable. People feared the rising violence, but the thought of a dismembered India was absurd. Many left their homes expecting to return once the violence had stopped.[6]

Partition forever altered the political and cultural landscape of South Asia. In the immediate aftermath, 17.9 million people migrated across the Indian subcontinent.[7] Muslims on the Indian side of the new borders, and Hindus and Sikhs caught on the Pakistani side, fled their ancestral homes.

Ninety-one-year-old Balwinder Kaur, whose family had migrated from the newly created Pakistan to India, and who now lives in Toronto, told me, 'It took me years to even accept that India had been cut up, no one could believe this had happened to us. The disbelief soon turned into silence. So much history is lost. Maybe if we had told the story of how our generation had suffered because of hate, we wouldn't see this new kind of hate spreading in the country.'

Nevertheless, when the British finally withdrew, the subcontinent was butchered into the twin nations of the Hindu-majority India and the Muslim-majority Pakistan. Freedom had finally arrived, killing the dream of an undivided India.

The British lawyer Cyril Radcliffe arrived in India on 8 July 1947 to draw the borders between an 'independent India' and a newly created Pakistan. Radcliffe had never been to India and had very little knowledge of the vast continent he was tasked to partition. The maps and the census data he worked with were out of date; there was no time to get the details right, and no time to inspect. In seven weeks it was done, the many frontiers were remade, and the territory was born. The boundary commission finished preparing their maps on 12 August, and the maps were made public on 17 August, two days after Partition.[8] Radcliffe burnt his papers, notes and personal copies, refused his fee of Rs 40,000 and left the broken continent, with its butchered freedoms, once and for all. Radcliffe, in an interview with the Indian journalist Kuldip Nayar, said, 'I had no alternative; the time at my disposal was so short that I could not do a better job.

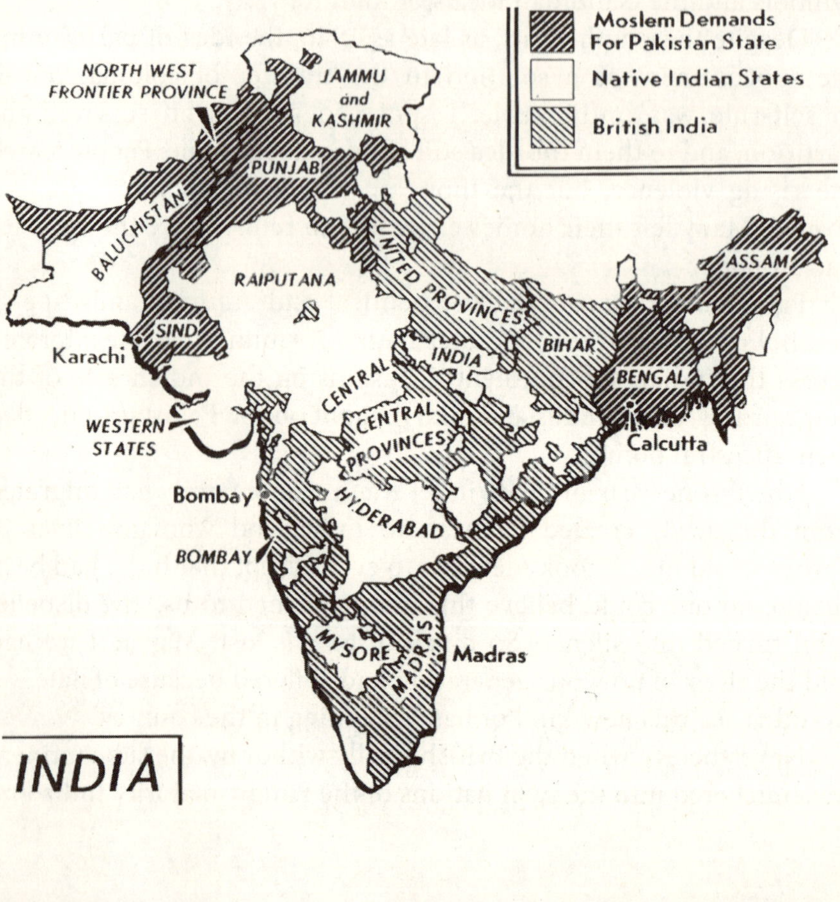

Given the same period I would do the same thing. However, if I had two to three years, I might have improved on what I did.'[9]

A new map and two nations were born, but the border was far from settled.

On 14 August 1947, Pakistan became free, and India declared her independence a day after. The old archival newsreels show India's first prime minister, Jawaharlal Nehru, addressing his people: 'Long years ago we made a tryst with destiny,' he begins with measured eloquence. 'At the stroke of the midnight hour, when the world sleeps, India will awake to life and freedom. A moment comes, which comes but rarely in history when we step out from the old to the new when an age ends, and when the soul of a nation, long suppressed, finds utterance.'

Nehru's speech embodied the grand ambitions of young India and painted a picture of a nation made of men and women equally protected by the law. Three hundred million people who had been considered less than subjects under the British rule, divided for years by religion, language, class and caste, would all be united under one book: the revolutionary Constitution given to her by Babasaheb Ambedkar, independent India's first law minister and the chairman of the Constitution Drafting Committee.

While Nehru was still declaring this victory, the slaughter began. Not everyone rejoiced in these new freedoms. Not everyone lived to see its promises. The estimated number killed between March 1947 and January 1948 ranges from 180,000 to 1 million. There were 3.4 million 'missing' members of targeted minorities in the 1951 census.[10]

Before India could find her voice, screams from massacres and riots reverberated throughout the country.

Dispatches from the front lines read like an instruction manual for creating hell on earth. Ordinary men and women became killers, forging weapons out of anything at hand. Hundreds of thousands of women were raped and then killed or disfigured. The ones who escaped with their lives were kidnapped and forced to marry their rapists. Every grotesque atrocity imaginable happened here. When the great migration came to an end and the killing ebbed, two million people had been murdered. Seventy years later, people are still living with the consequences. With India's new citizenship laws based on religions, appropriately described as the 'new Nuremberg laws' given their communal logic, the unfinished business of the Partition is playing out again. As I write this, I wonder what will survive of the 'world's largest secular democracy'.

The American photojournalist Margaret Bourke-White documented Partition violence and the great migration. She had been to a Nazi concentration camp just a year earlier, and in her memoir, Bourke-White writes that Calcutta looked like Buchenwald: 'There were heartbreaking subjects to photograph. Babies were born along the way; people died along the way. Thousands perished. I saw children pulling at the hands of their mother, unable to understand that those arms would never carry them again. There were scenes straight out of the Old Testament.'[11]

My grandfather, J.M. Kalyanasundaram, the printer and publisher of the Communist Tamil newspaper *JanaSakthi*, met Bourke-White in Madras and maintained a correspondence with her for a few years. They lost touch in the 1950s.

Bourke-White wrote in her memoir, 'The effort to understand India, with her centuries telescoped into a handful of years, had a very deep effect on me.' Reading her words, I remember wondering what then happened to the seventeen million people who still lived with the memory of these unspeakable acts. If just bearing witness had affected Bourke-White so much, what happened to those who had lived through the violence and inherited this loss?

Seventy years later, India and Pakistan are still in search of their identities. Even those who had supported the Partition could never have imagined the modern militarised border, land mines and bunkers. Each country has a state, a nuclear army and strong ideologies of patriotism. But are they nations? Do the people within those boundaries indeed belong within their borders or even respect them?

~

Today, the subcontinent's borders are usually categorised and studied with a focus on the three lines that gave birth to Pakistan, Afghanistan, Bangladesh and India: the Durand, Radcliffe and McMahon Lines, all named after British civil servants who knew very little of the regions they divided.

In 1893, Mortimer Durand and Emir Abdur Rahman Khan signed the agreement that created that Durand Line between Afghanistan and British India. The agreement, a single-page document with seven clauses, created a frontier without identifying structures. The Durand Line cuts through the Pashtun tribal areas and Pakistan's southwestern province of Balochistan, politically dividing Pashtuns, Baloch and other ethnic groups. The line was intended to be a buffer between the British and Russian empires—never a border. Pakistan inherited the line in 1947 following its independence.

The Radcliffe Line was demarcated in 1947 upon the partition of India. Today, the western line still serves as the India–Pakistan border, and the eastern line as the India–Bangladesh border.

The McMahon Line runs between India and China, resulting from a 1914 agreement between British and Tibetan representatives. China has refused to accept the McMahon Line, disputing India's control over the northeastern state of Arunachal Pradesh and often referring to this region as South Tibet. India, meanwhile, lays claim to part of Chinese-controlled northern Kashmir (ceded to China by Pakistan) and to the remote Aksai Chin area.

Another much-discussed line is the LoC—the Line of Control—that divides the Muslim-majority region of Kashmir between India and Pakistan. While not a true international border, the LoC is the 'effective boundary' between the two countries. The line initially marked the military front when the two nations declared a ceasefire on 1 January 1949. The military front was formally renamed the Line of Control after the Simla Agreement, signed on 3 July 1972. The lines that distinguish Indian-held Kashmir from the Pakistan-held territories have remained contentious and intractable for over six decades. This contested border keeps most of India's western and northwestern frontiers heavily militarised, with an ongoing demand for freedom and right to self-determination from the Kashmir Valley.

Unlike its militarised borders, India has an open border with Nepal, where, in principle, people may move freely. The border with Burma, while militarily sensitive, is not policed or militarised to the same degree as its northern neighbours. The India–Bhutan border, once as open as the Nepal–India border, appears to be evolving towards a militarised border resembling the contemporary Pakistan and Bangladesh borders.

These lines are far from perfect. Miscalculations, mistakes and cartographic confusions are foundational to the world's bloodiest property dispute.

The disputes that arose from the creation of new nation states in South Asia marked an unprecedented and disorienting rupture in the subcontinent. People found their identities and histories remade by new lines on the map, enforced by a standing army. Families, communities and ultimately entire societies have been damaged, destroyed or scattered by political upheavals and violence.

This book tells some of their stories, long forgotten and erased, to interrogate the nature of our contemporary borders. The people whose stories I have documented lived through displacement, economic migration, political exile, ecocide and, in some cases, extreme brutality and violence. Others lost their homes forever without physically moving.

Often, when I left interviews, I would hear a family member who had been listening say, 'I have never heard this story before,' or, '[He or she] has never told us this.'

If the story of human civilisation is about the creation and destruction of various walls, boundaries, frontiers and fences, what story does the present map of the world tell us?

In elementary school in Madras, as homework, we were told to trace the outline of India many times over to memorise it. The phrase 'Kashmir to Kanyakumari'—arbitrarily connecting the northern frontier with the southernmost tip of India—was used to signify the vastness of the country and the unity of its people.

When I started travelling in 2013, it seemed easy to trace the border and write about it. I started with Calcutta as my base; I got permissions, travel permits and a visa to Bangladesh. I briefly headed to the Sundarbans to the south before making the journey up to Sikkim and then India's northeastern states: first Arunachal Pradesh, and then curving down to Nagaland.

But in 2014, my visit to Kashmir complicated matters. Unlike the southern Bengal border, it was impossible to trace the fraught LoC or wander from one point to another. The militarisation, the butchered geographies, the minefields, the barbed wires and the bunkers made it impossible to travel along the line on the map. I had to prepare weeks in advance, make calls, and fix appointments. I could travel a few hundred miles, crossing checkpoint after checkpoint, and I still might not connect with the person I was hoping to meet or arrive at the place I'd hoped to see. Kashmir was also where my grammar of dissent found political and moral clarity.

In Kashmir I stayed in the largest city, Srinagar, and made multiple trips to the border villages and hamlets: Uri, Bandipora, Keran, Mundiyan, Pathan and back. I would leave Srinagar, head to the border villages, stay in the homes of those I trusted, travel shorter distances and return. The overarching surveillance in these spaces meant I couldn't stay long; I had to move quickly and constantly. In some of these villages, within hours of my arrival, the local police would be on alert. In some places, like Uri, I was quickly summoned to meet the local inspector.

During this time I also started questioning my images and my photographic practice. I wondered how images might function not as documents of truth, but as archives of memory, and if I could mould them to fill in the silences of narrative.

In 2015, my travel plans along India's western border with Pakistan came to an abrupt end. My father fell ill in March, and I raced home to Madras. On 21 July, he went into surgery, with my sister as his donor. Seeing two people I loved being wheeled into

surgery changed me profoundly. In August of that year, after his surgery, I travelled back to Kashmir before returning to New York. Within a month, I found out that I was pregnant. My dad's illness and my pregnancy changed the way I saw the world, wrote about it and encountered it. Confronted by the mortality of a parent and my impending motherhood, the book changed.

Those years were lonely and filled with anguish. I often came close to shelving this book, convinced that I would never finish the journey. But the images stayed with me: of the families that stood on either side of Teetwal—a small border village, divided by a river, located near the LoC in Kupwara—hoping to catch a glimpse of the other; a mother gathering from the newspapers images that resembled her now-disappeared son and pasting them into a scrapbook; and families holding photographs of the ones violently taken away from them.

In 2018, I left my eighteen-month-old daughter to finish the last leg of travel along the western border, before returning to the northeastern state of Assam to understand and document the violence in the detention camps that held people who were arbitrarily detained as foreigners.

This book, then, is not a straightforward chronology of travel. Instead, it is a series of encounters in towns, cities and abandoned ruins. The absence, silence and ambiguity of some of the geographical locations are intended to protect the identities of those who appear in this book and the contested spaces they inhabit.

Not all stories made their way to the book. When ambiguity could no longer protect people, I let their stories go. Not all stories need to be told.

It is not my goal to 'bear witness' or 'give voice to the voiceless'. Such writings have long been implicated in the history of colonial ethnographic practices—where native informants are poised to become the voices of the empire. The people in this book are eloquent advocates of their history and their struggles. My role, then, and this book's role, is to find in their articulations a critique of the nation state, its violence and the arbitrariness of territorial sovereignty. The stories in this book are a way to engage with how people live, struggle, fight and survive. Their stories challenge us to think; to consider whether it is possible to reject the idea that freedom, dignity and self-determination require territorial sovereignty.

The more I travelled along the border, the more I realised the books I had read were disconnected from the realities of the people I encountered. Local history and memory sometimes bore no resemblance to the political history I knew. I had to unlearn how I wrote, but more importantly, I had to unlearn the prejudices of the privilege I had.

Meanwhile, the India I was writing about was rapidly transforming into a violent, xenophobic Hindu state, waging war against its Constitution and so many of its people. An authoritarian India, deeply antagonistic to secularism, political dissent and pluralism, emerged as I travelled and wrote this book.

I was in the northern state of Rajasthan, just after a Muslim folk singer, Ahmad Khan, was lynched in Jaisalmer's Dantal village. Khan hailed from the Manganiyar community of Muslims who are known for their folk songs in praise of Hindu deities. A Hindu priest, a local faith healer named Ramesh Suthar, hired Khan, and then lynched him for 'not singing well enough'.[12] Over forty Muslim families fled the village following the lynching. Manganiyar folk singers once traversed the undivided deserts of the region, from Rajasthan to Sindh in present-day Pakistan, singing songs about Alexander the Great, old kings, conquests, local gods and goddesses, and beautiful singing girls.

A few weeks later, I saw the footage of a Muslim dairy farmer, Pehlu Khan, begging for his life before a Hindu mob in Alwar, Rajasthan. Despite video evidence, the men who killed him were acquitted.

Tabish, a young protestor I met during a 2019 protest against India's citizenship laws, spoke about the fear most young Muslims live with: 'We are so used to this fear, we think it is normal . . . I saw people circulating videos of Junaid, a sixteen-year-old boy, being lynched on the train.' Junaid had been travelling back to his village in Haryana after shopping in Delhi for Eid in June 2017. Tabish was in his ancestral village in Meerut when the news broke, and a week after, when he boarded the train from Meerut to Delhi, he travelled in fear: 'I shaved my week-long stubble . . . and kept to myself the entire journey.'

While violence against minorities in India has always been chronic, by the 1970s, winning elections by appealing to majoritarian sentiment against Muslim and other marginalised communities had become a well-honed strategy. This culminated in three events that fundamentally transformed India: the pogrom against the Sikhs in Delhi in 1984; the destruction of the Babri Masjid in 1992 at Ayodhya by a Hindu mob from Vishva Hindu Parishad, a militant right-wing Hindu nationalist organisation, and the slaughter of Muslims in Gujarat in 2002.

Since Prime Minister Narendra Modi came to power in 2014, Muslims have become disproportionate victims of violence, especially lynchings. There were forty-seven 'cow-related hate crimes' between May 2014 and April 2019. These attacks are perpetrated by local cow-protection groups, often affiliated with militant Hindu groups with ties to the Modi government. Seventy-six per cent of the victims of these attacks are Muslims.[13]

Since 2014, a rise in violence, threats and intimidation against minorities in India and a failing economy with no opportunities have resulted in thousands fleeing the country. Many fly to Central America, where they begin their long, precarious journey northwards, towards the US–Mexico border, on foot. The US immigration lawyers I spoke to confirm the rise in the number of Indian asylum seekers entering the country through the southern Mexico border since Prime Minister Modi came to power, and cite the increase in sectarian violence as one of the reasons, along with dwindling livelihood choices. In 2022, Indian citizens taken into US custody at the Mexican border almost doubled; the previous high was 8,997 recorded in 2018. The people fleeing persecution include members of the LGBT community, farmers from Punjab, Muslims, Christians and Dalits. Last summer, a six-year-old Indian girl named Gurupreet died in the Arizona desert after her mother left her with other Indian migrants to go in search of water, a medical examiner and the US Border Patrol said.[14]

Hate speech by Modi and his ministers has been widespread and ongoing; for instance, Amit Shah, India's minister of home affairs, has called Muslim migrants 'termites' and 'infiltrators'.[15] Numerous students, lawyers, professors, rights activists, protestors and others challenging the government have been charged with sedition.

I wondered if as a nation we were forever condemned to return to the violent moment of our birth. When I was younger, I believed that India was somehow different, that despite our many failures we were unique. I believed we were secular and democratic. Here, at the end of those seven years, I no longer hold such beliefs. But I am moved by the radical hope that we should continue to fight for a new world, remade by these values.

In the wake of Modi's re-election in May 2019, the government has aggressively implemented policies that seek to remake India into a Hindu nation. In its first one hundred days, the Modi government unconstitutionally revoked the special status of relative autonomy in the Muslim-majority state of Jammu and Kashmir, putting over eight million Kashmiris under an unprecedented information blockade; the Unlawful Activities (Prevention) Act (UAPA) was amended to designate individuals as terrorists unilaterally; and the Right to Information Act was diluted.

The Indian Supreme Court has essentially ruled that faith can now triumph over the rule of law. The Hindu belief, based on mythology that the god Ram was born in Ayodhya, can be invoked to resolve property disputes. When majoritarian beliefs become constitutional values, we retreat into an untenable ideology that this country can no longer be home to both Hindus and Muslims.[16]

On 31 August 2019, the National Register of Citizens (NRC)—requiring Indians to provide evidence of their citizenship, while those declared 'foreigners' would be held in detention centres—released a list of names in the state of Assam that effectively rendered 1.9 million people stateless, many of them Muslims. In response to this, Genocide Watch issued two alerts—first for Indian-occupied Kashmir and, later, for Assam—stating that 'Preparation for genocide is definitely underway in India . . . The next stage is extermination.'[17] In November 2019, the government announced that the NRC would be implemented nationwide.

Then came the Citizenship Amendment Act (CAA), the coup de grâce: a clear articulation of the government's efforts to systematically transform India into an ethnonationalist state, where millions would become stateless subjects stripped of rights. Passed in December 2019, the CAA is India's equivalent of the Nuremberg Laws. It violates the secular principles of India's Constitution and introduces religion as the basis of citizenship, allowing Hindus, Parsis, Jains, Buddhists, Sikhs and Christians persecuted in Bangladesh, Pakistan and Afghanistan to acquire citizenship, while excluding persecuted Muslim communities from the region. Ahmadis in Pakistan, Hazaras in Afghanistan and the Rohingya of Myanmar are also excluded from seeking citizenship, as are Tibetans, Sri Lankan Tamils, Chins from Myanmar and other vulnerable groups. The National Campaign Against Torture (NCAT), a Delhi-based rights group, has said that 'the CAA has made about 6,00,000 refugees in India forever stateless and vulnerable to refoulement'.[18] The Act, along with the proposed NRC, would require every Indian to prove their citizenship; an exercise that would deny citizenship to large numbers of Muslims and other marginalised undocumented communities.

When the CAA was first introduced, millions of Indians across the country took to the streets. I was one of them. Students at Jamia Millia in Delhi and Aligarh Muslim University in Uttar Pradesh had begun non-violent protests.

Within days, the police stormed both the university campuses. Students who hid inside washrooms fearing baton charges were beaten up. Tear gas was fired inside the library, and students were dragged outside, beaten and arrested. The siege lasted for over five hours, and more than a hundred students were wounded.

Attacks on students brought more people out to the street. Muslim women of varying ages, most of them from poor neighbourhoods, occupied an area called Shaheen Bagh for over three months, braving the rain, cold and attacks from right-wing groups. The women of Shaheen Bagh inspired over a hundred other women-led permanent sit-ins across India.

Sparks of revolution were in the air. Images of B.R. Ambedkar, Gandhi and Dalit activist Rohith Vemula appeared at protest sites. The protestors read the Constitution and sang India's national anthem. Coined in 1921 by poet and freedom fighter Maulana Hasrat Mohani, the slogan 'Inquilab zindabad'—'Long live the revolution'—once the rallying cry for Indian independence against the British, was reclaimed and shouted against the Modi government.

As the protests progressed, so did police brutality and hate speech. In Uttar Pradesh, thirty-six Muslim boys were illegally detained and tortured. Beginning on 23 February 2020, north-east Delhi's Muslim communities endured a series of violent incidents at the hands of Hindu mobs, including the destruction of property, attacks on mosques and desecration of graveyards. Armed mobs first marked, and then firebombed, Muslim homes and businesses. They chanted the rallying cry 'Jai Shri Ram'[19] as they set fire to a local mosque and planted Hindu-nationalist flags on its minaret. This is not the first time 'Jai Shri Ram' was used as a rallying call; since the 1980s, the chant has been used to create a divisive politics of hate, starting with the violence in Ayodhya leading to the destruction of Babri Masjid.[20]

The perpetrators dumped bodies and severed limbs into open drains. Messages with a grotesque photograph of a bloated body arrived in a WhatsApp group run by activists and alerted us that more bodies had been fished out of the drain in the aftermath of the pogrom. The unofficial death toll was sixty, and the confirmed number fluctuated as various newspapers misspelt names, counted the dead twice and sometimes erred in confirming the reports.

Eighty-five-year-old Akbari had survived Partition and other riots, but died inside her home when it was set on fire. Musharraf, of Gokalpuri, was lynched as his daughter pleaded with the mob for mercy. The bodies of sixteen-year-old Mohammad Hashim and his elder brother, Mohammad Amir, were dredged out of a drain.

On the third day of violence, 7,500 emergency calls were made to the police control room throughout the day, yet no one arrived to protect these communities. Instead, the first-person accounts and videos I logged suggested that the police worked with the rioters, and in some cases even attacked the victims. In the aftermath of the violence, many residents have fled their homes, and remain homeless. Almost all the student leaders who organised peaceful protests are now in prison, charged under the UAPA of being terrorists. This includes a nineteen-year-old student, Amulya Leone, for chanting the slogan 'India zindabad, Pakistan zindabad' during an anti-CAA protest meeting.

Once the world's largest secular democracy, India is now a Hindu Rashtra, an ethnonationalist Hindu state.

~

Through my travels, I attempted to trace the outline of a country that is part modern, part feudal and still struggling with democracy. By the end of my travels, I found myself not with one map of India, but many maps that looked far different from the one I thought I knew. I was taught to look at the fringes as from an imaginary centre—always looking outward from the mainland to a faraway frontier. But when I found myself at that frontier, I realised I was standing in a wholly different world, a wholly different history and a wholly different version of the country I called home. And yet, in this landscape of unmarked graves and buried land mines, and cries for freedom, I began to understand that we live in a world made of borderlands, that borders are being created everywhere.

While the stories in this book are from the Afghanistan–Pakistan border, and from India's borders, they could take place anywhere. It is not just the South Asian borders that are unravelling: borders around the world are enclosing and suffocating their people rather than guaranteeing their freedom. What happened in Bosnia was repeated in Rwanda, and what happens in Palestine is happening in Kashmir.

And it is not just violence and war that people are fleeing. Climate change will radically remake the borders of our world—what lines will you enforce with a standing army when water and fire have swallowed them? What sovereignty will you impose on a city erased by rising seas?

Edward Said wrote, 'The earth is in effect one world, in which empty, uninhabited spaces virtually do not exist. Just as none of us is outside or beyond geography, none of us is completely free from the struggle over geography.'[21] The stories in this book are part of a greater, universal struggle over geography, as individuals across the world navigate the imposition of arbitrary borders. In the words of the historian Romila Thapar, 'Borders only become borders when cartographies come into existence.'[22]

Today, we live in a world where commodities, capital and drones have far greater freedom of movement than people fleeing dictators or genocide. The borders we have established in many places cannot continue to exist as they are. We shape nations out of imaginary, non-existent lines—sometimes amputating communities or whole cultures to make way for a country—and we defend these lines with violence lest they cease to exist altogether. As the need to rethink the shape of the post-war and postcolonial world intensifies, and the world contemplates the future of democracy and the nation state in contested terrains, the stories from the borderlands need to be told. These real histories are intricate, contradictory and full of inconvenient truths that cannot be neatly sorted into the textbook categories of cause and effect. They hold immense pain, but they also reveal glimpses of a new world.

PART I

THE AFGHANISTAN–PAKISTAN BORDER

The British annexation of the Indian subcontinent occurred between 1757 and 1849, and the 'Scramble for Africa' started with the British occupation of Egypt in 1881.[1] In the intervening thirty-year period, another empire expanded southwards across Central Asia: Russia.[2] The Russian expansion has been described as one of the 'nineteenth century's most rapid and dramatic examples of imperial conquest'.[3] By the 1880s, the Russians had advanced close to Afghanistan.

Colonel Gerald Morgan, who served in the British Army and later wrote extensively about Anglo-Russian rivalry in the region, writes that from opposite directions two empires expanded towards each other without any agreed frontier, vying to rule 'over a backward, uncivilized and undeveloped region'.[4] British diplomatic dispatches from this time echo this language; local rulers and their people appear infrequently, except as savages and uncivilised caricatures whose land, history and wealth are seen as entitled-to objects of conquest and plunder.

It was the looming Russian threat to British control over India that gave rise to a 1,622-mile-long border that today marks the divide between Afghanistan and Pakistan. When this border—known as the Durand Line—was created in 1893, Afghanistan had been reduced to a crumbling empire ruled by Abdur Rahman Khan, and the nation states of Pakistan and India did not exist—only British India.

The Afghan government does not accept the Durand Line, viewing it as an agreement between the British and Abdur Rahman that no longer holds following Indian independence and the creation of Pakistan in 1947. Pakistan, however, regards the line as a well-established international border.

To understand this region, especially Kashmir, one must understand the events in Afghanistan, British India and the princely state of Jammu and Kashmir over 180 years ago. The Anglo-Afghan War and the Anglo-Sikh Wars, fought between the British East India Company and the Afghan kingdom, and between British India and the Sikh empire, radically remade the contours of the region. If the Anglo-Afghan War decided a frontier between British India and Afghanistan, the Anglo-Sikh Wars—two wars fought between the East India Company and Sikh empire between 1845 and 1846—affected the future of Kashmir.

In 1846, the British East India Company defeated the Sikh empire in the First Anglo-Sikh War, and the Kashmir region and its people were sold to the Dogras for a sum of Rs 7.5 lakh. The Dogra rule in Kashmir was brutal—it economically plundered the Kashmiris through a series of land taxes and forced labour.[5] Throughout the Dogra rule, there were a series of protests and an ongoing local resistance against the oppressive regime. In 1865, the Kashmiri shawl-weavers' protest was crushed brutally. The event is memorialised every year as the shawl-weavers' massacre.

It is under these conditions of repression by the Hindu ruler of Kashmir, and resistance by its Muslim-majority population, that one must understand how the events of 1947 played out.

After the Partition, the future of Kashmir hung in the balance. Amidst this precarity, in October 1947, militias led by the army of the Dogra king, Hari Singh, massacred thousands of Muslims in the Jammu region. The massacre triggered a wave of migration during which nearly half a million people fled across the border to Pakistan. By the end of the killings, Muslims, who had been a majority in the Jammu region, became a minority.

In an incident that is now referred to as the 'Pathan Invasion', mere days after the Jammu massacre, frontier tribesmen along the Afghanistan–Pakistan border, supported by Pakistan, rode across the Indian border towards Srinagar, then still a princely state in northern India, to capture the territory. In response, Maharaja Hari Singh signed a treaty of accession with India. The Indians then brought their troops to Srinagar to tilt the balance against the tribal fighters. A ceasefire was signed on 1 January 1949, by which time Kashmir was effectively divided between India and Pakistan, as Indian-administered Kashmir and Pakistan-administered Kashmir, the latter referred to as 'Azad Kashmir'. Today, Pakistan-administered Kashmir shares a sixty-six-mile border with the Wakhan Corridor in Afghanistan.

Major General Akbar Khan of Pakistan is often cited as having played a crucial role in starting the Pathan invasion, and is credited as the architect of Pakistan's policy of using, recruiting and aiding non-state actors.[6] Pakistan is accused of using this strategy by deploying non-state actors widely in Kashmir during the 1999 Kargil War and in Afghanistan.

In the 1980s, as the mujahideen fought against the Soviet occupation of Afghanistan, Kashmiri fighters joined their fight. During this time, Pakistan, aided by the US's Central Intelligence Agency (CIA), supplied material resources and training to the mujahideen. After the Soviet withdrawal from Afghanistan in the 1980s, the immediate power vacuum and a lack of political settlement in Afghanistan paved the way for the Afghan civil war and the emergence of the Taliban.[7]

Meanwhile, in 1987, when many Kashmiris considered the state elections in their region rigged, a series of protests broke out. This flared into an insurgency throughout the 1990s before exploding into a full-fledged resistance to Indian rule.

In February 1989, when the last of the Russians left Kabul, so did the mujahideen who fought against the Soviets—both Afghan and foreign fighters. Many of them made their way to Kashmir.

Since 11 September 2001, the Afghanistan–Pakistan border has acquired global attention in the aftermath of the so-called war on terror.

1

SAR HAWZA

TRAPPED IN THE COLONISER'S MAP

Located in Afghanistan's remote south-eastern Paktika province, along the border with Pakistan and the western edge of the Sulaiman Mountains, the Sar Hawza district is home to the infamous Route Jeep—a major infiltration route into Paktika and a gateway to Afghanistan's northern provinces. Hezb-e-Islami, the Taliban, and local insurgents all have power bases and strongholds in this region. Sar Hawza has seen battles, air strikes, night raids, drones, and the rise of local warlords and petty criminals who now work at the behest of the US forces. By the time I got there in 2010, US forces and their Afghan allies had been fighting for years to assert control over the traditional Taliban stronghold.

Gaining control of this crucial supply route was a significant, hard-won victory for the US military base in Sar Hawza. After a decade of small victories at an enormous cost, the outpost felt like a ghost town inhabited by an army that had lost the will to fight. The base commander remarked, 'It felt like we spent ten years trying to hold a stretch of road and have nothing else to account for [it] except bodies and IEDs.' The company was scheduled to leave in four months, and the commander wanted nothing more than to 'get [his] boys back home safe'. Fatigue, frustration and a long tally of tactical failures haunted the base. Bowe Bergdahl, the American soldier who was held captive by the Taliban from June 2009 to May 2014, went missing from a town near Yahya Khel in Paktika province, not far from Sar Hawza.

While the US counter-insurgency strategy was aimed at winning the hearts and minds of locals, the forces had limited influence and were viewed with suspicion, often patrolling no more than a six-mile radius around their base. The stretch between the towns of Sar Hawza and Orgun, both Taliban strongholds, was monitored remotely from the US base. The Americans refused to patrol or even enter certain villages without air support, leaving the task to the local Afghan forces working with the US military.

Afghan Local Police (ALP) Commander Mahmud was my guide in Paktika province. Mahmud had fought against the Soviets, the Talibs and a few others he called traitors. He was the kind of man whose stories changed every time he told them. The commander was the creation of a ruptured society that required a certain murkiness of character and malleability of beliefs. He had to negotiate alliances and friendships with an unlikely cast of characters, ranging from local warlords to the US military officers he was tasked to work with.

In his latest role, he recruited, trained and commanded the ALP. Created at the behest of and funded by the Americans, the ALP was meant to 'secure local communities and prevent rural areas from infiltration of insurgent groups'. It was not, however, a real police force, but a local armed militia created to fight the Taliban. These militias were mostly made up of poor, orphaned, uneducated men and boys who were forced to fight under the threat of violence.

While I was there, the local shura (governing council) organised a celebration for a group of ALP cadets who had just graduated from their training. Earlier that day, I had photographed the cadets wearing their newly issued guns and cartridges—all eighteen of them, one after another—against a faded mustard-coloured wall. Among them was a boy of barely thirteen who was wearing body armour with ammunition and holding a bag of M&M's. When he smiled, he tried to hide his chipped teeth, which made him look like the child he was.

Almost thirty years earlier, this region had sheltered young rebels fighting the Russians. Then the United States had given them AK-47s and American combat rations, like peanut butter. Jan Mohammed, now in his sixties, still had an unopened 1986 American peanut-butter sachet from his days as a guerrilla.

War mementos come in all forms.

These days, a soldier like Jan Mohammed gets a week of training, guns, a hundred dollars a month and M&M's candies to fight the Taliban.

One of the cadets, who looked no older than fifteen, said he often crossed into Pakistan to see his family, and stayed there every winter in search of employment. 'My maternal cousin joined the local Taliban,' he said. 'They pay well for doing nothing, and he has a gun.'

Pointing to his AK-47, he said, 'These guns are not bad, either.'

Forcefully conscripted into a war they had no interest in, these boys were being prepared for slaughter, and the accidental recruit was meant to fight the accidental terrorist across the border in Pakistan. The US sergeant at Sar Hawza denied arming underage boys, describing this as 'an Afghan solution to an Afghan problem'. When I repeated this to Commander Mahmud, he responded with silence.

Over the next three weeks at Sar Hawza, I heard stories of war, valour, exile and disenchantment in these border villages. Here, boundaries were messy and state sovereignty fragmented, creating overlapping and alternating allegiances. The map of belonging people used was drawn from history passed down by their ancestors. The newer political maps drawn by outsiders were something else altogether.

Such borders can humiliate and hurt.

~

In 1893, the British decided that formal borders needed to be established between Afghanistan and colonial British India to limit Russian expansion in the region. The British viewed Afghanistan primarily as a buffer state and believed that if it were to be conquered by the Russian empire, then British India would be next to be 'invaded'. In October of that year, the Indian foreign secretary, Sir Henry Mortimer Durand, was sent to negotiate and demarcate the border with the Emir of Afghanistan. Durand arrived on the heels of two previous envoys, Sir Alexander Burnes and Sir Louis Cavagnari, who were both murdered by angry Afghan mobs.[1] Cavagnari was massacred by mutinous Afghan troops inside his home in Kabul. Burnes was hacked to death by a mob, and the following day his head was placed on a pike and displayed in the public square.[2]

Mortimer Durand fared better, and he and Emir Abdur Rahman Khan signed the agreement that created the Durand Line between Afghanistan and British India. The agreement—a single-page document with seven clauses—created a frontier without any identifying structures, not a border. When the men tasked with the job of demarcating the precise line arrived, they found that there were areas represented on the map that did not exist on the

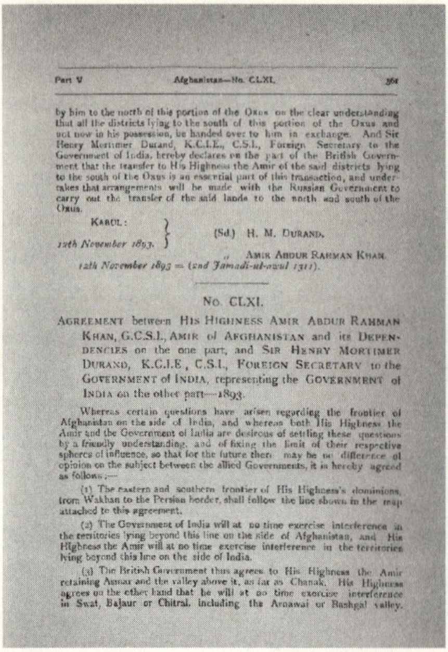

Part V Afghanistan—No. CLXI. 561

by him to the north of this portion of the Oxus on the clear understanding that all the districts lying to the south of this portion of the Oxus and not now in his possession, be handed over to him in exchange. And Sir Henry Mortimer Durand, K.C.I.E., C.S.I., Foreign Secretary to the Government of India, hereby declares on the part of the British Government that the transfer to His Highness the Amir of the said districts lying to the south of the Oxus is an essential part of this transaction, and undertakes that arrangements will be made with the Russian Government to carry out the transfer of the said lands to the north and south of the Oxus.

KABUL: 12th November 1893. (Sd.) H. M. DURAND.

" AMIR ABDUR RAHMAN KHAN.

12th November 1893 = (2nd Jamadi-ul-awul 1311).

No. CLXI.

AGREEMENT between HIS HIGHNESS AMIR ABDUR RAHMAN KHAN, G.C.S.I., AMIR of AFGHANISTAN and its DEPENDENCIES on the one part, and SIR HENRY MORTIMER DURAND, K.C.I.E., C.S.I., FOREIGN SECRETARY to the GOVERNMENT of INDIA, representing the GOVERNMENT of INDIA on the other part—1893.

Whereas certain questions have arisen regarding the frontier of Afghanistan on the side of India, and whereas both His Highness the Amir and the Government of India are desirous of settling these questions by a friendly understanding, and of fixing the limit of their respective spheres of influence, so that for the future there may be no difference of opinion on the subject between the allied Governments, it is hereby agreed as follows:—

(1) The eastern and southern frontier of His Highness's dominions, from Wakhan to the Persian border, shall follow the line shown in the map attached to this agreement.

(2) The Government of India will at no time exercise interference in the territories lying beyond this line on the side of Afghanistan, and His Highness the Amir will at no time exercise interference in the territories lying beyond this line on the side of India.

(3) The British Government thus agrees to His Highness the Amir retaining Asmar and the valley above it, as far as Chanak. His Highness agrees on the other hand that he will at no time exercise interference in Swat, Bajaur or Chitral, including the Arnawai or Bashgal valley.

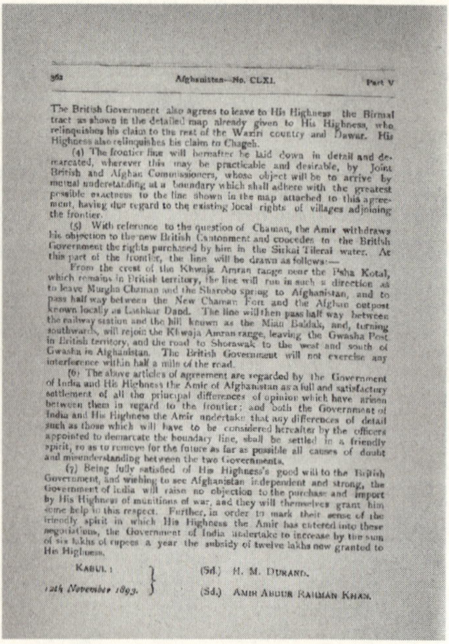

562 Afghanistan—No. CLXI. Part V

The British Government also agrees to leave to His Highness the Birmal tract as shown in the detailed map already given to His Highness, who relinquishes his claim to the rest of the Waziri country and Dawar. His Highness also relinquishes his claim to Chageh.

(4) The frontier line will hereafter be laid down in detail and demarcated, wherever this may be practicable and desirable, by Joint British and Afghan Commissioners, whose object will be to arrive by mutual understanding at a boundary which shall adhere with the greatest possible exactness to the line shown in the map attached to this agreement, having due regard to the existing local rights of villages adjoining the frontier.

(5) With reference to the question of Chaman, the Amir withdraws his objection to the new British Cantonment and concedes to the British Government the rights purchased by him in the Sirkai Tilerai water. At this part of the frontier, the line will be drawn as follows:—

From the crest of the Khwaja Amran range near the Psha Kotal, which remains in British territory, the line will run in such a direction as to leave Murgha Chaman and the Sharobo spring to Afghanistan, and to pass half way between the New Chaman Fort and the Afghan outpost known locally as Lashkar Dand. The line will then pass half way between the railway station and the hill known as the Mian Baldak, and, turning southwards, will rejoin the Khwaja Amran range, leaving the Gwasha Post in British territory, and the road to Shorawak to the west and south of Gwasha in Afghanistan. The British Government will not exercise any interference within half a mile of the road.

(6) The above articles of agreement are regarded by the Government of India and His Highness the Amir of Afghanistan as a full and satisfactory settlement of all the principal differences of opinion which have arisen between them in regard to the frontier; and both the Government of India and His Highness the Amir undertake that any differences of detail such as those which will have to be considered hereafter by the officers appointed to demarcate the boundary line, shall be settled in a friendly spirit, so as to remove for the future as far as possible all causes of doubt and misunderstanding between the two Governments.

(7) Being fully satisfied of His Highness's good will to the British Government, and wishing to see Afghanistan independent and strong, the Government of India will raise no objection to the purchase and import by His Highness of munitions of war, and they will themselves grant him some help in this respect. Further, in order to mark their sense of the friendly spirit in which His Highness the Amir has entered into these negotiations, the Government of India undertake to increase by the sum of six lakhs of rupees a year the subsidy of twelve lakhs now granted to His Highness.

KABUL: 12th November 1893. (Sd.) H. M. DURAND.

(Sd.) AMIR ABDUR RAHMAN KHAN.

ground, and there were parts that existed in real life that were not marked in the maps. For the Pashtun tribes actually living on the terrain being mapped, the Durand Line divided their lands, families and communities in two. Half of the Pashtun tribal region became part of British India, and the other half remained part of Afghanistan. The British historian Bijan Omrani writes, 'The people on the ground did not like the idea of being under any sort of British jurisdiction. The officers who were demarcating the Line soon found themselves the object of unwelcome attention, mainly in bullet form. By 1897 there was a general uprising all over the area, which it took 60,000 British regular troops to pacify.'[3] The British fought three wars in Afghanistan over a period of eighty years, finally granting Afghanistan independence in 1919.

The 1947 British departure from the subcontinent, and the resulting independence for India and Pakistan, called into question the legality of the Durand Line and Afghanistan's border with the newly formed Pakistan. On the eve of the partition of India, Afghanistan demanded that its former territories be handed back and the border revised. Afghanistan announced that all previous Durand Line agreements, including the subsequent Anglo-Afghan treaties, were invalid, since the treaties made between the British and the Afghans lapsed at the moment of independence.

The Afghans have always claimed that the agreements that created the line were obtained under duress. They questioned the veracity of the maps and suggested that the British fabricated both the map and the agreement after the fact (something the British regularly did). They also questioned whether the emir, Abdur Rahman Khan, and the British Crown actually intended the boundary to be a legal international boundary, instead of a less formal demarcation of areas of influence.

When the line was drawn in 1895–96, many British officials held the view that many Afghans share today: that the Durand Line was never meant to be an international boundary, 'it was a line that delimited areas of influence, not sovereignty'.[4]

No matter what officials believed, local history and the people here had no respect for the line. Yet, at the moment of Indian independence, the Pashtun tribes divided by an arbitrary line were not given any right to self-determination. They could only choose to join India or Pakistan—independence, or rejoining Afghanistan, was not an option.

Pakistan, for its part, claims to be the inheritor of the British agreements at the moment of independence, arguing that the frontier, the Durand Line, is a legitimate international boundary as of 1893, and was confirmed by later treaties in 1905, 1919, 1921 and 1930. What started as a line drawn to create a frontier between two imperial powers had become a border.

~

'If you fear loneliness, you cannot be a soldier or an honest man.' Masood said these words as he quickly smoked a small hand-rolled cigarette packed with a mix of hashish and tobacco. He was almost forty when I met him in the winter of 2012, in a remote border town in Paktika province. By then he had been many things: a smuggler, a fixer, a translator and a mercenary. These days, he called himself a 'businessman' and worked with everyone—the Americans, the Afghans, the Iranians, the Indians, the Pakistanis, the Haqqanis and the Taliban. He was one of the many minor strongmen with muscle and money that the decade-long US military presence in Afghanistan produced. He helped grease the wheels of military occupation.

It was six o'clock in the evening but already cold and dark. About twelve of us sat huddled in a room made warm by a fire and a couple of cheap Chinese heaters that had seen better days. I was the only woman among the men, who laughed, sang, ate chicken stuffed with raisins, smoked hashish, complained about their wives, exchanged video clips and retold stories from their childhoods. The men in that room were meant to be on opposite sides of the never-ending war on terror led by the US military and its Afghan allies against the Taliban. But on a frightfully cold night, among men with murky pasts and even murkier alliances, such absolutes don't exist.

After dinner, Masood showed me an old photograph of his father, folded and creased from being carried in his wallet. The back of the picture read 'Feb. 26th, 1980'. Masood's father, then a young man, stood in the middle of a group of mujahideen, guerrilla fighters in Afghanistan. He wore a smart winter jacket over his Pathan suit, a military uniform hat, a waist belt made of bullet cartridges and held a gun in his left hand. In May 1980, Masood fled to the Pakistani province of Peshawar with his grandmother. In August, the news arrived of his father's death—cause unknown. 'Hafiz,' Masood said, pointing to another man in the room, 'can tell you everything. He remembers everything . . . all the important dates . . . the fighting . . . I just remember being hungry all the time.' Masood went on,

'My great-grandfather and grandfather fought the British; my father fought the Russians. They were called heroes first, and then terrorists. I picked up my gun at fourteen. With a gun, I wasn't hungry anymore. Now they pay people like me to fight him.' He pointed to a younger man with a black turban sitting across the room. 'No one knows who they are fighting anymore. But I no longer fight other people's wars. I am not a soldier, I am a businessman.'

~

The day I left Sar Hawza, Commander Mahmud prepared a lavish meal of goat and rice and sent me away with words that betrayed his earlier silence: 'We take orders from an emperor who is a stranger to us . . . We have been sending boys to die to defend a line that doesn't exist. Sometimes they become cheaper than dried chickpeas, but orders are orders. Memory is a funny thing. It differs from the history you came here with.' He paused and added, 'It is the coloniser's map, and they had no respect for our land. Why should we respect their borders?'

For many of the older Afghans, now in their eighties and nineties, the racial memory of a border was not with Pakistan. For them, Pakistan did not exist. India, as we think of it today, did not exist.

They remembered British India, a contiguous, undivided land made not of borders but of frontiers. From an isolated command post on the Afghanistan border along Route Jeep, I could see Pakistan. The view confused me. There were no demarcating lines, border pillars or checkpoints. What had I hoped to find? A flat land perfectly divided like the lines on an atlas? It would take so little to find myself on the 'other side', and if I did, I would then be confronted with a wholly different view of history and memory. If Commander Mahmud were born on the other side of the Durand Line—a stroke of ink drawn by the departing empire but never truly marked on the ground—would the men he killed and the wars he fought be different?

On the first day of my embed with the International Security Assistance Forces, a US sergeant, Smith, remarked, 'Imagine, this shithole is the graveyard of empires.' The phrase and the book that carries this name—*In the Graveyard of Empires*—were ubiquitous during my time in Afghanistan. Every base I went to had a copy of this book; almost every American who lived there used this phrase liberally and unimaginatively, along with the word 'surreal', to describe a complicated country living through another cycle of war and violence. If I ever see Sergeant Smith again, I would like to tell him that the Afghans want their graveyards back and the new empire to leave, along with the borders they drew.

The young boy I photographed that winter with the M&M's did not live beyond the spring. Of the eighteen cadets, ten died and three crossed the border into Pakistan in search of work. When I Skyped with the interpreter who worked at the American base in Sar Hawza in the spring of the following year, he confirmed that the cadets had been buried in a new graveyard next to an old Sufi shrine. I asked him if he remembered the boy. He paused and said, 'I remember your photograph of him, but not him.' He ended the awkward silence by saying that the boy 'now [had] six feet of land to call his own, when alive, he had nothing'. I wish I had corrected him. Graves are usually four feet for children, not six.

PART II

THE INDIA–BANGLADESH BORDER

India–Bangladesh is a densely populated border, and cuts through farmlands, rivers and hills. The length fluctuates: 2,544 miles,[1] 2,582 miles,[2] 2,538 miles[3] and so on, depending on who keeps the record. An 8-foot-high fence, electrified in some stretches, covers 70 per cent of this border today. Smugglers, drug couriers, human traffickers and cattle rustlers from both countries continue to cross the border to ply their trades, often with the connivance of Indian and Bangladeshi border guards. The border—partly fenced, mostly porous—cuts through rivers, seasonal chars and hilly terrain. It crosses backyards, pastures and ponds. For some, simply moving from one part of your home to another means crossing an international border.[4]

The Indo-Bangladesh boundary is a contested colonial inheritance. Cyril Radcliffe, the man who was tasked with drawing the boundary between India and Pakistan, did not have a detailed map of the region. All he had to work with were revenue maps prepared by the colonial administration to collect taxes from various landlords, tax documents and the 1941 census.[5] It was assumed by everyone that the resulting lines were 'a makeshift border'—hurriedly drawn, and more useful 'for the purpose of transferring power' than for dividing the two countries. The prevailing wisdom then was that the two countries would at a later date 'agree to a mutual frontier based on people's wishes'.[6]

The lines on the new map decided by Radcliffe and the Bengal boundary committee had no resemblance to realities on the ground.[7] Some rivers identified in the Boundary Commission report did not exist, or if they did, it was hard to fix a boundary based on rivers that changed their path, making and remaking the border every day. In the newly created Indian Parliament, Nehru, then prime minister, spoke candidly about the difficulties of implementing the Boundary Commission's decision. He said, 'One side of the river is sometimes described as the other side. Maps are attached to this description but they do not tally. Sometimes a river is named and there is doubt as to which river is meant.'[8]

After Partition, the Radcliffe Line had left a murky distinction between the newly created independent India and what was then called East Pakistan. Later, the 1971 Bangladesh Liberation War ended with East Pakistan breaking away from Pakistan and becoming an independent nation. The Indian Army aided local Bangladeshi fighters in their fight for independence. In the aftermath of the war, it is estimated that over three million people died in Bangladesh, and nearly ten million Bengali refugees crossed the border into its territory.[9]

2

PANITAR

PLAYING CRICKET IN NO MAN'S LAND

My journey in India began in the West Bengal state capital of Calcutta. Calcutta is a city like no other. Nowhere in my travels felt so instantly like home as Calcutta did. In the evening, streets immediately became bookstores where you could find everything from Freud to Chekhov to Mishima in English and Bengali. The Bengalis I observed were partial to the Russian masters—Gorky, Tolstoy, Pushkin, Akhmatova and Dostoyevsky. A colloquium of men and women gathered in the city's coffeehouses and tea stalls named after Shakespeare. The old colonial buildings clinging to wisps of past glory coexisted with new buildings that smelt like mosquito repellent.

I spent a week there applying for and receiving the Inner Line Permit (ILP), an official travel document that 'allows travel of an Indian citizen into a protected area',[1] like the northeastern states of Nagaland and Arunachal Pradesh, for a limited period of time. The travel permits, originally a colonial practice, are still in place to regulate movement to certain areas located near India's international border. While in Calcutta, I was also working on getting permission to interview Border Security Force (BSF) officers and procuring a visa to Bangladesh.

My first move would be south, to the Sundarbans: a large mangrove forest in the delta of three major rivers at the Bay of Bengal, a one-of-a-kind ecosystem straddling the border between India and Bangladesh. No one thinks of the border when they think of the Sundarbans.

From Calcutta, I headed south by road before hopping on a short ferry ride to the village of Gosaba in Canning Subdivision of South 24 Parganas district, at the edge of the reserve forests. It is the last inhabited village before the Sundarbans start, but most tourists travel well past it. Gosaba is also home to the Daniel Hamilton estate archives. Hamilton was an eccentric man who once leased the Sundarbans, cleared it, created an agricultural collective as an economic experiment and issued his own currency. With the help of a friend who was then conducting fieldwork, I hoped to rent a small fishing boat from Gosaba and travel to the edge of Indian maritime frontiers.

There was a remoteness to this place, a lushness that came with decay and water and vegetation. The Sundarbans that I studied in middle school geography was wild, dark and disorienting, the home of the great Bengal tiger. For the people who lived there, it was a punishing labyrinth of immense mangrove forest and freshwater and brackish swampland. At the time of the Partition, Bangladesh received about two-thirds of the forest, and India holds the rest, fragmenting the natural reserve.

The tides in the Sundarbans are dramatic and whimsical, swallowing and spitting out over a third of the area's land each day. How could the Sundarbans, a forest that transforms with every rain, every high tide and monsoon, be partitioned? Today, there are BSF and coast guard units that patrol this silted delta in their dinky, rusted boats with tattered Indian flags affixed. There are three floating observation posts on the water there. The absurdity of the modern nation state is found even there, in the middle of an ocean that has midwifed civilisations for millennia.

In 2010, a news report began circulating that a 'Disputed Bay of Bengal island [had] disappear[ed] into the sea' as a result of climate change.[2] New Moore Island, or South Talpatti, was a small and uninhabited island on the Bay of Bengal near the Sundarbans. The island was born in the aftermath of the violent, destructive Bhola cyclone, and first emerged on satellite images in 1974. In 1981, India sent naval ships to plant a flag. But both India and Bangladesh claimed this tiny piece of land as theirs, initiating a thirty-year maritime dispute. Professor Sugata Hazra of the School of Oceanographic Studies at Jadavpur University in Calcutta, quoted in the original news reports, said, 'What these two countries could not achieve from years of talking, has been resolved by global warming.'[3]

The metaphorical dimension of New Moore Island stuck with me: an island born of violence, an object of contention throughout its existence, its disappearance heralded by the wrath of nature. I would hear this metaphor repeated in other stories I encountered, over and over again—of land so contentious, so soaked with blood, that water would reclaim it.

In another fifteen to twenty years it is likely that all of the Sundarbans, with its two hundred islands where some ten million Indians and Bangladeshis live, will be consumed by the rising ocean—a natural shift that will force an exodus of millions of refugees, creating enormous challenges for India and Bangladesh that neither country is prepared for.

~

As I drive away from the Sundarbans, BSF camps cover the landscape. Rolling tracts of farmland fall between a fence and an international border. Lush and parched, full of life and decay, the villages riven by the frontier nevertheless have a certain vitality, a rambling quality, despite the contingencies of the border that constantly remake this terrain.

I make my way to Panitar, one of the 250 hamlets that straddle India's border with Bangladesh, with the several armed BSF guards sent to accompany me. Panitar is notable for being home to a one-foot-high concrete block on the side of the Ichamati river marked 'Border Pillar No. 1'. Panitar's division is as cruel as it is arbitrary: here, the houses on either side of one dusty lane occupy two neighbouring countries. Where India ends and Bangladesh begins is a question confused by history, family and the border pillars themselves. Most of the other pillars that punctuate the border are older, faded pyramid-shaped blocks or newer rectangular blocks that appear as often in backyards as in the middle of fields. A number of the pillars have gone missing over the years. In some areas, you can still see 'Pakistan' marked on pillars—a remnant from the pre-1971 days when Bangladesh was East Pakistan.[4]

A few pillars have been lost to the river as it changes course. Most days, for the kids from either side of the border, Border Pillar No. 1 in Panitar is simply a handy cricket stump.

Each day I arrive at various camps and ask to speak to the officer in charge. Most officers are curious about the lone woman travelling the border and invite me in, serving me tea and biscuits. A few offer their own guards as local guides to 'show me around'; others refuse to speak, and demand that I return to Calcutta and come back with a permission or a press pass. In Panitar, the officer in charge insists that his men show me the lay of the land.

When they see me arrive with the BSF guards, a group of boys disperse from their makeshift wicket. The few that linger are hurriedly shooed away by a guard as he clears the area for a photograph of the forlorn Pillar No. One set against a cloudy afternoon sky.

'Take photo,' the guard tells me.

Afterwards, the BSF guards escort me into Panitar proper, and men from the village are summoned to answer my questions, while the women and children watch from a distance. In a matter of minutes, biscuits, cola and energy drinks arrive. My very tall BSF escort takes a large sip and grimaces in disapproval. 'This is Bangla cola,' he sneers. 'Not Indian.'

I ask the villagers the kind of forced, obligatory questions one asks when surrounded by armed guards. The villagers tell me it is 'great' living here, they have 'no problems', they have 'everything' and that 'the guards are good to us'.

The BSF keeps these villages under constant surveillance. Men and women are regularly called into the BSF camps for interrogation about the local smuggling networks, coerced into becoming informants and local spies. The BSF is an opaque, bureaucratic institution, which has a long history of using disproportionate force against the border population.[5]

I try to edge away and speak to other villagers, but I am quickly deterred. 'We can't leave you alone here,' one guard tells me, his voice elevated. 'It is unsafe, you might cross into Bangladesh by mistake, and if they catch you'—the guard dramatically lowers his voice and whispers—'that's it!'

On the way out of Panitar, I pass the BSF checkpoint near the village entrance. I see a young girl, probably around eight, walking a large bicycle along the road. After emptying the contents of her schoolbag and checking it, the guards let her pass. The tall BSF guard escorting me explains: 'Women and girls are the biggest smugglers. They smuggle food, cough syrup and cigarettes.'

After seeing the uncomfortable look on my face, he leans in and says, 'We have to treat everyone like a suspect.' As we leave, the gang of boisterous children resumes their game by the river, positioning themselves on the dusty pitch for another game of international cricket.

The indignities of daily life and the palpable sense of loss experienced during Partition are alive and well today. A few days later, still on the road, I meet a man named Gazi while asking directions to my next planned stop at Malda, a bustling border town 200 miles north of Panitar. He has a pleasant, sunburnt face and is quick to smile. Gazi's backyard is home to one of India's neglected border pillars with Bangladesh, and opens onto the river Ichamati. The river, born in Bangladesh and crossing through India, acts as a natural border between the two countries.

As we take a walk by the river, I see people from both sides crossing regularly. 'Yes, it happens,' Gazi says. 'How do you cut a river into two?' Like thousands who live along this densely populated border, he has a family that lives just a few feet away—in another country.

Sitting in his backyard, Gazi remarks, 'The Partition did not just happen, and the war did not just happen. It is unfinished, incomplete and ongoing.'

In this part of the world, the birth of this border, the bloody aftermath of the Partition, the war of liberation, the unknown pogroms and the many unreported riots are not history: they are family stories that one works very hard to either remember or forget. These family histories also become ways to untangle various threads and tales of migration—multiple arrivals, departures and returns. Gazi's great-grandfather is 101 and still alive, but he lives in the lower valleys of Assam, where he migrated over eighty years ago to work on a tea plantation. He was part of a wave of Bengali Muslim peasants and labourers who were brought to Assam as a part of the colonial economy. Gazi's grandmother was born when there was no border between India and Bangladesh, when both countries were part of British India. A few years into her life, she became a citizen of East Pakistan after the Partition. Of her three sons, two made India their home, but the third stayed in East Pakistan. Then East Pakistan became Bangladesh, leading to more border pillars and more treaties.

Gazi himself was born in a nearby farming village with porous land and a riverine border. Throughout his adolescence, he watched BSF camps mushroom along the farmlands. Fencing and floodlights, accompanied by aggressive and violent state intervention, rapidly transformed that once porous border into a harsh, militarised divide. Caught between two mighty states, the village of his childhood, once empty of men in uniforms and bunkers, doesn't exist anymore.

'Our homes are vanishing before our eyes.' Gazi says the most devastating things with a calm, even tone and a bright white smile.

When I ask him about illegal smuggling and trafficking, at first he dismisses my questions and denies all knowledge. As dusk approaches, a small round man in an ageing, ill-fitted brown safari suit walks into the courtyard and pulls Gazi aside for a quick chat. The man looks like a provincial bureaucrat. His sparse eyebrows give

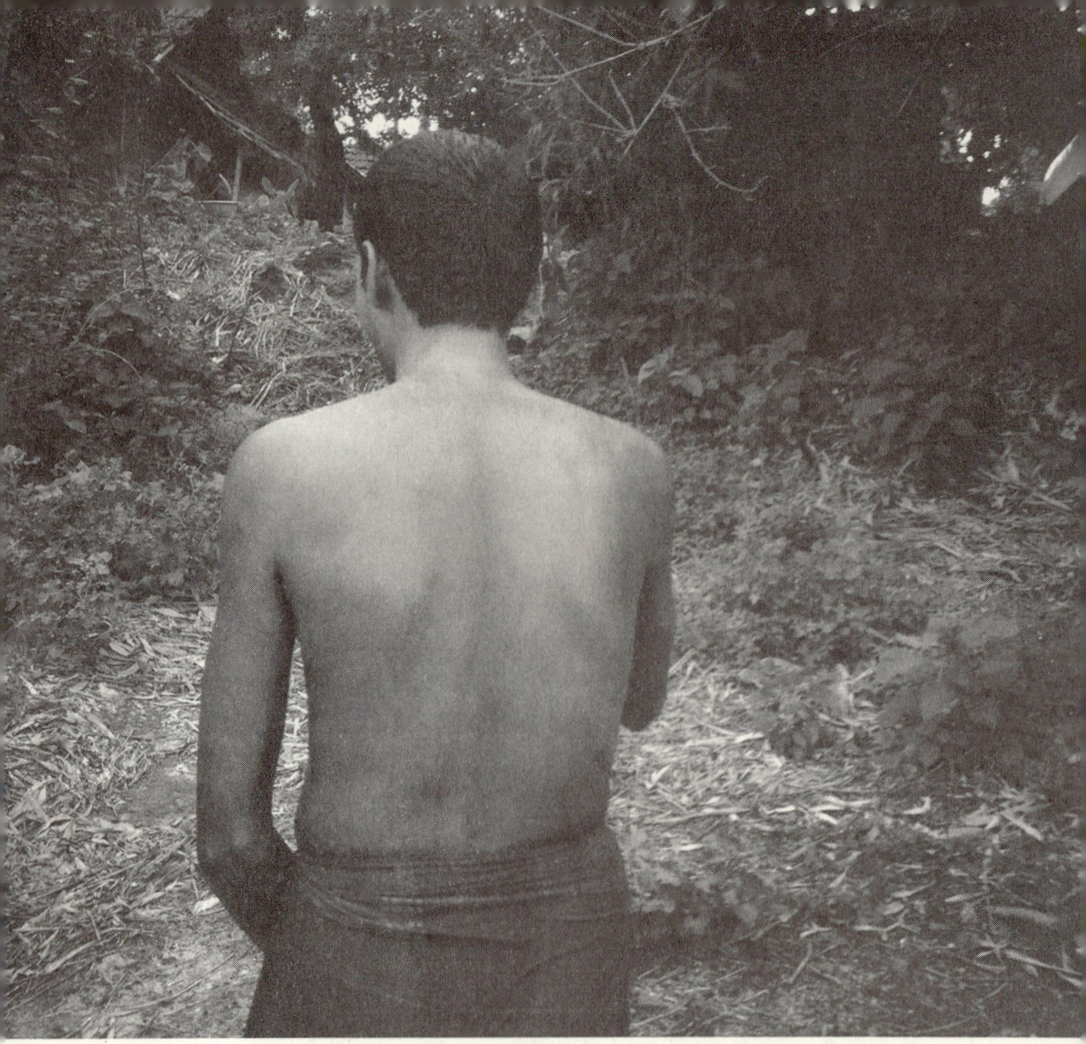

his face an incomplete look. As he talks to Gazi, he fiddles with a key chain and looks at me every few seconds, as if to indicate that I'm being discussed.

Gazi returns to our conversation annoyed. 'Someone must have told him you are here.' He pauses. 'He is not from here. He just moved here a few years ago. Now he is close to the BSF and keeps informing them about everything.' Gazi says that the BSF created an informal council with local representatives to discuss local issues and concerns, but had installed 'their' people, like the man in the safari suit. No one knows what this 'round man' really does all day, aside from circling the village like a menacing human drone, seeing, watching and informing.

After this visit, Gazi's aunt looks worried, demanding that he stop talking to me and resume his household chores. He shouts back at her to be quiet. The man's visit has changed Gazi. His smile disappears, and in its absence, his large eyes are filled with sadness, and anger remakes the contours of his face.

Gazi now speaks quickly, and confirms that smuggling happens, along with illegal barters and protection rackets. Smugglers are ruthless, and many of them work in close collaboration with the BSF guards and the local politicians.[6] The local elections, Gazi believes, are mostly a 'show' to decide every few years who will control the smuggling routes. He says that some of the killings, arrests and torture along the border have more to do with guards settling scores over smuggling cuts than any sort of border enforcement. Villagers live among smugglers, pimps and criminals, often provide safe havens for Bangladeshis crossing over, and sometimes turn a blind eye to women and children being trafficked. The clandestine economy thrives under the strong military presence of the state. 'You need money even [to fall in] love. Food first and the rules next,' he explains, justifying the complicated moral choices that people are forced to make every day.

No one chooses to become a smuggler, but people here go to great lengths to make a few extra rupees: 'You can build [a] strong wall, but cannot end the smuggling completely . . . You cannot tell people to stop feeling hungry. You can't stop people from doing things, even stealing or lying if it made life only a little better.'

Gazi rattles off a list of the commonly smuggled objects: electric fans, radios, batteries, milk powder, honey, sugar, salt, cattle, rice, cough syrup, clothes, tires, medicine to stop pregnancy, seeds and sometimes just green chillies. He quietly shrugs.

Towards the end of our conversation, Gazi mentions a young girl who was killed crossing the border two years back at Anantapur, in Kurigram district, located a hundred miles north. He doesn't remember her name, but he does remember the photographs of her lifeless body hanging on the barbed-wire border fence were widely shared on Bangla TV. 'People said they let her die without water. For them, we are not people,' Gazi says. 'They treat us like cattle. They see us as a herd.'

An internal BSF training manual from 2013 describes the so-called 'key attributes' of the Bengal border population: 'Predominantly Muslim', 'Illiteracy, backwardness and poverty', 'Inclination of youth towards easy money' and 'Hostile towards the forces'. Many of the officers and guards entrusted with protecting the border see the people they are supposed to safeguard as reductive stereotypes. Along the India–Bangladesh border, where acts of coercion and violence have become the new normal, this logic is used to justify treating 'barbarians barbarically', a sentiment I hear from many officers.

An officer at a border checkpoint in Petrapole remarks, 'They don't drink, so they use cough syrup.' In the eyes of the state, the locals are not citizens to be protected but subjects to be watched, disciplined and punished.

The longer we speak, the more comfortable Gazi feels with my presence. We walk to the river behind his house, and he wades into the water to retie the ropes that anchor his little catamarans to the riverbed. He relaxes his early hesitance to complain. Gazi does not describe himself as a victim of BSF brutality, but he seeks to explain how this peculiar place is cannibalising itself in an attempt to survive. In the process, the necessities of everyday civility are being eroded.

In Gazi's world, complaints, complicity, resistance and accommodation go hand in hand. Everyone abides by an informal treaty between unequal partners who nonetheless contaminate each other's existence.

Gazi's village could be any village along the India–Bangladesh border. This is everybody's daily life, and everybody's disaster. The BSF constables in Gazi's story do not have names. I notice this same detail in all the other stories I hear over the next month along the border with Bangladesh. The BSF men from other Indian states are 'foreign' for all purposes. They speak languages alien to this place and come from unfamiliar, distant parts of India. Though part of the same nation, they are foreigners in the local imagination.

~

Back on the road, I headed north towards the medieval city of Gauda, home to scattered fifteenth-century ruins and a significant border checkpoint between India and Bangladesh. To reach Gauda, I had to first head to Malda. The trip would take at least a couple of days and cover about 200 miles from Basirhat, so I made multiple stops along the way, trying to meet and interview officers and guards in as many BSF camps that dotted the border along the road to Malda and Gauda as I could.

On my second day, I finished my interview with an officer named Trivedi and left the BSF camp I'd stopped at. Our long, difficult interview felt more like an interrogation, and ended with the officer accusing me of being a 'spy'. This was at the beginning of my travels in 2014, and I was still learning how to interview officers, soldiers and men who held immense power in these liminal spaces. The years I had spent interviewing American and NATO soldiers in Afghanistan did not seem to help me here.

A few hundred feet outside the camp, I saw a group of young recruits gathering for their evening tea and cigarettes. When I heard Tamil being spoken, I ordered my cup of tea and responded in Tamil, hoping to break the ice. Many of these BSF recruits were from rural Tamil Nadu and Andhra Pradesh. The fact that I could speak the two languages of those regions—Tamil and Telugu—endeared me to them. Mohan, who was from Kanyakumari, asked me, in shy, fragmented sentences, how I learnt them, and where I was from.

Stories flowed both ways. I told them about my parents, who had met in college, fallen in love, and waited seven years to get married—a great love story about two young people in the 1970s who came from different castes and social classes, spoke different languages, and ended up together despite the odds. In a country like India, to fall in love with the 'wrong person' can still get you killed. I was living proof that love had triumphed. The recruits' willingness to speak so candidly came from the intimacy, familiarity and kinship that language had created in an alien terrain far from home.

Most of the recruits looked like teenagers. Harish, for one, had graduated from grade ten and spent a year without work before he went to a recruitment rally in a nearby town. This was the farthest he had ever travelled from home. He was no stranger to state violence: the village he grew up in lies in the infamous Red Corridor along the Andhra–Odisha border, where, at the height of the Naxalite-Maoist insurgency, the state burnt down entire villages in counter-insurgency operations. The Red Corridor covers the eastern, central and southern parts of India affected by the insurgency. The most affected areas are among the poorest in the country, with significant economic inequality. The insurgency has been ongoing since the late 1980s, and more than 6,000 people have died in this twenty-year fight. As a young boy who grew up seeing how violent and ruthless police officers can be, Harish almost venerated the power his BSF uniform gave him.

Harish said he was lucky to have found this work and others who spoke Telugu there. He and other young boys like him stayed inside BSF camps and spent little time off the clock. His world was filtered through his immediate superiors and commanders. As a new recruit, his job was to wait, watch and learn by example. His phone was his main conduit to the outside world. He called his mother often. Harish told me he was in love with a girl, Sandhya, from his village, and was trying to get her mobile number through friends who were still back home. 'This week I will have her number,' he assured me, and his friends cheered him on. He had poems he had written for her on his phone and hoped to send her these as a declaration of his love.

He showed me movie clips and pictures of movie actors and actresses he had stored on his phone. I told him that he resembled one of the young actors in a photograph and he blushed.

I asked Harish and his friends if they had heard about the fifteen-year-old girl who was killed while climbing over the barbed-wire fence that Gazi had told me about. Harish and the other recruits drew a blank. Since first hearing the story, I had found and read news reports that at least established the basic facts.

Felani Khatun and her family, like hundreds of thousands before her, crossed over into India a few years ago. Felani's father, Nurul Islam, was taking her back to Bangladesh to have her married. They crossed the border at night by climbing over the barbed-wire fence in Anantapur, Phulbari. Reports say Felani's clothes caught on the barbed wire and she screamed in panic. A BSF constable fired at her, wounding her fatally. What happened next is disputed, but in Gazi's gruesome version, Felani struggled to stay alive for four hours, begging for water before dying.

I told Harish that her killing happened only a few hundred miles from there, in Phulbari. He was shocked that the constable was charged. 'How can you punish someone for doing their job?' he wondered. He started speaking quickly, defensively. 'The local population is not friendly to us. The human rights cases and complaints are fake,' he asserted.

I tried to describe the crossing, the shooting, the wounding and Felani's eventual death. The brutality of it all escaped my audience.

Frustrated, I showed Harish the macabre image of Felani's body hanging from the fence with two guards in the background, which I had saved on my phone. Seeing that image on the phone created a visceral intimacy. Death soured the conversation.

Harish asked me to write down the girl's name so he could look it up on the Internet later. He seemed disturbed, and our conversation ended in awkward silences and a few stilted comments about new fences being built along the India–Bangladesh border.

As I travelled through the region for the next few months, I asked several more BSF guards and officers along the Bengal frontier about Felani. Like Harish, most had never heard of this incident, and often replied stating how impossible it was to protect the borders along my route without 'coercive force' or 'some kind of violence'. Another young officer at the Amudia border outpost, farther north along the border, said, 'These women cross illegally and cry rape; they smuggle goods inside their purdah . . . Some are Indians only in name; all of them have relatives in Bangladesh. Family means more than the lines.' He went on to show a video on his phone of his team apprehending two women smuggling in Nike shoes.

By the time I returned home from this leg of my trip, Felani's trial had taken place in a court set up by the BSF. The accused, Constable Amiya Ghosh, was acquitted of culpable homicide, and the evidence against him was deemed 'inconclusive and insufficient'.[7] Constable Ghosh and thousands like him are responsible for the preservation of the state's grip on these places, where they are vested with the power over life and death without any accountability to the law. These men are not inherently evil, wicked, sadistic or vile. Yet, they are terrifying in that, with all this power, they are trained to act, not think. The constant reinforcement that the borderlands are a different space, a contentious space, or an exceptional space where order must be established through force, enables exceptional acts of coercion and violence. In Felani's case, the most clinical argument in defence of her killing was that 'since Felani and many others like her were illegally transgressing into Indian territory—often at night, paying touts and traffickers—they were "not innocent" but "legitimate targets"'.[8]

At the border, the dominant narratives about illegal migration, national security, counter-insurgency and illicit trade can be difficult to see past. Yet, daily life constantly undermines these stories. The use of violence has not stopped migration or illicit trade, nor has it secured the border. Instead, the social and personal cost of the crossings has simply increased.

When I asked this question of a BSF guard in Taki, a small town situated on the Ichamati, he acknowledged the difficulties of guarding the border: 'They all look the same, speak the same.' Then he added, 'That is why we need to keep a close watch.' His response was the perfect distillation of Indian nationalism, a foundational myth about the nation's beginning and who belongs within its boundaries and who doesn't.

'There is no end to the ideology of difference,' said Pakistani political scientist and writer Eqbal Ahmad.[9] Along the borders, people are regularly reduced to their religious and cultural categories. Bengali is divided into Hindu Bengali and Muslim Bengali. Within Muslim Bengalis, individuals are further classified as locals or Bangladeshis. Sorting people into categories is accomplished quickly on paper and in policy. But in practice, how do you differentiate between local Muslims and the Muslims from Bangladesh, who speak the same language, follow the same customs, and are part of the same cultural and literary lineages?

~

I finally reached Malda in the evening, having come a little over 200 miles from Basirhat over the course of three days. I stayed in the clean and sufficient government-run guesthouse, run by the Ministry of Tourism. The next day, I rented a car arranged by the guesthouse manager and left early towards Gauda, with my driver and guide, Asim bhai. The manager at the hotel that I stayed at back in Calcutta had given me Asim bhai's number after I'd mentioned that I wanted to see the ruins. The people I met, spoke to and interviewed often looked out for me—introducing me to people they knew and safe places I could stay at, or, when I couldn't find a place to stay, opening their own homes to me.

Asim bhai reminded me of my father when he was younger. Tall, dark, mustachioed, with an interesting hooked nose and a curious face. He had studied history as a young man and abandoned his career as an archaeologist when he failed his first semester at the Institute of Archaeology in the 1990s. After working as an insurance salesman for twenty years, Asim bhai returned from Delhi and became a tour guide. He told me that when Radcliffe's boundaries were published, Pakistani flags were hoisted in Malda and the other Muslim-majority districts from the morning of 14 August 1947 until 17 August. The Muslim League and locals alike had assumed that these districts would be given to Pakistan, but they became part of India instead.

Gaur, or Gauda—once ruled by the Gupta and Pala empires, and later by the Delhi and Bengal Sultanates—was the ancient capital of Muslim Bengal circa 1450 to 1565.[10] The fifth most populous city in the medieval world, Gauda was reduced to ruin and decay by the end of the sixteenth century.[11] Located southwest of present-day Malda, it survives only as these abandoned ruins, now divided by an international border. Most of the ruins lie in India, and a few lie in Bangladesh. The Kotwali Darwaza, or Kotwali Gate, that was once part of a great fifteenth-century fort, now marks the border checkpoint between the two countries.

I first saw images of the Kotwali Darwaza, and the other ruins of Gaur, in the British Library. Joseph Beglar took the images in

1870 for the Archaeological Survey of India (ASI). John Henry Ravenshaw, an amateur photographer and a British civil servant who also photographed Gaur, described the arched Kotwali Darwaza 160 years ago: 'Even in its present ruined state, this gateway is one of the most imposing sights in Gaur; tamarind trees overhang it on all sides, while large pipal trees may be observed springing from the center of its walls.'[12]

The ethereal prints of the Kotwali Darwaza I saw preserved at the British Library bore no resemblance to the border crossing with trucks, hawkers and throngs of people waiting to pass through. The arch had fallen, and the tamarind and peepul trees were gone. The flanks of the arch remained but were in the last stages of decay, held by new walls on the sides and barbed wire. A newly constructed tar road ran through the gateways, and two wooden gates acted as the makeshift doorway. A bright blue metal sign next to the monument compressed the gateway's seven centuries of history into four sentences, in all caps, and used two different spellings in the same text—Gaur and Gour:

> KOTWALI DARWAZA
> About 30 feet high and 12 feet wide. This arched gateway now in ruins was the southern entrance into the outer ramparts of Gaur. Approximating in style to early Delhi architecture it was probably built between the earliest inscriptions at Gaur (1235 AD) and Alauddin Khilji's death in 1315 A.D when influence of Delhi predominated at Gour.

With three photocopies of your ID and permission from the local BSF post, you could climb to the top of the ruins. The guard took turns staring at my voter ID and my face, and said, 'You don't *sound* Indian.' After I showed him my passport, still unconvinced, he asked me, 'Why are you here . . . alone?' The guard demanded that Asim bhai present his driver's licence, car documents and border ID card. He returned from the car with these documents and his tourist-guide licence issued by the Ministry of Tourism, with the words Incredible India written on the top left corner. The guard asked Asim bhai if I was his girlfriend, and 'if this was our day out', with a creepy grin. Bhai responded with a stern face—'She is a writer'—and said nothing more. After more questions, and another thirty-minute wait, we, along with a newly married Gujarati couple, were allowed to climb the ancient gate reinforced by concrete.

A BSF guard climbed with us and stood next to me as I looked around. The husband asked his new bride to film him from his phone, as he shouted: *'Bharat mata ki jai'*, *'I salute our armed forces'* and *'Our soldiers will take back what was denied to us in the Partition'*.

He proceeded to narrate to the camera that this was once a 'Hindu temple that the Muslims had pillaged and built on top their forts'.

Asim bhai ignored the diatribe, while the guard who had accompanied us looked bewildered, refusing to be in the video. The guard asked that the man read the ASI sign at the base, and reminded him that this was not a temple, but part of a structure built during the Delhi Sultanate, as a gateway to the medieval city. The man ignored the guard and started his descent down, with his new bride still filming the tirade. From the top of the Kotwali Darwaza, I saw India and Bangladesh spread out on both sides. I looked at Asim bhai and asked him if he was okay; he smiled. Here, the past did not graciously extend an invitation to the present. And I feared for what the future held, when history was so quickly rewritten one social media video at a time.

From the gate at Gauda, we headed to Gunamanta Masjid, another set of ruins a few miles away, completely empty of tourists. The decaying mosque built in 1484 stood in silence, surrounded by lush green forests. As the evening light turned yellow, I could see the intricate designs on the columns and vaults that resembled the rib-vault churches of Catalonia and Andalusia. These relics had survived the plunder of the city by the Afghans in the sixteenth century CE, the coming of the British and then a struggle for freedom, followed by the Partition that divided unequally between the two countries the history, the Sultanate past and the ruins. Asim bhai told me that tourists don't come here, given that it's farthest away, and lesser known. The last time he had driven a British couple here was almost four years ago. He knew intimately the history of the ruins and its various encounters with outsiders. Yet, he didn't think of these decaying structures as ruins or even as history. The stones of Gunamanta have been interpreted in many ways. For the British explorers, these ruins became a way to not only document the colony but also reconstruct its history. For the present-day Indians, they are either tourist destinations that mean very little, or contested sites, the histories of which are being quickly rewritten. Asim bhai told me that, in many of these ruins and lesser-known shrines, he now regularly saw vandals place images and idols of Hindu gods and goddesses.

When we rewrite history, we exclude people. We violently cast Muslims, who are equal inheritors of this land and its past, as foreigners. When we exclude them from our history, we can quietly exclude them from this land. If we could preserve these ruins and see them as part of our shared history, then perhaps we could live in a present that makes space for multiple ways of life to coexist.

~

The next day, I left for the village of Phulbari, a seven-hour drive from Malda, where Felani Khatun was shot next to Border Pillar No. 947. Phulbari lies right next to the border fence, less than a thousand feet from Bangladesh. Through the Bangladeshi rights organisation I was in touch with, I connected with a local teacher, who met me a few miles outside the village. From there, we walked to the village and through the narrow lane that Felani and her father Nurul passed through to cross from India to Bangladesh. It was evening, and I stood a few yards from where Felani had been killed. The earth was wet, and the smell of the recent rain was still in the air.

Ashraf Ali, a witness to the murder who lives two minutes away from the spot, joined us and pointed to where he saw Felani hanging for hours after she died there.

Felani was the eldest of six children. Her father, Nurul Islam, and his family lived in Bongaigaon in Assam. When he first crossed the border with his mother, it was still porous. He was very young, and his father had just died. They moved so they could earn a living. He worked as a ragpicker, pulled rickshaws and worked in brickfields. All his children, including Felani, were born in India. Nurul Islam had arranged Felani's marriage with her maternal cousin Mohammad Amjad Ali, who worked at a garment-manufacturing factory in Dhaka. To cross the border for the wedding, Nurul made a deal with the Indian smugglers Mosharaf Hossain and Buzrat for Rs 3,000. Felani never made it to the other side of the fence. When her clothes got tangled in the barbed wire, she started to scream. In response, the Indian border guard Amiya Ghosh opened fire at her. The bullet hit Felani's chest, and she fell on to the barbed-wire fence. In an interview with Odhikar, a human rights organisation, Nurul said that 'he . . . began to scream out for his daughter, but when the BSF aimed their guns at him, he had to move away'. After this, 'he lost consciousness'.[13] Five hours later, Felani's body was brought down.

That day, standing just a few feet from where Nurul Islam lost his child, I saw two children running around and playing with an orange-and-purple kite. I picked up my camera to take a picture, but Ali requested that I don't. The children here had known Felani. Here, lullabies and bedtime stories are cautionary tales of how to not stray too close to the border fences. Their images don't need to become a part of an archive of violence. Let them be children playing with kites, not bodies photographed next to a site of violence. I apologised immediately, and watched the children chase the kites.

Some moments do not have to become a photograph. As I watched these children play, I didn't quite know what I had expected to see. What memories of violence can a physical border fence hold? I saw one little girl, no older than four, pluck some purple wildflowers growing near the fence. Flowers bloom here regardless of the ruined lives, anguish and trauma, and children chase orange-and-purple kites. Life prevails over death. If only freedom could as well.

~

From a one-floor hotel in Taki, Basirhat district, I walk over to have tea where the truck drivers wait to cross into Bangladesh through the Bhomra–Ghojadanga border crossing. The boys from both sides of the border start an impromptu game of cricket in no man's land. Unlike Panitar, where the border pillar was the wicket, here, the boys use sticks discarded on the street to fashion the wicket.

I sit and watch them play. Within a few days, I become an acceptable fixture. After a week, a small, lanky boy named Dotty walks over and sits next to me. As we speak, somehow making do between his Bengali and my patchy Hindi, he greedily flicks through the images on my camera, trying to find himself in the photographs. I ask Dotty where he lives. 'The other side,' he says, pointing off in a vague direction. A couple of men slow their walk, clearly eavesdropping on our conversation. When Dotty spots them, he falls silent. He later told me that one of the hoverers was a feared and loathed informant for the local police.

To put the boy at ease, I ask him about his favourite cricketers. After a minute, he relaxes and starts speaking about cricket and the players he likes. Soon, other boys join in. When the eavesdroppers move on, Dotty asserts himself as the ringleader and introduces the other boys, offering colourful one-sentence biographies.

'Gollu, who ate too much rui fish.'

'Tutu, who has failed Class Three, twice.'

'Bulbul, who has never scored more than ten runs.'

Cricket remains the theme the next day. As I pick up my evening meal of spiced tea and deep-fried bread rolls from the tea stall, the owner, without much prompting, says he has a newspaper clipping from India's 1983 World Cup win. I ask him why he saved the clipping, and he says that everyone did back then. The win was not about cricket—it was about hope.

India was the underdog, and no one expected her to win against the mighty West Indies. The win was just what the nation needed, he says. The Emergency years of the 1970s had broken the nation's soul. Prime Minister Indira Gandhi had declared this 'Emergency' on 25 June 1975. It lasted for twenty-one months, into 1977. This is often referred to as the 'darkest period' of the Indian democracy, when civil liberties were suspended, resistance was brutally crushed, and students and all dissenters were jailed. Jobs were scarce, and the village was on the verge of a drought. He says it was like holding on to a piece of a miracle.

As I sip my tea, Lefty, one of the older boys I met with Dotty last night, smiles and walks over. He, like several others, crosses the border both ways almost every day to play a game of cricket, catch a film, visit family, shop at the markets or, occasionally, attend a wedding. For a time, his frequent crossings had been easy, but over the past decade, barbed-wire fences have gone up, floodlights have been installed and the number of uniformed men patrolling their dusty roads has increased.

A moment later, Dotty joins us at the tea stall, wearing a long blue cricket jersey that hangs all the way to his knees. The front is emblazoned with India, and on the back is Dhoni 7 in yellow. The bright blue is fading on the sleeves, and small holes dot the hem. The jersey, Dotty says, is his prized possession and a gift from his father, who has migrated to find work.

'When is your father coming back?' I ask. Dotty shrugs and says he doesn't know. The land here is getting harder to farm, and the border-fencing project cuts right through many farmers' fields. In some cases, the villagers can only reach their land through a gate between 8 a.m. and 5 p.m. The last time Dotty's father was home was over a year ago, but he had returned with enough money to pay off the family's debts. He left again a week later for Kerala, almost 1,500 miles away, with an 'agent' who promised better pay of Rs 300 a day—three times more than what he would make here as a day labourer.

Lefty says he's heading north the next day to run some errands, and I should come along and meet Sharif. Lefty assures me that the old man, originally from Noakhali (now part of southeastern Bangladesh), speaks 'good English', 'watches English news' and 'knows a lot about everything'.

No one knows precisely how old Sharif is, just that he came from Kolkata forty years ago to run a small restaurant and a couple of telephone booths. His empire of tea and telephones serves as a local meeting point, where Sharif holds court each night on the state of the republic, Tarkovsky films, Bollywood and politics. So, the next day, Lefty and I huddle into a rickshaw and head north. After a little more than two hours, we arrive at Sharif's eclectically furnished tea stall, full of metal-beamed wooden furniture in earthy, seventies-orange tones, with red-and-yellow leather cushions that have seen better days.

Sharif is a distinguished-looking man with a full head of white hair and a day's growth of beard. Lefty introduces us in rapid Bengali, and I catch the word 'cricket' in the quick banter between them. When Lefty leaves to run his errand, Sharif addresses me in English. 'People started calling me Sharif after *Doctor Zhivago*,' he says with a chuckle, 'because I looked a little like Omar Sharif.'

He speaks with the clipped accent of India's English-speaking elite of another era. He quotes Wodehouse and Orwell, sometimes adding his own lines to their famous passages. Sharif would have fit right into the clubs of Raj-era Calcutta, sipping gin at three in the afternoon, but in this porous border zone, his diction and disposition are anomalous.

As we sip our tea, Sharif says, 'Tell me about yourself,' adding, 'How can I help, my dear?'

I tell Sharif about my travels along the border with Bangladesh, explaining that I plan to make my way along India's borders with Burma, China, Tibet, Pakistan and Nepal. I tell him about my conversations with Lefty and Dotty, and how a question about a game of cricket made a little boy comfortable in a place where even children are being spied on.

The game of cricket, says Sharif, has changed beyond recognition. Sportsmanship no longer drives the sport, he laments. Cricket has become the embodiment of bourgeois nationalism, performed for commerce and politics.

Sharif tells me about his years in Calcutta as a student, listening to the All India Radio (AIR) cricket commentary: 'Many of us learnt English diction listening to these greats speak.' Until the late 1950s, the commentary was in English. He adored the commentator Bobby Talyarkhan and spent hours in front of the mirror practising lines from the commentary he had committed to memory. It was a different time and, in many ways, a different world, one where princes and scions of crumbling dynasties were the guardians of the game. Cricket was not yet open to the masses. The Presidency matches played before Independence and Partition were mostly communal games featuring teams based on religious groups, where Hindus, Muslims and Parsis played against each other. Sharif shakes his head. 'Imagine, on one hand, the country was caught up in the growing demand for freedom, and on the other, we were playing communal gladiatorial matches, pitting Muslims against Hindus.'

The communal games continued until 1946, when Pakistan became a political reality. For many like Sharif, Partition ushered in an unforeseen future.

'Perhaps I was too young, but no one could have predicted the turbulent months that followed Partition—the riots, violence and mayhem that was unleashed. Calcutta felt like hell's playground on earth. And there was so much anger and pain. So much was lost, and so quickly. Some of us got to choose, and others had no choice. When people first came here, we called them refugees, and now we call them illegals. But a Bengali is a Bengali no matter where the line is drawn. He was a Bengali when Pakistan was created and is still one when it became Bangladesh.'

News travelled slowly in 1946. It had taken weeks for Sharif, in Calcutta, to hear about the riots that killed the last of his family and the fire that burnt down his ancestral home of Noakhali.

It took a long time for Sharif to come to terms with Partition, but nothing marked the new country's existence more decisively than India and Pakistan playing each other in 1951, when the newly minted Pakistani team toured Delhi, Bombay and Lucknow. Sharif remembers celebrations on the streets when India won the matches in Delhi and Bombay, as well as the violent reaction in Lucknow when India lost. The sport had become a battle between the two nations. Just a few years earlier, they had shared one cricketing history and the same players, but the wounds of Partition had carried over to the game.

'Do you know that Pakistan's first cricket team captain, Abdul Hafeez Kardar, had played Test cricket for India first?' Sharif smiles. 'The father of Pakistani cricket started his career playing for India. Imagine what he must have felt? Only years ago, he had played for India, and now he was back to a place he had once called home, to play against men he had once played with on the same team.' Such were the irreconcilable ambiguities of life.

Sharif has never returned to Noakhali, and he couldn't go if he wanted to: in 1951, the local river consumed the town. 'There was too much blood for the earth to soak up, so the water consumed it,' he says. Like Kardar's India, Sharif's Noakhali is a mythical home built on imagination. He remembers nothing about it. What stories will Lefty, Dotty and the rest of them tell in the years to come, and where will their stories begin?

'It feels like Partition is still alive,' says Sharif, of living on a border becoming ever more fortified. 'We pass its memory on from one generation to another.'

3

NEAR JALPAIGURI

'THEY STOLE MY DREAMS'

Without consideration, without pity, without shame
They built around me a great towering wall.

And now I sit here and despair.
I think of nothing else: this fate gnaws at my mind;

for I had many things to do out there.
When they were building the walls, how could I not be aware?

Yet never did I hear the clatter of the builder, or any sound
Imperceptibly they shut off me from the outside world.

– Constantine P. Cavafy, 'Walls'

Ali was thin. His eyes had sunken in, and his cheeks clung to his face.

When I met him, he hadn't seen or spoken to another person in over three weeks. His house was dark and dilapidated. All the windows were closed and sealed, and all the light was snuffed out. Old newspapers were stuck together and plastered onto the windows; another thick layer of duct tape held these papers together and sealed any gaps around the edges. The darkened windows reminded me of photographs I had seen from wartime Sarajevo. The borderlands had become a different kind of a battlefront.

Ali was fighting the light, and he had lived in this darkness for almost two years now. He refused to allow candlelight inside his home, so we sat in blackness. His house had nothing except a worn-down mattress, and two shirts and a pair of dark grey trousers that hung right next to the main wooden door.

Ali's childhood friend Jamshed ran a small hardware store, and convinced me to travel with him to see Ali. He had heard from the local teacher whom I had interviewed days earlier that I was 'speaking to people about the border'. So Jamshed found me at the hotel where I was staying, bringing a small plastic bag full of images of himself and his friend Ali. I told him I wasn't a journalist, and this wouldn't be in any newspaper.

'The border runs through him,' Jamshed told me. 'You have to speak to him. You have to. He is almost gone, but I don't want his story to be gone too. Will you write this down?'

Two days later, Jamshed picked me up early in the morning, and we drove to Ali's house. Jamshed lives near the hamlet of Murikhawa, cradled by the river Mahananda, which acts as a natural border between India and Bangladesh here. The town of Tetulia, or the 'City of Dreams', in Bangladesh, is only 600 yards away. The Murikhawa border outpost in Jalpaiguri, West Bengal, was one of the first places to install the border fence and floodlights.

When the boundary was announced in 1947, this section of the border was forgotten and left unmarked due to an administrative oversight. Some villages that lie within Indian territory remain off the official map. Some appear as part of Bangladesh. Conversely, some villages on the Bangladesh side appear within the Indian map.[1]

From here, we drove another forty miles east towards Ali's house, and it took us almost half a day. We passed through three BSF checkpoints, and were stopped at each for over an hour. At the last checkpoint, the guard made the biggest fuss.

After much back and forth, Jamshed convinced the guards to let us through. I left my Nikon DSLR camera with them as collateral, and after more negotiations, a box of Cadbury chocolates I happened to have with me finalised the agreement. They would allow us to pass, but we had to return before sundown.

Ali lived right on the edge of the India–Bangladesh border. His village, once porous, was now almost completely sealed off and floodlit by the enormous lights on the borderline. Once the village thrived on the cross-border markets and cattle trade, but now it was almost empty. In the last sixty years, agriculture had become unsustainable, fish disappeared from the rivers, almost everyone slid into debt, and people were forced to move because of cyclones and the constant flooding of the region. In some cases, people moved after bouts of violence. 'It gets worse each year,' Jamshed told me, as we walked towards Ali's house. No one reports on these 'small pogroms', Jamshed said, alluding to the steady rise in violence against Muslim communities that lived there. We walked another twenty minutes down the winding road that took us past a small seasonal river. The border fence was visible from this small country road, ugly and menacing, submerged in at least a foot of marshy water.

Jamshed remarked that 'all this land was once rivers and chars', remade after every rain. Large parts of these rivers were reclaimed to build these border fences. But the men who put these fences here forgot that the river always finds its way back and, because the fences hover over soft marshes, people can easily duck under to cross back and forth.

Unlike the Punjab border, where the area was cleared of people, the Bengal border was messy. How do you remove twenty million people from their homes?

A few minutes later, I saw a floodlight emerge between the lush green trees. Jamshed pointed to one of these floodlights, and told me, 'Below the light is where Ali is.' The terrain became wetter and marshier the farther we walked. The last two houses we passed before Ali's were abandoned.

As if in a panopticon, a large floodlight stood just a few feet behind Ali's house. The floodlights had been erected almost three years before, and the bases of these structures were already turning crimson red from the rust. Ali's home appeared on no maps. It lay on one of the last remaining stretches of porous, unfenced international border left over from an administrative error. There are still parts of the border where no one quite knows where India ends and Bangladesh begins. Even the BSF soldiers sent to guard these arbitrary lines often ended up on the wrong side by mistake.

Jamshed went inside to greet Ali and convinced him to come out for a bit. Ali then stepped out of his house with his hands stretched out to touch the walls for support. It took him a few minutes to adjust to the light.

Jamshed had brought his friend some local cookies, flavoured with rose water.

Ali looked famished and small. The handsome young man I had seen in Jamshed's pictures a few days back had clearly changed.

I would compare many photographs from the past to the many people in front of me as I travelled the length of the border. Those who stood before me as I listened to their stories were vastly different from the images of themselves they showed me. The photos became an aide-mémoire to a time they could no longer return to. In those moments, the photograph became a cruel reminder of possibilities that were lost, and the people before me looked like a faded copy of their former selves violently dragged into a nightmare.

Ali managed a smile and offered to make tea. Jamshed started a fire, in the open stove on the right side of the courtyard, to boil water. We sat in silence for a while.

Ali requested that we go inside his house. 'I don't like the light anymore,' he told us. The water boiled with the loose tea leaves, sugar and milk that Jamshed had carried with him.

'What do I tell her?' Ali asked, looking to Jamshed as we sat inside his house in darkness. We finished the tea with the too-sweet rose water-flavoured biscuits as Ali recounted the first time they ate these cookies as boys.

I had got used to the dark, and I thought I saw a faint outline of a smile on Ali for the first time. Jamshed spoke, holding his friend's hands lovingly with care. Ali mostly nodded, and sometimes managed a smile, only interrupting when he thought Jamshed had some detail wrong.

The pair told me stories from their childhood: swimming in the nearby pond, catching fish and making the first trip as young men to the nearby town to see movies.

'In the middle of the pond runs the zero point,' Jamshed told me.

The 'zero point' is where Bangladesh and India meet, the official demarcation between the two countries. But this border is peculiar in that the zero point differs from where the actual border fence stands.

In 1959, a military subcommittee of Indian and Pakistani delegates agreed that, once the boundary was demarcated, neither side would 'have any permanent or temporary border security forces or any other armed personnel within 150 yards'[2] from the boundary line established by Cyril Radcliffe in the Partition twelve years earlier. The agreement between the Government of India and Pakistan was referred to as the 1959 Ground Rules, and listed a series of procedures to end the disputes and incidents along the Indo-East Pakistan Border Area.

The Radcliffe Line cut through villages, markets, rivers, farms and even houses. The border turned neighbours into citizens of different countries—India and Pakistan—in 1947. After the Liberation War of 1971, East Pakistan became Bangladesh, and these rules were confirmed again in the 1974 Land Boundary Agreement between India and Bangladesh.

In 2007, India began the construction of a border fence 150 yards from the zero point, which left substantial areas of Indian farmland, villages and families living close to the border outside of the fence. According to some estimates, 890 families are still living outside the border fencing and 200 of these are in Barak Valley, all waiting for the monetary compensation and rehabilitation package the government had promised them.

Bangladesh objected to the construction of the fences within 150 yards from the international border, alleging that the fencing and border roads violated the guidelines of the Ground Rules. Bangladesh has neither border fences nor border roads.

Officially, the land between the zero point and the border fence is Indian territory. But the construction of the fence created a no man's land within the national territory.

Ali was trapped in this no man's land.

The farmlands and houses caught in this purgatory can be accessed only through gates built along the border fence. Every time a person crosses these gates, they need to present their identity card. An estimated 150 million people live in 111 border districts along India's land border and many don't have any form of ID card, and often face harassment on account of not being able to prove their identity. In this part of the world, living in a country does not necessarily entail possessing documents that confirm it.

~

Ali got married in 2004. When he turned twenty-one, his mother arranged for him to marry K., a girl of sixteen, from across the border in Bangladesh. Ali first met his wife on the day of their marriage, and Jamshed had hired a photographer to document the ceremony. For a small wedding, it was a grand affair.

'I brought him a green suit, he looked like a cinema hero,' added Jamshed, still holding Ali's hand.

Cross-border marriages are common, and women from both sides relocate to get married. Ali told me that when K. made the trip with her family to be married, she had never encountered the border or its guards. 'I don't think she knew that she was crossing "illegally" to be married.'

The marriage was organised through a network of brokers in Bangladesh. A large number of women from Bangladesh have crossed into India since the early 1980s as brides, living in villages across the border, or taken to states as far away as Uttar Pradesh, Haryana and Gujarat. K.'s sister had travelled the breadth of the subcontinent—from a small village in Bangladesh to India's westernmost state of Gujarat, which shares a border with Pakistan—to be married. The villages around the border of Kutch, in Gujarat, have a substantial

Muslim population, and migrant Bangladeshi brides have settled there.

When you live so close to it, it is hard to understand what a border really *is*. 'We used to cross the border all the time before. I remember my mother and I wading through shallow waters during low tide to reach the other side,' Jamshed said, pointing in the direction of Bangladesh. 'No one here thought travelling to see our family was "illegal". I never thought I was crossing an international border; I was going to see my aunt.'

K. hadn't realised that by crossing to get married, she had become undocumented. By becoming someone's 'wife', she had lost her country. It is an odd thing to understand, harder to come to terms with. One of the only documents Ali ever saw of K.'s was a paper from her middle school that said she had passed grade seven. Another was the photograph of her entire family—all seventeen of them—grandparents, uncles, aunts, cousins, nieces and nephews, with all their names meticulously written down on the back. K. was twelve when the image was taken at her sister's wedding. Her name was spelt differently in each of these identifying documents, the only two she had: one with an *e* instead of an *i*; one with a *bhi* in the place of a *bi*.

When they got married, K. crossed the border, with sixteen of her family members. If they had married only a few years later, they would have had to pay 6,000 taka (roughly Rs 5,200) in bribes each way to cross over, and even bribes no longer guarantee for safe passage. The border itself started becoming more violent, with the border guards now ready to shoot to kill on sight. Fences started coming up, and smugglers regularly clashed with the border guards on both sides. Ali and K.'s village became a point for trafficking young girls and cattle into India, and their border became one of barbed wire, bribes, machetes and guns.

After two years, K. wanted to return home to see her family. Without passports or official documents, Ali did not know how to make the journey to Bangladesh and back. Often, police and the local BSF guards sympathised with the local families and their 'foreign brides', and left those families alone.

But even this started changing. In 2007, rumours spread that a truck full of illegal Bangladeshi women and girls had been repatriated by the local police officers from a nearby district. For two days, K. hid inside their house, refusing to come out.

This figure of the 'illegal Bangladeshi' in India became polarising election rhetoric. The explosive mix of security, immigration and religion was turned into vitriol-filled political and cultural campaigns. People can be undocumented, they can be migrants, but can they be 'illegal'? The language of the 'illegal' and the 'infiltrator' dominated public discourse. Words are powerful, and they have the capacity to normalise hate. To call a human being illegal is not only racist and inaccurate, but also dehumanising. No human being is illegal. Existing is not illegal.

Even more absurdly, while K. had no ID or documents to prove who she was, India, since 2007, has been trying to issue photo ID cards for its cattle population. The BBC reported that year that Indian border guards had 'started photographing cows in villages in the eastern state of West Bengal and issuing them with identity cards'.[3] A decade after that first report, another appeared in 2017, from the *Telegraph*. 'Prime Minister Narendra Modi,' it said, had 'initiated a plan to assign unique 12-digit identification numbers to 88 million cattle in India by the end of 2017.'[4]

~

Ali's family owned a small piece of land, caught in the middle of a no man's land. But with his ageing mother to care for and debts to pay, he started to work for a local tout smuggling cough syrup into Bangladesh.

'Everyone was doing it then,' he said with a sigh.

The tout convinced Ali that it was easier for women to hide 'small items' carried across the border, and promised to help Ali and K. procure documents and passports that would allow them to travel to Bangladesh and back legally.

K. would smuggle cough syrup into Bangladesh and smuggle back fake 'Reebok' shoes. She started making these trips every few months. The trips across the border were short, and she would leave early in the morning and return by night. They made enough money to get by, until K. returned home from one of her trips with bruises on her face.

Her cheeks had turned dark purple. She cried in pain all night and drank the codeine-laced cough syrup that she smuggled to stop the pain.

K. never told Ali what had happened. Violence against women, especially sexual violence, was routine in these spaces. Perhaps Ali knew, and he must have had his own suspicions, but he didn't want to speak to me about that night. His sentences became shorter, and he relied on Jamshed to finish his thoughts.

After the incident, the next few months were difficult. K. refused to leave their home and stopped smuggling goods. Rumours spread about the attack on K. Women in the village said cruel things. 'They had poison in their eyes and tongues,' said Ali.

They started receiving regular visits from the local police. Sometimes the men asked for bribes and threatened to arrest K. Because she was married to Ali, K. could not be deported back to Bangladesh, but that did not stop the threats from the local police. The local tout also threatened the couple and demanded that K. resume smuggling goods across the border. A month later, at night, two drunken men arrived at their door, demanding sexual favours from K.

Ali mumbled, with tears running down his cheeks, 'I fought them off that night, but I knew it was no longer safe here.'

The next week, Jamshed gathered some money, and helped Ali arrange for K. to cross the border again to go live with her parents. They contacted a smuggler who would help her cross the border and accompany her back to her village six hours away.

Ali never had a passport. There was no way for him to take K. back home 'legally'.

'We had no money left to bribe the guards, just enough for K.,' he told me. 'I thought she might be safer there.' Ali paused and said that if he had had the money, he would have accompanied K. to Bangladesh.

That was the last time Ali saw his wife. K.'s family was too poor to support her, and soon she moved to the capital city of Dhaka. She found work in one of the city's many garment factories, sewing buttons on designer dresses, working ten hours a day for less than Rs 2,000 a month. K. pleaded with Ali many times over to come to Dhaka, to start a new life together. But Ali wouldn't. Once she sent him a picture wearing a pretty blue dress she had stitched. 'Her friend Nazma took the photograph. She looked happy.'

'I know many men travel far and wide. They risk their lives. But I couldn't. I have always lived here. This is what I know. I did not want to be a fish out of water.'

'She would call at night and ask if I was okay. Every time she would ask if I could come to Dhaka, I would say I will think about it and then she would cry.' In 2012, a garment factory in the district where K. worked caught fire. Over a hundred people died working in inhumane conditions. K. saw the building burn and lost friends to the fire that day.

'That night she called and pleaded again. I said nothing . . . and the calls stopped. She is better without me.'

~

By 2010, the border fence encircled Ali's home and his land. His small plot, caught between the zero point and the fence, had plummeted in value. He sold it for Rs 18,000 to pay for his mother's medicines. Compensation was only given for the patch of land where the fence was erected. People like Ali received nothing for land that became no man's land, or for the income they lost by being cut off from their workable land.

In 2012, Ali's mother died. He had by now spent close to a decade struggling. 'All this struggle makes no sense. Is life so difficult for everyone? Or is it just me?'

In 2008, the Indian Ministry of Home Affairs confirmed in a press release that floodlights had been installed on 172 miles of the most frequently crossed sections of the border.[5] By 2012, the lighting project was expanded to cover another 1,765 miles of the border with Bangladesh, at an additional cost of US$ 275 million.[6] As the geographer Reese Jones writes of the border, 'the panopticon of the Indian state need not be imagined; it shined bright all night long for many of the Bangladeshi borderland residents.'[7]

A few months after his mother's death, Ali was summoned to the BSF camp. The floodlights had been installed without much care or consideration for those who lived next to them. Through a local 'leader', they convinced Ali to sign papers saying he was okay with the lights. He was even paid for that concession. For Rs 20,000, of which he received only Rs 13,000 in hand, he said, 'I gave away my right to protest.' Ali isn't sure what the documents were, or what was written on them.

Ali had forgotten all about the lights, until one night, he returned home and found this house filled with bright orange light. 'I tried sleeping, but it was difficult.'

Within a week, he felt tired and depressed, and started feeling mild pains in his body. Two weeks later, he fainted at the brickkiln factory he was working at and was fired soon after. He tried to approach the local BSF to seek help, but he wasn't allowed inside.

In the weeks and the months that followed, Jamshed says Ali's words started slurring; he experienced mild paralysis of his left arm and started getting panic attacks.

Then came the hallucinations and nightmares. Ali wasn't sure if what he saw and experienced was real. He dreamt of wild dogs mauling his mother, the BSF torturing K., and the smugglers humiliating him by stripping him naked and parading him on the street. He stopped eating.

In the middle of the night, Jamshed got a frantic call from Ali, saying hounds were hunting him. When Jamshed arrived, Ali was lying face down, naked, outside this house. Jamshed called for help, but no one came. By now, Ali had come to be ostracised as a cursed madman and his neighbours stayed away. Jamshed cleaned and bathed his friend and put him to bed.

Jamshed went to the local store and got newspapers, and dark fabric to cover the windows. When Ali woke up, he felt calmer.

'After a long time, I felt safe, and I found a small piece of home in this darkness,' Ali said, grabbing the sides of his mattress.

After that temporary breakthrough, Ali became obsessed with this darkness; he got more paper, duct tape and fabric. Every crevice in his home was plastered and sealed. He started staying in, more and more.

When he did step out, Ali became disoriented even walking around his village. Small tasks—like buying food, washing clothes or fetching water from the nearby pond—felt like an adventure into the unknown.

Then one day, the nightmares stopped, along with all of his dreams.

'I can't dream anymore. I haven't for almost a year. They took my land, they stole my life, they stole my future, they took my nightmares and they stole my dreams too.' It was getting dark, and Ali looked tired and anxious. 'I never thought I would miss my nightmares.'

'The lights will come on soon. I need to lock everything,' he said.

Jamshed took out a few packets of biscuits and potato chips from his bag, and stacked them against the wall next to Ali's mattress. He hugged his friend lovingly and carefully, like he was worried he might break Ali if he hugged him harder.

Ali asked Jamshed if he had the pictures from his wedding day, and he quickly pulled them from his plastic cover. Ali touched his image and smiled. 'I used to be handsome,' he said. 'What happened to me?' Jamshed held Ali's hand tight again, kissed his friend on his forehead lovingly and said goodbye.

As we walked away, we could see the border lights come on.

When we reached the car, I leant against the door on the driver's seat. Like he had done with Ali, Jamshed reached out and held my hand for a few seconds.

We got inside and drove back towards the first of the many checkpoints we had to cross that night.

~

In 2018, Ali was reported missing by Jamshed. Ali remains missing, to this day.

I called Sharif, whom I had met in 2014 in my first leg of journey along the India–Bangladesh border, to read this finished chapter to him. His number rang for days but no one picked up. After two days he called back, and I read him the chapter. 'They did steal his dreams,' he told me. 'They stole mine too.'

In December of 2019, Sharif passed away. I found out through a text message from Lefty.

PART III

THE INDIA–CHINA BORDER

The border between India and China remains contentious and has never been clearly demarcated. The Line of Actual Control (LAC) between India and China—named by the Chinese premier Zhou Enlai as part of an informal ceasefire after China invaded the region in 1962—is part of the disputed border region, currently claimed by both countries, known as the North East Frontier Agency (NEFA). The India–China border is divided into three sectors: western, middle and eastern.[1] The disputes in the western sector pertain to the Johnson Line, which was mapped by the British in the 1860s.[2] The western sector included Indian-administered Kashmir and the Chinese provinces of Xinjiang and Tibet. After Independence in 1947, the Government of India used the Johnson Line to establish its western boundary, which included Aksai Chin, which lay within the territory of the princely state of Jammu and Kashmir. A.G. Noorani writes, 'After Independence, the Ministry of States, headed by Vallabhbhai Patel, published two White Papers; in July 1948 and February 1950. Both showed the entire northern boundary from the India-China-Afghan trijunction, the subject of the Sino-Pakistan agreement, to the India-China-Nepal trijunction as "undefined", in contrast to a clear depiction of the McMahon Line in the east.'[3]

Following Independence, India laid its claim based on boundaries inherited from the British.[4]

China disagreed. Although the existence of the LAC was

confirmed by an international treaty in 1993, certain stretches of its 2,167-mile length are not mutually agreed upon.

Initially, in the early 1950s, China did not object to India's claim. Today, Aksai Chin is claimed as part of Xinjiang by China and as part of the Himalayan Ladakh region by India. The region is incredibly inhospitable, with temperatures regularly below freezing, and the average altitude there is 14,000 feet.

The middle sector is the only part of the line where India and China have exchanged maps on which they broadly agree.[5] The eastern sector of the India–China border, marked by the McMahon Line, is highly disputed.[6] Here, China claims significant areas of Arunachal Pradesh, which it refers to as 'Southern Tibet' in its maps.[7]

At the Simla Convention in 1913–14, China, British India and Tibet met to discuss an agreement to settle boundaries between Tibet and India, and Tibet and China. Chinese representatives subsequently refused to accept it. Nearly seven decades since, the border issue remains unresolved.

4

TAWANG

CARTOGRAPHIC CONFUSION

After two months of travelling along the India–Bangladesh border, I continued north to Sikkim and the border with China. I was intent on going to Tawang, a Buddhist monastery town near the India–China border located in India's northeasternmost state of Arunachal Pradesh. The sixth Dalai Lama was born there in 1683, and it houses what is considered the most important Tibetan monastery outside of Tibet. It takes about twenty hours on the road to drive the 300 miles to Tawang from Itanagar, the capital of Arunachal Pradesh—a reflection of the crumbling road networks in the region. The border roads are maintained and built by the Border Roads Organisation (BRO), a notoriously corrupt agency[1] that employs thousands of migrant wage labourers from the rest of the country. Despite their efforts, the road to Tawang is a muddy, rocky, unpaved single lane dotted with army camps. As the driver of the car I hired struggled to navigate this dangerous road from Itanagar to Tawang, we were passed by army trucks, convoys and shared jeeps crammed with local passengers.

Tawang is about sixty-two miles from the LAC in the eastern sector. Since the 1962 conflict, the region has been increasingly militarised. In the eighteenth and nineteenth centuries, NEFA was neither Indian nor Chinese. Even after the British took control of nearby Assam in 1826, most of what is now NEFA was left 'unadministered'.

The British historically viewed the northeast frontier as foreign, forgotten and neglected. As late as 1900, this area was considered outside the control of the British dominion in India. In the 1930s, a British soldier touring the Kameng Frontier Division, present-day Arunachal Pradesh, described the territory north of the Sela Pass as 'forbidden, because it belonged to Tibet'.[2] While Tibet cast a shadow of influence over the area, the region was composed of independent indigenous tribes too small and unorganised to form 'states' by any imperial measure.

Today, the Sela Pass is a transformed place. No longer empty and uninhabited, it is now heavily militarised and home to the notable shrine to Jaswant Baba. As the story goes, Jaswant Baba or Jaswant Singh Rawat was a brave Indian soldier who died in the Sino-Indian War of 1962 after fending off the invading Chinese troops for three days—cementing his reputation as a revered local deity. Soldiers and tourists alike travelling through Sela visit the shrine to pay their respects to the hero.[3]

Shrines to fallen soldiers are scattered throughout this region, and new ones emerge all the time. The names of the soldiers commemorated in these shrines differ, but the stories follow a similar arc. The soldier always single-handedly fights the Chinese and keeps a marching army at bay for up to three days, sometimes longer. Often a local girl helps him; she is called Sela, Nuranang or Bumla, after whom these passes were named when the war ended.[4] The soldier and the local girl fall in love, only to be betrayed by the girl's father. It is this betrayal that leads to the soldier's final capture and death. Without that betrayal, perhaps he would have prevailed.

In remote Achingmori, a village in the Upper Subansiri district in Arunachal Pradesh, lies the shrine of Sher Jung Thapa. The plaque describes him as 'a valiant soldier of the Indian Army' who stood his ground against a major assault by the Chinese in 1962, adding, 'Alone, with only a light machine gun, he killed several Chinese soldiers.'

Most of these shrines have no historical basis, and many fall outside the actual theatre of the 1962 war. And, of course, no single unit or individual ever engaged the Chinese troops for three days.[5] But a heady mix of folklore, Indian mythology and romance create a potent nationalistic fantasy. In these tales, the soldier represents India, and the local girl, Sela, embodies the region. The father's betrayal captures some of India's mistrust of a region with ties to China.

When I first got to the Tawang region, I was introduced through a local journalist to 'all the people I must meet'. He handed me a premade checklist stocked with army officers, NGO workers and a few locals 'who had witnessed the 1962 war'. As I sat down to interview them, it became apparent that there was a script in place. In my experience, people speak faster than they think, and often stories retold from memory are fraught with false starts, confusion and a sense that the person is trying to fathom the past in words. Here, everyone I spoke to responded in perfect sound bites. In these, an old war was being retold—the facts changed a little, timelines meandered and, by the time I was done with the interviews, it felt like India had indeed won the 1962 war.

I asked the local journalist why he wanted me to speak to these specific people. He responded that this was the same list that went around when new journalists from Delhi arrived every few years on the anniversary of the 1962 war. 'I mix it up,' he said. 'That way it's not the same, but similar. Same difference.'

'Same difference' sums up much of the Indian republic's minimal engagement with this part of the world.

Even after the Simla Convention, the Government of Tibet continued to exert influence over Tawang for another twenty years.[6] In 1959, the Dalai Lama passed through Tawang as he fled Tibet and went into exile in India. Today, China claims sovereignty over Tibet and Tawang, referring to the region as 'South Tibet' on its maps. Since the 1962 war, the area has remained at the heart of the China and India territorial dispute and has become highly militarised, including by massive military presence in the town of Tawang. More than a quarter of the land in Tawang district has been taken over by the Indian Army and paramilitary forces.[7] Another quarter has been acquired by the civil administration.[8]

In the Indian-mainland imagination, Tawang remains an untamed frontier, with stunning landscapes emptied of people and their history. There is very little understanding or consideration about how many lives have been remade by the escalating military presence and territorial disputes. Local histories of protest, discontent over development projects, and concern over the destruction of sacred lands, loss of local languages, oral histories and traditions seldom make it to the news.

~

While Indian national history obsesses over the 1962 war with China, it rarely remembers the earlier events that ultimately set the stage for the war to come a decade later. In 1951, the Indian Army set their sights on Tawang, under the command of Major Ralengnao (Bob) Khathing of the Second Assam Rifles. Khathing, the man 'sent to take over Tawang, was a Naga'.[9]

The orders given to Major Khathing by the prime minister's office were unequivocal: his task was to occupy the area and act as if Indian administration there was 'the most natural order of things'.[10] He was to make 'it clear to all Tibetan officials that the jurisdiction in the area vested with India and not in them'.[11]

Two years later, a dominant tribe in this region, the Tagin, massacred an Assam Rifles platoon in Achingmori in the Subansiri Frontier Division. Forty-seven soldiers were murdered, and a dozen were taken hostage.[12]

Why the attack happened remains a mystery. India blamed the incident on the Tagins' savagery, while dissenters argued that the earlier military expedition and occupation had angered the locals. Before the massacre, the Tagins were rarely mentioned in official state sources.

Following the Achingmori attack, an important question was put to Prime Minister Nehru in Parliament about his NEFA policy: 'Would the Prime Minister be justified in taking action against the Tagins who did not consider themselves as Indian citizens and lived in an unadministered area outside the control of the Indian state?' Nehru answered that, while the Tagins might not see themselves as Indian citizens, that did not mean the area was outside Indian territory.[13]

Rhetorically, the Indian government had unilaterally designated the Tagins as citizens, and called their territory 'integral to the Indian union'.[14] But in practice, they treated the locals as savages to be tamed.

The official Indian account concludes that the incident and subsequent state response successfully won hearts and minds in the newly acquired Indian borderlands. In his book *Enchanted Frontiers: Sikkim, Bhutan, and India's Northeastern Borderlands*, Nari Rustomji, who served as a bureaucrat in NEFA for over ten years, describes the Indian response to the Tagin rebellion as a 'benevolent grand strategy' that allowed the Indian state its much-needed inroads into the region.[15]

S.M. Krishnatry, who joined the British Indian Army in 1942 and remained posted in the northeastern frontiers for almost thirty-five years, paints a more sobering picture. He writes that the Tagin areas were treated 'almost [like] a war zone', adding that when the Indian Army arrived at a Tagin village three weeks after the massacre, 'the only things they could find were abandoned houses, chicken, and pigs, which of course were slaughtered, and houses burnt'.[16] Clearly, this was neither benevolence nor grand strategy. It was more like a state out of its depth, unprepared and lacking basic knowledge of the people it was encountering. The incident exposed the fragility of India's position in the eastern Himalayas. Matthew Edney, a geographer and historian, writes that 'to govern territories, one must know them'.[17] But can one govern knowing just the territory, and not its people?

During my time in Tawang, I discovered many parallels between the state's narrative of the Achingmori incident and the 1962 war as remembered by the locals. In the Tawang monastery, I spent long hours speaking to the older monks, who had lived through the 1962 war, and the younger monks, who felt strong sympathies to the Arab Spring protests and the acts of self-immolation in the Tibetan resistance, and many of whom were also part of local protests against the new dam constructions. Since 2011, Tawang witnessed a series of public protests against the Indian government's decision to set up fifteen dams across the district. Concerned about environmental and ecological damage to sacred lands (and the ongoing practice of confiscating local lands for military and administrative use), the local Buddhist monks and people from the local Monpa community came together to stop the construction. In these protests, the monks were regularly beaten and injured by the local police.

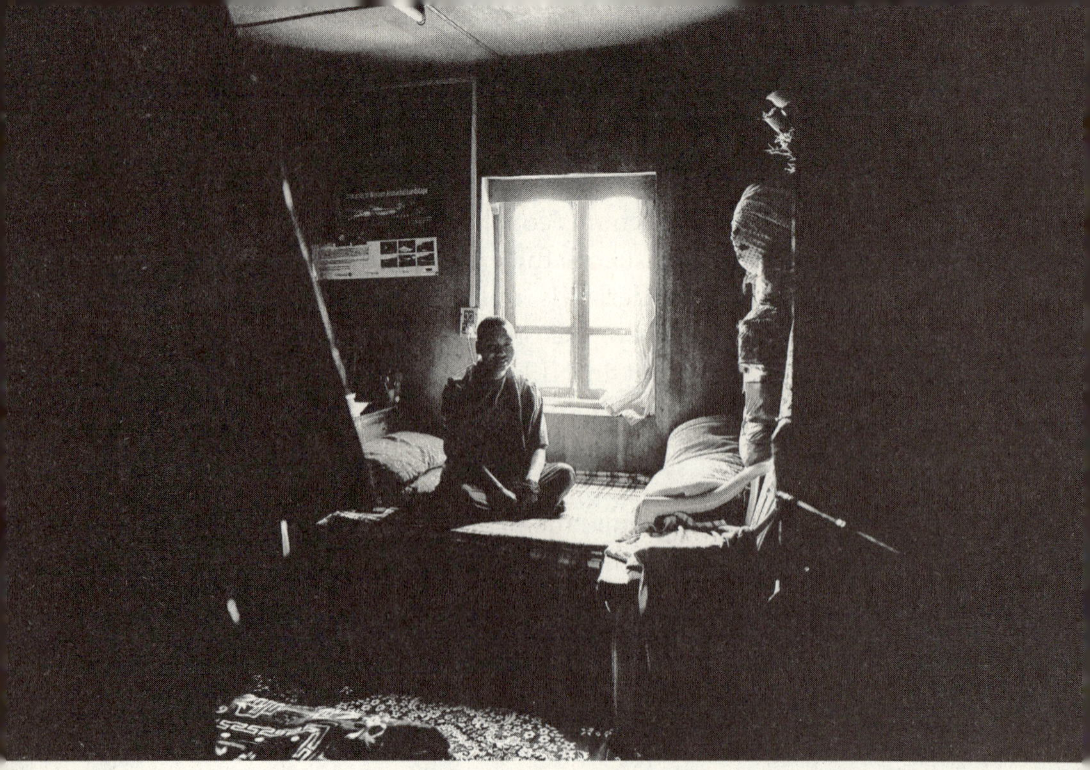

Those who witnessed the 1962 war and suffered its aftermath have not forgotten the Indian Army's humiliating defeat at the hands of the Chinese. By the time the Chinese marched into the Sangti valley, nine miles outside Dirang, on the Bomdila–Tawang highway in the West Kameng district, the Indian Army was long gone. A seventy-eight-year-old monk recalled seeing the decaying bodies of many Indian soldiers on the slopes of Dirang. In his words, 'You can raise Indian flags and call us Indian. But people do not forget that the Indian Army deserted us. [The] Chinese occupied parts of this land and [these] people. We lived under occupation.' The occupation lasted for a month, and was somewhat benevolent, with the Chinese throwing lavish feasts with dancers and entertainers. But those who survived have not stopped feeling abandoned by India.

Of course, the word occupation is never used in official Indian descriptions of the story. Today, the narratives of what really transpired during the 1962 war continue to conflict. In India, the 1962 war is regarded as an 'unprovoked surprise attack by an expansionist China.'[18] In response, China has maintained that the 1962 war was a response to perceived Indian aggression.[19]

Given China's continued occupation of Tibet, and India's inability to fortify the border infrastructure—leaving ill-equipped soldiers and a lack of decent roads, hospitals and schools even after all these years—many in Tawang believe that China will attack again and fear that history will repeat itself, only more violently.

Before I left Tawang, I made a trip to Bumla Pass, located about twenty-three miles from Tawang in Arunachal Pradesh at the India–China border, a full 15,200 feet above sea level. The People's Liberation Army (PLA) of China invaded through Bumla during the 1962 war. To visit, Indian citizens require special permission from the army.

As I entered Bumla, the breathtaking sight of the Himalayan frontier—and a small board that says, 'no civilian beyond this point'—greeted me. The pass had been recently opened from the Indian side and made into a tourist destination, but I saw few tourists around, except families of soldiers on holiday, being driven back and forth to the base. Next to the actual border stood a small peace memorial where people could leave pebbles by the flags with Tibetan prayers.

At the post, I met a young officer from the Indian Army's relatively new Naga Regiment. It drizzled a little that day, and he showed me around the pass with an umbrella in hand. We spoke about the insurgency in his home of Nagaland, at the Myanmar border, which, like much of India's borderlands, has a fraught relationship with central India.

Calls for Naga nationalism still ring strong among certain groups of people, so upon meeting this soldier I was curious about his experience working for the Indian military when many people in his homeland consider India an 'occupying force'. Recruiting men from one troubled, rebellious region to police another has a long colonial history that the Indian state continues to employ.

In the course of the conversation, the officer made regular references to Brigadier John Dalvi's memoir *Himalayan Blunder*. Dalvi was an Indian Army officer during the Sino-Indian War of 1962 who commanded the Indian Seventh Brigade in NEFA before he was taken as a Chinese prisoner of war on 22 October 1962, and held in a prisoner of war camp in Tibet for nearly seven months.

Dalvi's book has never been studied academically. India's foreign policy establishment continues to ignore it. Yet, the book became the basis of our lengthy conversation about the officer's experience of growing up in the heart of Naga insurgency, only to be recruited to fight 'unruly' tribes in other states in the name of India's counter-insurgency practices.

When I first spoke to him, I wondered if the young officer's constant return to Dalvi's book was a way to steer the conversation elsewhere. But when I returned to the transcripts from our discussion, I realised how closely he quoted John Dalvi. Perhaps what connected these two men across years, race, class, privilege and training was the meditation on the inherent absurdity of war and the recognition that most of soldiering involved cynical subordination to ideas that no longer made sense.

Himalayan Blunder is no longer banned in India, but even today there are unspoken rules within the army about openly reading or discussing the book, because it contradicts the official version of the India–China war written by its commanding officer, Brij Mohan Kaul, in his book *The Untold Story*.

Dalvi's book opens with the lines, 'This book was born in the prisoner of war camp in Tibet on a cold, bleak night.'[20] But its most haunting line comes a few paragraphs later when he writes, 'This is a record of the destruction of a brigade without a formal declaration of war.'[21] *Himalayan Blunder* is a story of the calamity of the border, and the lengths men in power would go to enforce these absurd lines, knowing well the human cost. But it is also a story about how truth is silenced, and how in its place acceptable lies form the basis of a national history.

The Naga officer pointed to the paragraph in the book where Dalvi discusses his return to India:

> We deplaned and were greeted with correct military protocol, tinged with chill reserve. It was only later that I found out that we had to clear ourselves of the charge of having been brainwashed . . . Without a doubt, the prisoners had been declared outcasts. Apparently, we should have atoned for the past national sins of omission and commission with our lives. Our repatriation was embarrassing as the national spotlight had again been focused on the Sino-Indian Conflict.[22]

A real accounting of the 1962 war has never occurred, at least not in India. For such an accounting would also lead to the important

question of Indian culpability, and require the country to reflect on its ongoing propaganda practices.

In the early 1980s, Karunakar Gupta, a London-based scholar who was studying the India–China border, presented his thesis that the ongoing strife at the border stemmed entirely from the suppression of facts, distortion of history, possible alterations of maps and withholding of official documents relating to the frontier. He also argued that there was a deliberate and even official incitement of nationalistic emotions in India to justify the series of political blunders that led to the 1962 war.

As a young student in London, Gupta had started researching the origins of the McMahon Line, the border between British India and Tibet. The legal basis for the McMahon Line rests on the negotiations between British, Chinese and Tibetan representatives, which took place in Simla between 1913–14. The precise nature of what transpired in these negotiations remains unclear, and the validity of the Anglo-Tibetan agreement they produced is dubious. During the meeting, the Chinese refused to sign or ratify any of the conditions discussed.

Aitchison's Treaties, a collection of British Indian treaties published in 1929–33, reported that the Simla Convention was of no political or international significance because of China's refusal to sign it.[23] A few years later, the same volume was reprinted with very different and altered information, this time portraying the negotiations that led to the Simla Convention as significant and binding. Gupta discovered both versions of *Aitchison's Treaties*, and proved that the British Indian government, mainly on the advice of Sir Olaf Caroe, a British administrator and the governor of the North-West Frontier Province, arranged for the records to be falsified by republishing the original volume with different information. Gupta argues that the documents were forged in an attempt to confuse the matter, perhaps to gain some leverage in future negotiations, but later the falsified version became an accepted fact.[24] The newly independent India inherited a fabricated border, and Gupta believed that Prime Minister Nehru was misled by his reliance on the forged British papers about the McMahon Line. Gupta's argument and conclusions brought into question India's historical claims along the Sino-Indian border and reveal the danger of flawed and forged maps—the same maps India went to war over in 1962. Gupta, almost twenty years after the 1962 war, wrote that 'Distortion of history, suppression of facts, and withholding of official documents relating to the frontier from independent historians have been as much responsible for the aggravation of the Sino-Indian border conflict as the deliberate and even official incitement of "nationalistic" emotions in India.'[25]

Gupta continued to write, research and publish his work, but was increasingly isolated from state-funded institutions. The British diplomatic historian Sir Alastair Lamb foresaw Gupta's future in his 1976 review of *The Hidden History of the Sino-Indian Frontier*: '[Gupta], indeed, is one of the very few Indian scholars to have published in India, observations on the nature of the Sino-Indian conflict, which disagree in fundamentals with the received official opinion enshrined in the writings of Dr. S. Gopal and his cohorts. For this, he may well win neither fame nor fortune in his own country, but elsewhere his courage and integrity deserve every commendation.'[26]

Gupta died in the 1980s, and as predicted, while he was admired overseas, he never received recognition in India. Students of history or current affairs do not teach, cite or reference his scholarship.

Today, much of Gupta's thirty years of meticulous research has simply disappeared.

If Gupta is to be believed, much of the Sino-Indian Frontier, the war, the current militarisation of the region and the increasing nationalistic jingoism might all be premised on a lie fabricated by a departing colonial power and forged maps.

PART IV

THE INDIA–MYANMAR BORDER

India and Burma have been culturally and commercially linked since the fifth century. Later, both countries came under British colonial rule: India first in 1824, with Burma following at the end of the Anglo-Burmese War in 1885. After occupying Burma, the British ruled it as a part of British India until 1937.

Colonial rule brought a number of Indians to Burma. The Rangoon police were entirely Indian by 1861, and in the decade after 1885, some 18,000 Indian soldiers were stationed in Burma. During the Second World War, Japan occupied Burma, and forced many Malaysian and Burmese Tamils to labour on a 200-mile railway track between Thailand and Burma. Over 150,000 Tamils died during the occupation, and many survivors fled to India. Following Japanese occupation, Burma underwent its own freedom movement and was granted independence in 1948. Since then, the country has been mired in a long-running civil war between various ethnic and political minorities and the military junta that ruled Burma for over forty years. The first democratic elections since 1990 were held there on 8 November 2015. The National League for Democracy won the elections; however, its leader Aung San Suu Kyi is constitutionally barred from the presidency, as the Burmese Constitution prohibits those with foreign spouses or children from holding the presidential office. To circumvent this, in April 2016, a new position—the state counsellor—was created to allow Suu Kyi to govern, with her long-time aide, Htin Kyaw, sworn in as president.

Like India's, Myanmar's multi-ethnic, religiously plural society suffers from the rise of xenophobic nationalism (in Burma's case, infused with Buddhism). The Burmese security forces regularly persecute minorities, like the Rohingya and Kachin tribals, many of whom have left Burma to seek asylum in India and Bangladesh.

The porous India–Myanmar border is 1,020 miles long. The McMahon Line, agreed upon by Britain and Tibet as part of the Simla Agreement in 1914, became the basis of the boundary demarcation between India and Myanmar. The border was officially declared through an agreement between Prime Minister Nehru and Prime Minister U Nu of Burma through an aerial survey in 1953. But the Nagas, Mizos and the region's other indigenous groups have never accepted this border imposed on them.

5

NAGALAND

UNIMAGINED BY MY NATION'S CARTOGRAPHY

Scattered over miles of desolate country,
where the villages have been literally pulverized,
and the shell-pocked land is like the surface of a rough sea,
there are many colonies, containing thousands of India's working classes.

– YMCA worker's account, India Office Records (IOR),
British Library, London[1]

Nagaland was one of the first places I visited in 2013 when I started travelling through the border. On the border with Myanmar, Nagaland lies at the farthest eastern end of the official Indian maps. The landscape is mountainous, made of never-ending rivers and forests; the Naga Hills rise from the Brahmaputra valley. An Incredible India brochure calls Nagaland 'the land of the festivals', and next to it are images of an ageing tribal head-hunter from Longwa village on the international border—reinforcing orientalist stereotypes of the people as noble savages who inhabit Eden.

It was here that I first heard people tell me with not a trace of doubt that they are not part of India, and that they are waging an everyday war to protect what is left of their identity, dignity and history. I had been on the road for two months. After travelling along the southern Bengal border, and making my way up to Sikkim and Arunachal Pradesh, I turned back southwards to Nagaland via Dimapur.

To enter Nagaland, I had to visit the Nagaland House in Calcutta before I began this journey to obtain an ILP.[2] As I waited for the documents to be stamped and signed, one of the officers at the Nagaland House, after looking through my documents, remarked, 'It is a disputed territory. I don't see why Indians want to go there. You act as [if] it is yours.'

At present, travel to Arunachal Pradesh, Mizoram, Manipur and Nagaland requires an ILP. The permit is a colonial relic originally implemented through the Bengal Eastern Frontier Regulations, 1873, and is still used in independent India, with the minor difference that 'citizens of India' replaced the words 'British subjects' in 1950.

Generalised as 'the Northeast', this region includes eight different states, namely Arunachal Pradesh, Assam, Manipur, Meghalaya, Mizoram, Nagaland, Sikkim and Tripura. Orientalised, and disparagingly referred to as India's 'last frontier' or the 'Mongoloid fringe', it is a postcolonial region carved out in the aftermath of the partition of the subcontinent. Here there are a thousand imagined homelands that have struggled to become reality.

The phrase 'northeast' arrived with the coloniser and his map, in which over 255 tribes, and their history, their memory and their land, were violently clubbed together into a fictional region for political convenience, administrative ease and the purpose of surveilling the border regions. Unrest and violence have been ubiquitous here. The result has been six decades of armed conflict, ranging from demands for self-determination and greater autonomy, to the assertion of more rights, to complete secession from India. These demands are rooted in a violent past that has never been acquitted.

As I started my travels in Nagaland, a friend—a musician raised in both Shillong and Calcutta, who now gives piano lessons in Kalimpong—had given me a collection of poems he had collected from writers in the region over the years. Every time he encountered a writer or a poet, he saved their poem in a document and sourced them.

When no translation existed, he crudely translated the words he could, and asked his friends for help with other languages. When he started collecting these writers and poets almost twenty years ago, there were no anthologies or collections of poetry from this region.

When I asked him what I should read, he sent these poems as a pdf along with this email:

> We have lived through so much, my dear S. Here, we struggle to find our chronologies. What book should I give you? Where would this history begin? 20 years ago? 50? 130? Or 400? What book could explain to you my Tamil friend whose history is alien to me, and mine to her?
>
> Sometimes I feel poetry is a much better signifier of our loss, hope and butchered freedoms. Read as you travel. Call when you return, else stop by in Kalimpong on your way *back.*

My friend was right; I knew nothing about curfews, martial law, or growing up around guns. I knew less about the people who lived here. We carried the same navy-blue Indian passport; we spoke about the peculiar smell of the passports, which my friend dubbed as the smell of the 'mainland imprinted through the bureaucracy'. But beyond this passport, we had nothing in common. We were strangers bound by the territorial limits of a nation that struggled to contain us. I knew nothing about his people's history. My school textbooks and the newspapers I read growing up taught me nothing of the many histories of Indian state violence.

These were places unimagined by my nation's cartography.

The poet and writer Kynpham Sing Nongkynrih, one of the most important contemporary writers from Meghalaya, appeared in my friend's pdf of poems. His prescient phrase captures this: 'Somewhere in a forgotten little corner of the world a hill tribe of one million, fearful of its extinction, waged an arms insurrection against a nation.'

My friend's other advice to me was, 'Don't orientalise the beauty of this region.' Beauty and violence coexist, but never as a binary. This stuck with me. I was here not to tell their stories, but to critique a state that was complicit in silence, violence and erasure.

~

Nagaland is home to one of the longest-running conflicts in the world. Nagas were the first to insist on independence, a separate homeland from India. Active as early as the 1950s, the Naga insurgency is the oldest and most potent resistance in India today. This region has seen insurgency, separatist movements, tribal and non-tribal conflicts. Here violence, bloodshed, conflict and corruption have spilt over into everyday life. It was not just boots on the ground that they feared; they also feared an absolute annihilation of their history, language and identity.

Before British colonisation, the Nagas had very little contact with the outside world. Like the phrase 'northeast', the word 'Naga', too, was an arbitrary grouping of otherwise distinct tribes, communities and people. The first British incursion into Naga territory took place in 1832. Captains Francis Jenkins and R.B. Pemberton attempted to map the land route from the Manipuri kingdom in Imphal to the British headquarters in Assam. What followed was a series of violent engagements that stretched over thirty years.

Most accounts from this time—missionary reports, ethnographic writings and personal diaries of British officers—all casually erase the brutality of colonial violence. The banning of headhunting, the annexation of territory, the imposition of Western-style education through newly arriving missionaries and the papering-over of complicated local rivalries were all seen as necessary aspects of a 'backward' and 'uncivilised' people's transition towards becoming one nation under the British Crown. In a letter, the secretary to the Government of Bengal writes, '[They] need to restrain the savage tribes which infest the frontier . . . existing only as pests and nuisance to their neighbours, and to wean them gradually from their present habits of plunder and outrage against inhabitants of British territory.'[3] Colonisation was described as 'the most precious gift for all those caught in the state of barbarous disorder.'[4] A certain kind of violence was not only allowed, but justified.

Eighty years later, Naga forces were enlisted and sent to France as part of the Naga Labour Corps in the First World War. The journey from the hilly frontiers of the empire to the battlegrounds in France had a profound effect on Naga political identity. A new consciousness was born, and in 1918, some of the men who returned from the war formed the Naga Club in the Naga capital of Kohima. There, three decades before India's independence, the Naga Club petitioned the British government for the right to self-determination.

As the call for self-determination in the Naga homeland grew, the world once again prepared to go to war.

In April 1944, the Japanese Army laid siege to Kohima and its surrounding villages. Kohima district became one of the last and bloodiest theatres of the Second World War. Caught between two imperial armies, many families fled and took refuge in the forest or elsewhere. Almost eighty years later, the last of the disappearing generation that lived through the war still remembers the Allied bombing campaigns and air strikes that destroyed large swathes of the district.

Eighty-five-year-old Vijunuo, in Kohima, still remembers the beginnings of the long line of violence from the Second World War to the present—from the time the Japanese forces reached Nagaland to the years of insurgency and brutal Indian violence that followed.

Here, family histories are inexorably linked to histories of loss, often told as repetitions of the past. The families that fled or lost their homes when the Indian Army burnt their villages down in the 1950s and '60s also have stories of British troops burning down their homes nearly a hundred years earlier. Like Vijunuo, families that fled during the bombing of Kohima also remember fleeing again in 1956 as the Naga fight for independence grew.

When Vijunuo returned to Kohima, after the Allied bombing, the streets were littered with bodies, and she still remembers the stench of rotting corpses. She saw people packing dead bodies into bags and burying them in the war cemetery. 'Not many people know or even remember these battles,' she tells me. For her this was a 'forgotten war' fought by a 'forgotten army'.

Khonoma village, about ten miles outside the state capital, was once the heartland of the Naga insurgency. The bloody years may have passed, but a large stone memorial built in the memory of Khrisanisa Seyie, the first president of the Federal Government of Nagaland, stands undaunted. The plaque on the monument quotes President Seyie: 'Nagas are not Indians; their territory is not part of the Indian union. We shall uphold and defend this unique truth at all costs and always.'

It was from Khonoma that Angami Zapu Phizo, founder of the Naga National Council (NNC), launched the struggle for independence from India. Nearby, another memorial commemorates General Mowu Gwizantsu, commander-in-chief of the Naga Army: 'Khonoma gratefully remembers him and the dauntless men he led in far-flung battles to defend the right of their people as a nation.'

Gravestones in most Naga villages, especially areas scarred by the insurgency, bear the name of their war dead, how they were killed and which Indian regiment killed them.

'In loving memory of Methavi, who was put to death on 29th April 1955 by the Sikh regiment,' says one grave. Another says:

> ZASIBITUO NAGA
> ZOTSHUMA VILLAGE
> A NATIONAL LEADER
> DIED IN THE FREEDOM STRUGGLE
> OF THE NAGA INDEPENDENCE
> MURDERED BY INDIAN
> ON SATURDAY 18TH OCT. 1952
> AT 10:30 AM
> 28.4.1953

A simpler gravestone in the remote Khiamniungan region bordering Burma reads only, 'India killed my son.'

Indian counter-insurgency practices often meant that the bodies of Naga fighters were deliberately left to rot. 'We have specific burial customs,' Vijunuo says, 'and in so many cases, the army refused to hand over dead bodies to the family.' She tells me the story of her friend's brother who joined the underground and was later tortured and killed. When the army refused to hand him over, the family made a small memorial plaque in their backyard, with just the date of his disappearance. According to her, beyond the Second World War, all the battles, massacres and 'emptied bullets to lay claim to this region' have been forgotten.

These many little epitaphs and plaques throughout Nagaland serve as memorials to the many dead, and to the 'little massacres', as Vijunuo refers to them, that have devastated various communities.

Here epitaphs exist where the historical record has not yet recognised the past. Each family in Nagaland has a story like Vijunuo's to tell, and with time, these stories will die quietly without epitaphs. It's not just broken bodies: stories and memories can also be buried in unmarked graves.

~

On my second visit to Nagaland, a retired teacher and former rebel, N., took me to see Garrison Hill's War Cemetery. Now in his eighties, he had lived through the brutal years of the war that he described as an era 'when a gun was pointed at you from every direction, from everyone'. He had, like Vijunuo, seen the Japanese battle for Kohima, and remembered the aftermath of the war, Phizo's declaration of Nagaland's independence and the first gunshots for freedom that were fired. He saw the Indian convoys roll into his city, and saw the first of the bunkers being built.

The violence here was generational. N. spoke about the many silences that people carried within them: 'Many of us haven't spoken about what we saw, some of us have chosen to move on, others don't even think of the great violence done to us as violence anymore . . . It is all so normal now.'

When every family here has lost someone, so cruelly, with so much violence, no one thinks of this as extraordinary. He added, 'We think it is normal . . . What do we talk about after sundown with our neighbours? Exchange notes on our dead—my family lost three, yours lost four. In these cases, one is left to nothing but regret . . . no justice.'

When you are powerless, time will acquit every crime committed against you.

In the early afternoon, as Kohima's light turned into hues of blue and orange, we walked through the war cemetery, lined with epitaphs and under a heavy silence. We came to one that said, 'An unknown soldier is buried here.' Looking down at the city, N. remarked that so many unknown civilians throughout the region were buried in small, shallow graves. They had all deserved better. 'I have lost so many people, so many, in the name of freedom. Yet now what we are left with is nothing but "reconciliation".'

By 'reconciliation', he meant the peace deal currently being held between the Government of India and the various factions in Nagaland to resolve decades-old disputes. The Nagaland Peace Accord was signed on 3 August 2015, but the exact details of the agreement remain vague.

The real loss, he told me, was that no one had asked them.

'No one has bothered to ask us what we lived through and what we lost, or what we want. In all these years.' N. told me that this was the first time he had openly talked about the past. '"Past" has become a dirty word here. I haven't told my children, grandchildren or their children anything. They will grow up without their language and their history. They will not know who robbed them of their future because we refused to teach them our past . . .'

The older he got, N. said, the more his memory faded. What he did remember was visceral: the sound of bullets—no, not quite the bullet, but the muted sounds of the 'thud' the body makes when it hits the ground.

Overlooking Kohima, the war cemetery lies on the battleground of Garrison Hill. Now a lush and serene tourist destination, this is where one of the bloodiest battles during the Second World War was fought. Due to its strategic location, controlling Kohima was crucial for the Allied troops to hold on to vital supplies needed for waging the Battle of Imphal. For the Japanese, Kohima represented the foothold it would need to implement their plan of invading India.

The cemetery contains 1,420 epitaphs of soldiers who perished in the Battle of Kohima in 1944. Their ages ranged from late teens to barely twenty and into their early thirties—what should have been their prime of life. Some were listed with their regiments, units or ambulance corps; sometimes, their parents' names were recorded beneath. I wrote down the names of as many men as possible, from as many corners of the world. Darwar Khan, born in Peshawar; William

Mackinion Currie, born in Calcutta; Henry D'Souza of Peramanur; Sepoy Eleyasar from Malabar; Hassan Gul from Kohat; Jamkishei Kuki from Naga Hills; Lance Corporal Rupert Bennett Redden, born in Kharagpur; Kabal Zar, born in Tangai, South Waziristan, in current-day Pakistan—

They fought and perished on this hill. They were Scots and Englishmen born in India, they were Khans, Dars, Pillai, Singhs and Zars. A few epitaphs contained almost no detail, simply noting that 'a soldier of the Indian Army is honoured here' or is 'known unto God'. The war records list all these men of various races, born across the undivided subcontinent, as 'Indian'.

Along with these 'Indians', American, Canadian and Australian airmen, Nepali and African soldiers, local Nagas, the Japanese and their allies all died fighting in a forgotten imperial war in an alien land.

The cemetery was almost empty except for a handful of visitors. A Ms Keanne had made the long trip to Kohima from Devon in Britain. Her father had fought here as a nineteen-year-old. Now, twenty years after his death, she emptied his ashes on the grounds. Next to her stood a man who was explaining the cemetery's history. Keanne had just spent a week in Uttar Pradesh trying to locate her great-grandmother's tomb without much luck. Her family had a long connection to the subcontinent, her maternal great-grandmother arrived to be married to a British officer, and her paternal great-grandfather had served in the North-West Provinces, and there were 'rumours', she said, 'of mixed origins'.

But this was her first trip to India, and the country was 'overwhelming', she told us. She was ready to head back home to Devon, where she had started volunteering for UKIP—the UK Independence Party—a right-wing, racist, anti-immigrant and populist party in the United Kingdom. 'We are,' she said, 'worried about the Islamification of Britain. I hear you have the same problem.'

N. quietly asked who this 'we' was, reminding her that she was standing in a cemetery with epitaphs of men born Christian, Muslim, Hindu, Jewish, Sikh, Parsi and Jain—who died fighting in an imperial war in an alien land.

Ignoring him, Keanne looked at me and said, 'We are not racist,' but continued, 'We feel we are losing our British sensibilities . . .' After another pause, she added, 'You are not Muslim, are you . . .? I don't mean to offend,' and walked away with her guide. That Keanne—whose country had colonised, plundered and made India their home—was now 'worried about Islamification' further drove home how normalised and ubiquitous anti-Muslim bigotry had become.

An American visitor named Andrew Jackson had a grandfather who had served in the 823rd Aviation Engineer Battalion—an African American unit that built the Ledo Road that stretched from Assam all the way into present-day Myanmar. Having heard our conversation, Andrew walked up to us while we were still talking to Keanne. 'The English always leave a bloody mess,' Andrew added as he saw her leave.

Andrew had travelled to the small town of Ledo in Assam and was making his way through the region. Not much is left of Ledo Road now, except for Stilwell Park with decaying plaques that tell a short history of the road. In 2010, the BBC reported that 'much of the road [had] been swallowed up by the jungle'.[5]

Andrew had come in search of old graves of the many African American soldiers who perished here. Kohima was Andrew's last stop before heading to Calcutta, and then home to Chicago.

N. told Andrew that Alberta Hunter, the legendary jazz musician, had sung her blues in Assam in a 1944 performance for the US troops that were building the Ledo Road. Andrew was thrilled to hear that Hunter had performed, but knew little about the war. His grandfather had died in the 1980s, before he was born. All he had were a few military papers and vague family history. 'No one asked him about this, no one cared to write what he went through, and I don't think he spoke about it either. Black folk don't speak about the military at our homes,' he said.

African Americans have served in every war the US has ever fought, and still, even the dead soldiers were segregated. Andrew knew stories of black veterans who had returned from serving in the Second World War who had been lynched. Andrew himself had served two tours in Iraq, the second soon after the Samarra bombings, which unleashed an urban war on the streets of Baghdad.

'I don't think Americans really know what we saw there, and did there. We just blew up a country for no reason,' he said, and added, 'I travelled so far to fight someone else's war.'

When we parted ways with Andrew, N. and I continued walking towards the top of the hill, where we met J. Sato, and saw another perspective on the war. Now in his forties, Sato was in Kohima, accompanied by his grandfather's friend, Mikio Kinoshita. At ninety-five, Kinoshita had survived the battle and returned home, but Sato's grandfather was one of the 50,000 missing Japanese war dead. The Japanese lost their entire Thirty-First Division in the single battle of Kohima. At least 70,000 Japanese soldiers lost their lives in Manipur and Nagaland when they invaded British India, and many went missing and remain buried in unknown, unmarked graves. Sato translated the frail Mr Kinoshita's words: 'We left the bones of our brothers here.' Most Japanese soldiers were buried in the villages of Jotsoma, Riisoma and Kigwema in Kohima district, and Sato and Kinoshita were here to visit these places. There were now regular tours arranged for Japanese descendants to visit these sites.

Kinoshita found Kohima and many of the theatres of engagement unrecognisable; he had hoped to remember something. For Sato, this was a pilgrimage he had wanted to make for a while. He grew up in the shadow of loss. His grandmother and mother never got over his grandfather's disappearance. For a long time, they hoped he would return.

As we said our goodbyes, Sato asked that we take his picture next to the plaque that said, 'When you go home tell them of us and say; "For your tomorrow we gave our today."'

After the photo was taken, N. remarked, 'This is the lie they sell each generation of men. Some of us don't have a home to return to; our todays are done. I shudder to think what tomorrow we have left for our children.'

~

Nagaland remains one of India's most highly policed states, and the army maintains a permanent presence and surveillance to control all local factions. Votes work on the barter system and remain the most valuable currency. Despite the value of votes, the rule of law has very little currency. Travelling through Nagaland, I found myself in the midst of the two 'parallel governments' oppressing their people in perfect coordination and complicity: the National Socialist Council of Nagaland's (NSCN-IM) Isak-Muivah faction has a Naga Army and there is the Indian Reserve Battalion. The NSCN—a modern Naga separatist group—was formed on 31 January 1980 to oppose the Shillong Accord of 1975, signed as a peace agreement between the previous separatist group, the NNC, and the Indian government. Drug trafficking from Myanmar is reported to be a major source of income for the NSCN-IM, and I heard many stories of extortion and smuggling in regions where the group carries influence. Illegal taxation is rampant. Petty crimes are policed by communities, which take the law into their hands. This is what India has to show for itself after seventy years of rule and presence in the region.

The Naga city of Tuensang, difficult to access and situated right on the border with Myanmar, is where the Naga government was first established in 1954. The people of Tuensang continue to find themselves in the crossfire of three opposing and fighting groups—the Indian Army, the Naga underground and the Burmese armed forces. During the height of the insurgency, the Indian Army came in search of Naga underground fighters. The Burmese Army also made incursions into Naga areas to weed out armed groups. The Naga underground groups targeted those they suspected were collaborating with the Indian and Burmese armed forces.

The way to Tuensang was paved with bad roads, and interrupted by blockades and stray dogs. The young man who drove me here the second time said that, when he was young, they named these dogs after the Indian Army soldiers—Mishra, Natarajan, Singh and Mukesh—and chuckled.

I travelled through Nagaland at the height of the Bodo agitations. Members of the separatist Bodo people, who have been demanding a separate statehood in Assam for decades, were renewing the attacks on refugee Muslims that had begun in the 1990s. As a result, the main roads had been blocked, and essential vegetables, fruits and pulses usually transported across state lines were in short supply. Smaller hotels and restaurants were closed. I had to buy lentils, rice and spices, and carry them with me on the road—often offering rice and lentils to a family in return for use of their kitchen. A three-day shutdown and roadblock had completely paralysed the state.

The church's presence was ubiquitous; each small hamlet and village came with a quaint church and local school as 90 per cent of Nagaland is Christian. I spoke with a local pastor in the remote

Tuensang area who wondered if India sought to keep this region as a buffer state, backward and underdeveloped: 'Look what happened to Tibet and Afghanistan, "buffer" means we are merely pawns, we are not a working part of the country. It also means that we are dispensable. Many of our children leave for the mainland but never quite fit in. They face so much racism.'

The government abuses of the 1950s and '60s right up to the '90s became the many circles of the inferno. There were cases of beheading, burning people alive, torture and mutilation. Some of these tortures and killings were committed publicly in front of the whole village. Three years later, I would hear the story of a schoolteacher in Kupwara, Kashmir, in a border village. He was beaten to death in the village square in the 1980s. Public executions and extrajudicial killings of civilians are a tried and tested counter-insurgency strategy of inflicting terror, and have been used across time and geography in India and elsewhere. Modern states, including the United States, Israel, France and many others, continue this practice to date.

As the resistance and rebellion spread into Naga Hills, in April 1956, the 'responsibility of maintaining law and order' was handed over to the Indian Army.[6] In 1956–57, the Ministry of Defence defended the violence, stating that 'due to hostile activity by misguided Nagas, the law and order situation deteriorated in the Tuensang area of the North Eastern Frontier Agency'.[7]

The 'grouping' of villages began immediately and continued into 1957. In February that year, the whole population of Mangmetong and Longkhum were moved into an enclosed area. Families of individuals who had joined the rebellion were further segregated from the 'general' population.[8] The grouping was often followed by 'burnings'.

The soldiers would inform the village headman that his village was about to be burnt.[9] In Mokokchung district, almost every village was burnt, several times over.[10] Mongjen village was reportedly burnt seven times, and Mamtong nineteen times, before the villagers finally surrendered.[11] This method was justified as being used to cut off access to food and shelter to the insurgents and those resisting the Indian state, but it resulted in mass starvation and homelessness. Multiple search operations and curfews accompanied the grouping and burning operations.[12]

Sometimes, the regrouping took place long after the village had been burnt, and the villagers spent the intervening period in the jungles or fields around their former homes. We walked to some of the remote border villages, many inaccessible and only reachable by a long trek. Many of the women we met refused to speak, and many had never encountered an outsider, except the Indian soldiers.

Ya was close to eighty when I met her in a remote border village in Tuensang district. Almost sixty years ago, as she was on the way to her fields, an Indian Army patrol convoy raped her. She doesn't remember how many men there were, or their faces. They all became one violent, faceless nightmare. When she recovered consciousness, she discovered many 'marks' on her body, and she was bleeding profusely.

'They had left me to die alone.'

The story of her rape soon spread. It was one of the first known instances of rape by Indian soldiers, and she was left to die on the street by the soldiers to send a message. She remained alone her whole life: 'No one was willing to marry me, I got no help.'

'I am not the only one,' she told me, her face still stoic.

Every family had these gruesome stories. And many of the women lived in shame and pain because of what was done to them.

It was late afternoon when I left Ya's house, and my translator friends walked ahead. I walked towards a border pillar across the old helipad built by the Japanese during the Second World War. Without realising, I found myself on the Burmese side of the border.

I knew I was in Myanmar because the Burmese border security guards I ran into informed me that I had crossed the border, and I was quickly taken into their custody. The men spoke in a mishmash of English and a language I didn't understand. They explained that they had to inform their Indian counterparts on the other side of the border, the Assam Rifles, who would come and pick me up. I was not allowed to walk back unaccompanied, even though I was just ten yards away from 'India'. When I protested, I was told that the penalty for border crossing was three years in Burma. I had to choose—they could take me to the nearest police station inside Burma, a day's drive away, where I would face charges. Or I could wait for the Indian soldiers.

INDIA
146 B.P.
1970-71

Mere hours before, I had heard Ya tell me about her ordeal, and the women who sat next to her had listed their own dark encounters with the Indian military. A few weeks earlier, Toyoba, a Rohingya refugee I met in Calcutta, had told me about the brutality that the Burmese border security force, the Nasaka, had inflicted on his family. He had told me stories of raped women, dismembered bodies and burnt-down mosques.

I felt an unexplainable emotion—sickness in my gut, a mix of disbelief and disgust. I had never felt this specific fear before. When I felt a hand on my backpack, I froze. Were they about to grab me, like they had grabbed Ya? I shuddered.

The fear made me heavy, and I found it difficult to move.

The men spoke politely, offered me pork stewed in pickled bamboo shoot. I waited patiently for the soldiers from India to arrive and take me back. Two hours later, five soldiers arrived, looking excited. I was told this was the most exciting thing that had happened here in a long time.

The soldiers from opposite sides of the border greeted each other like old friends. The Indians offered to make tea with the firewood, and the Burmese set their radio to the AIR station. In this part of the world, the radio frequencies and cell phone towers could pick up signals from both sides. The soldiers complained about their commanding officers and drank their tea.

There was no official handing-over ceremony: once the tea was finished, everyone got up to leave. Before we went, the Burmese soldiers alerted the Indian soldiers to a body they had spotted recently while scouting the no man's land between the two countries. 'Not ours,' the Indians responded. 'Must be the locals settling scores.' With quick banter, the matter of the unidentified dead body was settled, and I was escorted back across the border. The soldiers dropped me off at the guesthouse and told me to stay out of trouble.

I went inside and locked myself in. When I reached for my notebook, it was gone; I had left it across the border in Myanmar. I flung my phone across the room in rage and broke into tears. I did not know why I was crying.

I showered and lay on the little cot, exhausted; I still had my friend's collection of poetry that I had printed weeks before. In it was Manipuri writer Robin Ngangom's poem 'Native Land':

First came the scream of the dying in a bad dream,
then the radio report, and a newspaper:
six shot dead, twenty-five houses razed,
sixteen beheaded with hands tied behind their backs inside a church.
As the days crumbled, and the victors
and their victims grew in number,
I hardened inside my thickening hide,
until I lost my tenuous humanity.
I ceased thinking of abandoned children inside
blazing huts still waiting for their parents.
If they remembered their grandmother's tales of many winter hearths
at the hour of sleeping death,
I didn't want to know, if they ever learnt the magic of letters.
And the women heavy with seed,
their soft bodies mown down like grain stalk during their lyric harvests;
if they wore wildflowers in their hair while they waited for their men,
I didn't care anymore.
I burnt my truth with them, and buried uneasy manhood with them.
I did mutter, on some far-off day:
'There are limits,' but when the days absolved the butchers,
I continue to live as if nothing happened.

I underlined 'when the days absolved the butchers' and 'live as if nothing happened'.

I drew a large breath and started rewriting my notes.

6

NELLIE

STUCK BETWEEN REMEMBERING AND FORGETTING

Massacre is a dead metaphor that is eating my friends, eating them without salt.

Massacre opened the door to them when other doors were closed, and called them by their names when news reports were looking for numbers.

Massacre is a dead metaphor that comes out of the television and eats my friends without a single pinch of salt.

– Ghayath Almadhoun, 'Massacre',
translated from the Arabic by Catherine Cobham

Nellie is one of the small villages in the northeastern state of Assam's Nagaon district. It carries the heavy history of having been ground zero of one of the bloodiest massacres in India. More than 3,000 Muslims—mostly women and children—were massacred there and in the surrounding villages on a single day in February 1983. Local eyewitness accounts of the massacre report a much higher number of fatalities.

Newspaper reports appear sporadically on the anniversary of the massacre, repeating the same information and always referring to Nellie as the 'forgotten massacre' in which 'illegal Muslim immigrants' were killed. But those who buried their dead and returned to live next to these graveyards have a different memory of these events. And after three decades of silence, they now bear the burden of explaining, repeating and narrating what happened in Nellie over and over.

~

With Guwahati, the capital city, as my base, I travelled throughout Assam. Each day, I would travel out to the villages where the communities I wanted to speak with lived, and return to the guesthouse. In my earlier journeys along the borderlands, I would travel along the border for months at a stretch and return home when I ran out of money. I lived in cheap hotels and government guesthouses, and sometimes even slept in the car when I couldn't find a place for the night. When I returned in 2018—thirty-five years after the historic massacre—much had changed for me and this book. I had given birth and left my eighteen-month-old daughter behind. As the rhythm of my life and my body had changed, the way I travelled and moved in the world also changed. I felt sure that this trip was my last chance to finish the journey that I had started almost five years earlier.

The last five years had also affected the politics, moods, rhythms, joys and sorrows of the people of Assam. Two realities dominated daily life: the ebb and flow of the mighty Brahmaputra and Barak rivers, and the battle to establish who was 'Assamese'. Almost all the people I encountered there were either made or broken by the rivers, as well as by the battle to establish who they were.

A third of Assam's border with Bangladesh is porous—about 162 miles of the border are fenced, and about fifty-nine miles are along the river Brahmaputra. The river is dotted with 'char chapori' or 'chars', shifting sand islands that are created and remade each time the river Brahmaputra ebbs and flows. These shifting chars are also homes that people leave every time the land erodes. Every three or four years, when the chars become unliveable, its inhabitants move in search of the next liveable char.

Independent India inherited the former British protectorate of Assam, a region that today shares borders with Bangladesh, Bhutan, Burma, China, Sikkim and Tibet. If history had taken a different turn, Assam might have been given to Bangladesh (then East Pakistan) in the Partition scramble. In the 1950s and '60s, Bengali Muslims were deemed 'illegal infiltrators' from East Pakistan and regularly

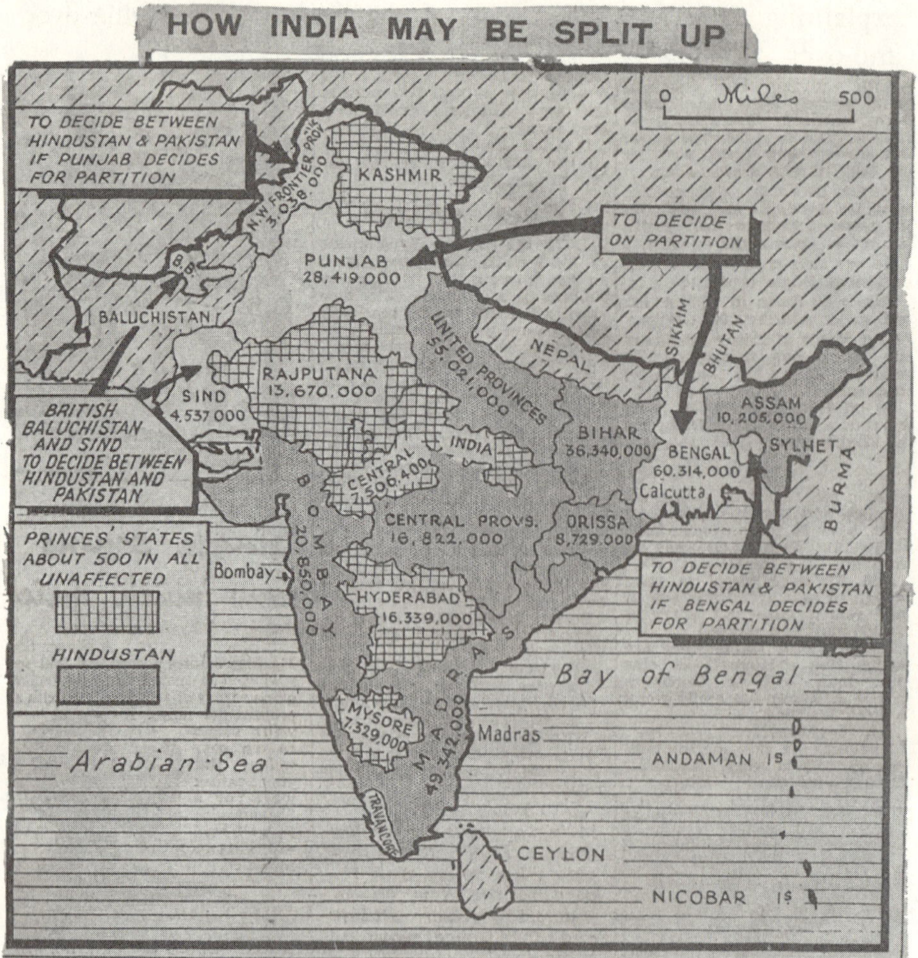

expelled en masse from Assam. When Bangladesh became an independent country in 1971, popular anger against Muslims in the region intensified. It was often reported that 'Bangladeshi Muslims' were illegally migrating into Assam through the porous border to escape poverty, and the news reports often exaggerated the numbers. Almost anyone who was Muslim, even if they had lived in Assam for generations, was viewed as a foreigner and illegal immigrant. In Assam, the term 'Miya' is used as a slur to brand Assamese Muslims of Bengali heritage as migrants from West Bengal, or worse, illegal immigrants from Bangladesh—a grave accusation that can lead to the loss of Indian citizenship.

By 1980, the All Assam Students' Union (AASU) led an anti-foreigner movement. The students' union called for an election boycott and threatened Muslims with violent consequences if they voted. Many believe that the Nellie massacre was orchestrated to punish the Muslims for defying the election boycott and voting in the February 1983 contest. It started in Borbori village on the morning of 18 February 1983. Nellie and fourteen other villages were surrounded by a mob armed with guns and machetes.

~

Nobin Hussain waited on his bike at the head of a small forked road that leads into the village of Nellie. I followed in my car. Over three decades after the massacre, Nellie had not changed. I had expected it to have transformed like the villages I'd seen in Bosnia, Rwanda, Palestine and Kashmir in recent years. Instead, it looked just like the images I had seen from the 1980s. Nellie had clutched its memories and retreated into itself. There were no memorials or sites of mourning. And nothing in the village suggested that it had borne witness to one of the worst massacres in modern history. As we drove past the village shops and the houses, people stared in confusion. A local journalist named Ahmed, who accompanied me on the trip, said, 'People here are not used to outsiders. No one comes here anymore. No one goes out unless it is absolutely necessary.'

Nellie was not remote: it was just a few miles off one of Assam's main roads. Its isolation was a choice.

In the other villages I visited in Assam, I observed something similar. Most communities were self-segregated by religion. People drew circles around their existences and, with each successive bout of misery, violence and heartache, these circles became smaller. So did their territory of belonging. Towns shrunk into villages, villages into streets, and streets into homes.

The world went on around them, but violence had rendered it incomprehensible. In many of the Muslim villages I visited, people hadn't seen an outsider in over a decade. Now, when outsiders did arrive, it was usually the police rounding up residents accused of being foreigners or illegals by a local tribunal. These tribunals function 'to detect and deport non-citizens', officially referred to as 'foreigners', staying in Assam.[1] Once accused, the burden of proof is on the individuals to establish that they are citizens who belong.

As we drove into the village, the tar roads became gold-coloured, single-lane sand tracks. On both sides sprawled lush farmland, dotted by small ponds.

The village was getting ready for the evening when we arrived. People were leaving the farms and returning home from work. Nobin Hussain parked his bike on the side of the road, crossed the street and pointed to a mostly empty plot of land surrounded by farms. Overlooking the ground was a small mud hut where children between the ages of three and ten were playing hide-and-seek and imaginary games with a yellow ribbon. The area was called Dohotia Habi: a mass grave where, thirty-five years ago, Nobin buried close to 350 children between the ages of two months and ten years.

As we stood on the edge of the open space and spoke, the family that lived near the grave brought out plastic chairs for us to sit. Some people walking by recognised Nobin and stopped to share their own story. Their losses fit together like a puzzle connected by the burden of having been left behind. Most Muslims in the area claim to have lived there for generations, and hold on to crumbling paper documents that establish their claims to citizenship.

A woman in a light green sari, with large fish motifs printed on its edges, said of the 1983 massacre, 'I had left for a wedding and when I returned, everyone was gone.'

An older man returning from the fields added, 'I lay under a corpse for two days before they found me.'

A younger man in his thirties whose family then lived on the other side of the river added, 'We saw bodies float by the river.'

The men and women also sang, remembering their dead through music. As I sat and listened to this spontaneous communal mourning, I felt like a tourist of emotional pain, recording and cataloguing the memories of those who had lost everything. I had been a stenographer of other people's tragedy all my life. Yet, what had this chronicling achieved?

I thought of a book of Russian folktales I was given in my youth. In one of those stories, the old woman has a cautionary tale for her granddaughter, who keeps asking for more stories. The grandmother says that everyone can only carry so many stories during their

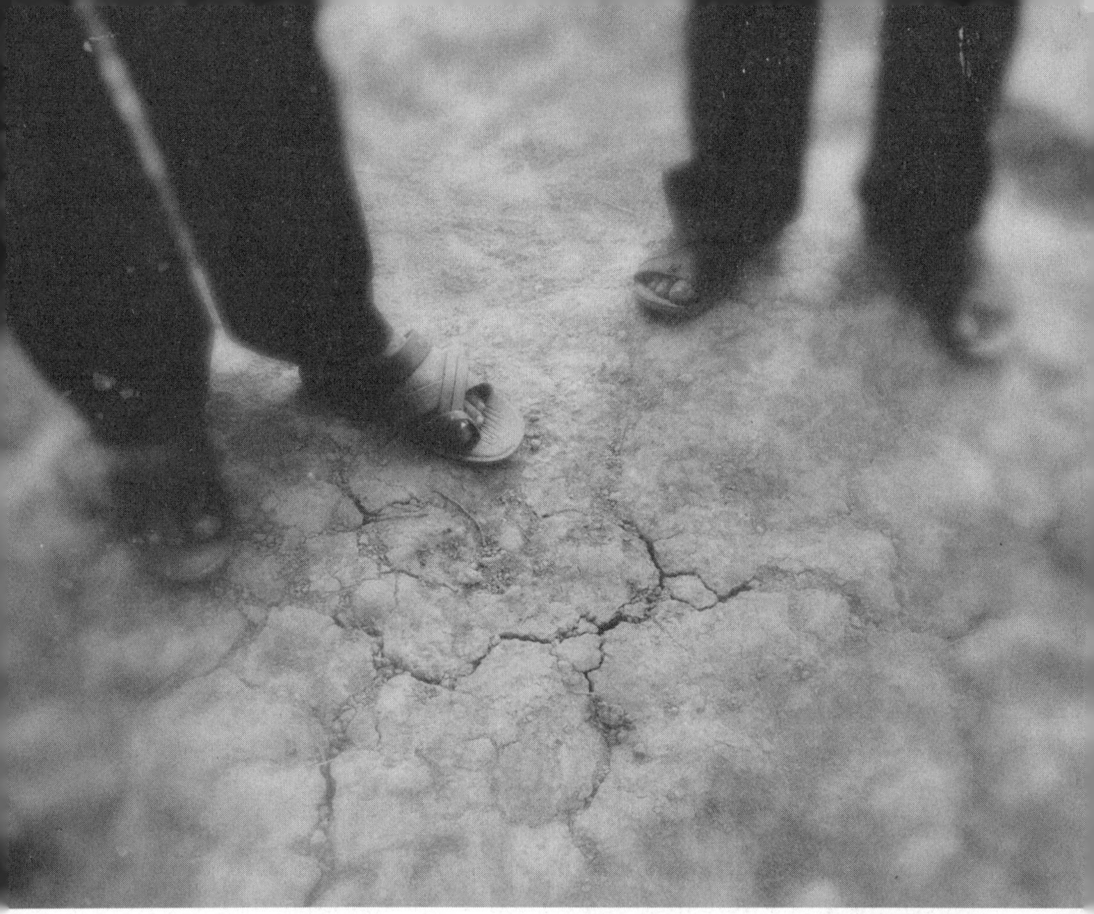

lifetime, and when the earth becomes heavy with them, the stories will either explode into stardust or float away quietly into the sky.

By now I had reached the number of stories I could hold. I wanted some of them to float away into the dark sky so that I could see them from a distance.

Nobin, now fifty-eight, has lived his entire life in Nellie. He was twenty-three when the massacre happened. Around eight in the morning, mobs of a few hundred men from outside the village gathered and started torching the houses. As the fire spread, people started running. When they poured into the streets, guns and machetes confronted them. The mob, Nobin tells me, was made of local Tiwa tribals, Hindu Bengalis and local Assamese.

Nobin was attacked and shot at. With a wounded leg, he ran towards the local Central Reserve Police Force (CRPF) camp, hoping to get help. The men who attacked him were not his neighbours, yet they seemed to know the landscape of his village well. They had strategically placed themselves around the perimeter of the village and blocked all the paths leading out. When people tried to run to safety, the mobs were waiting to slaughter those who fled. These were men who enjoyed killing and had come prepared to inflict the most damage.

Anyone who managed to outrun them was hunted down and brutally hacked to death. Young men who tried to fight back were 'finished off' first. Once the men were 'taken care of', it 'became easy to slaughter the women and children'.

With his wounded leg, it took Nobin a few hours to reach the highway on foot. He ran towards the first Muslim home by a mosque that had not been torched. With the help of that family, he tried to inform the police in Jagiroad, the precinct in charge of Nellie, and the troops from the CRPF.

When he finally met the police officer in charge, the man accused Nobin of being one of the rioters and threatened to arrest him instead. While Nobin was still pleading with the police officer, the CRPF troops finally arrived. The soldiers did not speak the local language, and Nobin struggled helplessly to convince them to come to the village and help.

'They didn't believe us. They just ignored us.'

Two more hours passed before Nobin and another young man,

Abdul Muttalib, who had also escaped the mob, finally convinced the CRPF to go to Nellie.

By the time the CRPF arrived, the last of the mob had dissolved into the dusk. Neither the police nor the CRPF made any attempts to arrest the rioting men. Over 3,000 people were killed in Nellie and the fourteen other Muslim-majority villages nearby in one day.

When Nobin returned in the evening, he found his home partly destroyed. In his absence, his eldest sister, Jamila Khatum, had been shot dead. He found her at the entrance of their house, still clutching her two children, who had been hacked to death.

That evening the survivors gathered at a local school and held vigil all night. They started searching for other survivors the next day, amid fear that the mob would return (and in some places it did, roaming the streets with machetes). For the next three days, they looked for people who were still alive. They found some camouflaged under dead bodies, too afraid to leave. Nobin's own mother had hidden in the pond beneath the water lilies.

When the fear of the mob's return lessened, they worked to gather the dead and pile them in groups waiting for burial. It took another two days to recover the bodies of all the children. With two other men, Nobin dug shallow graves and buried 350 children on this piece of land. They laid the bodies side by side in a hurry and buried them at five in the evening. As they started covering the bodies, Nobin found a little toddler, still breathing but barely alive. They had got lucky with him. That boy, Abdul Rashid, now thirty-seven, lives in the same village.

Answering a question I asked earlier about the lack of markings at the grave sites, Nobin now added, 'Abdul is our walking headstone.'

Nobin buried the children in this grave and two other graves, each holding around a hundred bodies. He said that there are at least a hundred different grave sites scattered across the fourteen other villages where the massacres happened. These graves varied in size. Diagonally across from the mass grave where we stood, Nobin pointed to a large sturdy tree surrounded by bushes.

'There are three bodies there. Sometimes we buried them where we found them.'

The police and the CRPF returned a few days later to provide relief materials—expired biscuits and blankets—but left the locals to 'clean up' themselves. No rescue operations were organised. When locals found injured survivors, they took them to local medical camps and hospitals, where in many cases, they died a slow painful death without any medical assistance, since the camps had no doctors.

A year later, the government gave as compensation Rs 2,000 for the injured and Rs 5,000 for a life lost. 'No one came to help,' Nobin repeated. 'There is no justice. They say there is a book, a Constitution. I want to know whom it is for . . . The government also gave money to the rioters and murderers who were injured by the police. In the next village, the CRPF fired at the crowd to disperse. These men have become martyrs. But they are murderers.'

None of the local newspapers in Assam carried the news of the massacre or published the images. The only official inquiry report that was commissioned by the state remains unpublished. To date, no one has been convicted of these murders.

Every year, Nobin and others from the village commemorate the massacre in a quiet ceremony. People gather in silence and leave. The men who buried these bodies, like Nobin, remember the number of bodies in each grave, but don't know who is buried in them. Many remain unaccounted. People were buried in a hurry; some were disfigured beyond recognition. The graves remain unexhumed. When Nobin's generation is gone, there will be no proof.

Before I left, I asked Nobin the names of his two nieces who had been killed. He said the six-year-old was Fazila. For a moment he struggled, and then said that the three-year-old was called Rashi. He had no photographs of the children. A few years earlier, he had given a journalist from Guwahati a picture of his sister. The journalist never wrote about his family and never returned the photograph. Nobin and millions like him deserve justice, but at the very least they deserve respect and empathy from those who claim to tell their stories.

As we spoke, Ahmed, the journalist who had accompanied me, showed me a black-and-white picture on his phone of children laid on the ground before the burial. He pointed to the photograph and said that this image was taken here. Nobin confirmed this. He remembered a lone photographer who stayed on for twenty days after the other journalists had left. He didn't know this photographer's name. But many in the village knew the images well. Almost everyone had his pictures, cut out of magazines, and now saved on their phones.

The stories I had heard for the past five years were beginning to weigh me down. I worried that I might become that journalist from Guwahati who took Nobin's photographs, that I would abdicate my responsibility to write, or that I would write in ways that would obscure their stories.

That night, I returned to the guesthouse and called my photographer friend Ritesh Uttamchandani. We had been friends for over a decade. Ritesh and I often struggled with the same questions and doubts—what did it mean to photograph and document other people's experiences with violence? What function did that image serve? What roles did photographers play in the business of bearing witness? I wanted to speak to the photographer who had recorded the massacre, to know what he saw, but more importantly, to learn what his photographs failed to capture. Unlike the writer, the photographer is a merciless editor. No other act of documentation starts with the explicit decision to capture the frame, by an act of eliminating everything else around it.

Ritesh helped me find Bhawan Singh, the lone photographer who had photographed the Nellie massacre. I reached him through his son, Virender Singh. Over the phone, Virender invited me to their home in Delhi to meet his father. The day after, I left Guwahati and went to Delhi to talk to the photographer who stayed behind in Nellie.

Bhawan Singh, now in his seventies, had spent close to fifty years documenting the Indian republic. He won the World Press Photo Award for his work on the Nellie massacre. I told him that, for the people I met in Nellie, who have never even planted a stone marking their mass graves, his images were the sole proof of their loss and of the unimaginable violence they had endured.

Bhawan went quiet. He didn't know his images had left the pages of newspapers and magazines to become memories and evidence in these peoples' lives.

He was in Guwahati in the 1980s, working on a long-term project on rural India, when news of the massacre spread and he was dispatched to Nellie by his editor. Bhawan had never heard of the hamlet before. He corroborated everything that Nobin had told me about how the people were left to fend for themselves, while the police and the CRPF did nothing to help. Days after the massacre, he saw a group of men return to the villages, looking for survivors. Sitting with me in his room, he said, 'I have never seen anything like that, and I have spent my entire life photographing this country . . .

'Sometimes I look at my images, and I have immense love for the people of this country, and then I see an image that makes me angry, afraid and even fearful for our future . . .

'Where did all this hate come from, where is it going to take us . . . ?'

The magazine that sent him, *India Today*, was one of the few publications that reported on the Nellie massacre. When the prime minister at the time, Indira Gandhi, arrived, she was a bit shocked to see Bhawan there, waiting to photograph her. He said that the prime minister spent no more than five minutes in 'the devastated village' before returning to a nearby field where her helicopter waited.

'I saw the most powerful people in this country, who could have done the right thing, do nothing. They treated the people who lost everything with so much disregard. They were annoyed that the dead bodies were laid out and photographed. But they had no empathy or the decency to try and understand why this had happened. Or what could have been done to stop this.'

Prime Minister Indira Gandhi, when asked why she had not acted promptly to stop the violence during the Nellie massacre in 1983, replied, 'One has to let such events take their own course before stepping in.'[2]

The only other photographer at Nellie in the aftermath was a staff photographer for *The Telegraph*, who took a few images and left for Calcutta the next day. Bhawan described a moment when the other photographer focused his lens on an old, frail man reaching for a partly destroyed Quran on the ground. He asked the other photographer to stop, and the two got into a disagreement. For Bhawan, reducing this trauma to yet another image of a Muslim man with a Quran amidst the carnage was its own form of oppression.

'Photographers also "shoot"; we can kill people over again with our cameras. We can slowly destroy their humanity by making them into a herd.'

I spent the rest of the day with Bhawan Singh, looking at thousands of his contact sheets from over the years. It was his magnum opus—the culmination of forty years spent recording rural India, her villages and her people. Bhawan had visited every state in the republic to record a nation in transition. I had never seen images like these.

~

'Illusion is the most tenacious weed in the collective consciousness,' Antonio Gramsci wrote in 1921. 'History teaches but it has no pupils.' The lines we draw, the fences we build and the borders we enforce are illusions. They are not real, but they give birth to violent consequences, and have become a part of collective consciousness. Humanity's most significant moral and political failures of this century begin with these lines. At the border, even the most civilised among us begin to make excuses for repression, brutality and violence. At the border, we eschew all that we otherwise celebrate under the demands of freedom, progress, liberty and secular ideals. If we are to learn from history, we must begin by imagining the possibilities of freedom without nation states, without borders that kill.

Amidst the chaos of the Partition, in 1951, India employed an NRC. This is the official record of individuals who qualified as citizens of India as per the Citizenship Act of 1955. The register was prepared after the 1951 census but was never maintained—until recently, when it was revived for the state of Assam.

According to Article 5 of the Citizenship Act, all the people that were residents of India when the Constitution came into effect were citizens of India, along with those born in India. The Act was amended in 1986 to restrict citizenship by birth. Now, at least one parent had to be an Indian citizen for the child to qualify for citizenship. This placed severe limitations on the birth-right citizenship principle adopted in the Constitution and the original Citizenship Act.

The register, meant to be a definitive list of genuine Indian citizens in Assam, was updated for the first time since Partition in 2019. Many villagers I met in and around Nellie, who were victims of the 1983 massacre, were excluded from the final NRC list. Citizens for Justice and Peace, an Mumbai-based rights organisation, reported that close to 90 per cent of those in the village of Borguri (a larger village that surrounds Nellie), where the massacre took place, were excluded.[3] In the same month, Genocide Watch issued a genocide alert, citing the citizenship exercise had created conditions in which a 'genocidal process [was] underway'.[4]

In the 1960s, a special police force was created in Assam with the sole purpose of identifying undocumented immigrants alongside the creation of 'Foreigners Tribunals'. From 1997 on, the Election Commission started identifying voters as 'doubtful' and arbitrarily purged them from the electoral rolls. Around 370,000 persons were declared 'doubtful' and put on trial before the Foreigners Tribunals, quasi-judicial bodies set up under the Foreigners (Tribunals) Order of 1964 to adjudicate who is a citizen and who not. Out of an estimated 370,000, only 199,631 cases were referred to the tribunals for verification. During the initial trials, 3,686 persons were found to be foreigners, and their names were removed from the electoral rolls.

Nobin Hussain and many others from his village have been summoned to more than a dozen such hearings to prove their citizenship. Between 1985 and 2019, the hundred-plus Foreigners Tribunals in Assam had deemed 117,164 persons as foreigners. Out of these, 63,959 persons (or 58 per cent) have been declared foreigners 'ex parte', meaning that they were declared foreigners without even being given a hearing. An overwhelming percentage of them are Muslims.

Nobin Hussain's name was also left out of the final NRC list; we don't know what awaits him and the 1.9 million people who are currently excluded. If they are declared non-citizens, it would create the world's largest underclass of stateless subjects. These people who were left off the register are at risk of being imprisoned in the detention camps currently being built. The first camp, which was under construction when I was travelling, is the 'size of seven football fields',[5] and the workers who helped build it may well end up within its walls.

As the Indian government has passed legislation to extend the NRC to the rest of the country, it seems certain that the largest crisis of manufactured statelessness in human history is forthcoming.

7

GUWAHATI

TALES OF THREE DETENTIONS

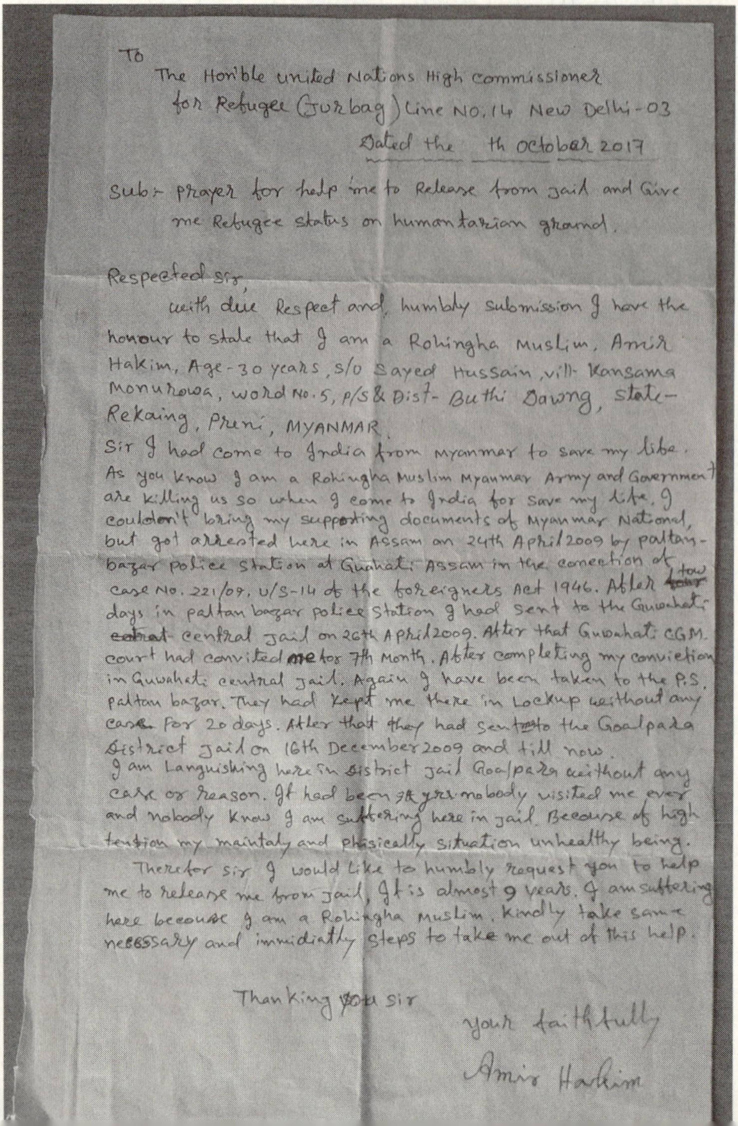
To
The Hon'ble united Nations High commissioner
for Refugee (Jurbag) Line No. 14 New Delhi-03
Dated the th October 2017

Sub:- prayer for help me to Release from jail and Give
me Refugee status on humantarian grand.

Respected sir,
with due Respect and humbly submission I have the honour to stale that I am a Rohingha Muslim, Amir Hakim, Age-30 years, S/o Sayed Hussain, vill- Kansama Monurowa, word No. 5, P/S & Dist- Buthi Dawng, State- Rekaing, Preni, MYANMAR.
Sir I had come to India from Myanmar to save my life. As you know I am a Rohingha Muslim Myanmar Army and Government are killing us so when I come to India for save my life, I couldn't bring my supporting documents of Myanmar National, but got arrested here in Assam on 24th April 2009 by paltan-bazar police station at Guwahati Assam in the conection of case No. 221/09, U/S-14 of the foreigners Act 1946. After tow days in paltan bazar police station I had sent to the Guwahati central jail on 26th April 2009. After that Guwahati CGM. court had convited me for 7th Month. After completing my conviction in Guwahati central jail. Again I have been taken to the P.S. paltan bazar. They had kept me there in Lockup without any case for 20 days. After that they had sent to the Goalpara District jail on 16th December 2009 and till now.
I am Languishing here in District jail Goalpara without any case or reason. It had been 9 yrs nobody visited me ever and nobody know I am suffering here in jail. Becouse of high tention my maintaly and phisically situation unhealthy being.
Therefor sir I would like to humbly request you to help me to release me from jail, It is almost 9 years. I am suffering here becouse I am a Rohingha Muslim. Kindly take same necessary and immidiatly steps to take me out of this help.

Thanking you sir

Your faithfully
Amir Hakim

I

Amir Hakim wrote the letter on thin, fragile paper, folded many times over, and Imrul Islam smuggled it out of Goalpara District Jail in Assam that also doubled as the detention centre. The letter was a plea, a petition for help to the outside world. Amir is a Rohingya refugee who has been held in Goalpara District Jail since 2009. There are over 300 Rohingya refugees in Indian jails, all of them arrested for illegally entering India. Their crime: fleeing violence and Myanmar's ongoing genocide against their people, and entering India without legal documents. Since the late 1970s, nearly one million Rohingya are estimated to have fled Myanmar. Various waves of Rohingya refugees have arrived in India, fleeing violence, since then.

When I read Amir's letter for the first time, I wondered what legal documents he could have possibly carried. Since the 1990s, the only proof of identity that most Rohingya have had was a 'white card' issued by the Myanmar government that conferred on them neither citizenship nor rights. The only other proof of their partial existence was a 'household list' provided by Myanmar authorities as part of the annual census. The census exercise was a bureaucratic 'cordon-and-search' operation, done through the list-making and census-taking. Each year, the exercise was used to harass, intimidate, surveil and threaten communities already living in fear.

The household list records only names and dates of birth, not even places of birth. The Rohingya are systematically denied any evidence of their birth in Myanmar, and their undocumentedness is a precursor to their statelessness.

The Burmese state has consistently denied and prevented the Rohingya from obtaining official documentation, like the national registration cards that would confer rights and access to public services. Denial of citizenship to Rohingya has been an official state policy since the country's 1982 citizenship laws were passed. The plan to erase the Rohingya identity, history and language is integral to the project of creating a vast Buddhist majority in Burma. The Rohingya face forced labour, arbitrary confiscation of property and restrictions on their freedom of movement. They do not have access to schools beyond primary education, since the government reserves secondary education for citizens.

I met Imrul in Guwahati after his release, and his face changed as he spoke about his time in prison—a place, he said, that 'made everything feel a little less human and not deserving of any kindness'. Imrul was tall, with kind eyes. Born and raised in Assam, he was a local businessman and contractor. In September 2017, he was arrested and detained in the Goalpara prison after a fight about his failure to pay the loan instalments on his car. As many as two-thirds of the inmates in India's prisons have not been convicted. Imrul, like many of them, was sent to prison for his pretrial detention. It was here that Imrul first met Amir Hakim and other men who continue to languish in India's prisons, with no recourse to lawyers or any due process. 'Many,' Imrul said, 'have lost the faith of ever being released.' The food in these centres is terrible, the surroundings unhygienic and torture routine.

There are currently six such detention centres—at Goalpara, Silchar, Kokrajhar, Tezpur, Jorhat and Dibrugarh—all located within larger prison facilities. In the past few years, the prisons have transformed into detention centres for those the state has declared 'foreigners', and for people awaiting trial before a Foreigners Tribunal. These detention centres were set up between 2009 and 2015 on the direction of the Gauhati High Court to house those declared foreigners by the hundred Foreigners Tribunals in the state—till they are deported or released.

Undertrials, petty criminals convicted for stealing less than a dollar, people accused of 'terrorist activities' and those considered 'foreigners' and detained indefinitely were all housed under one roof.

In addition to these prisons, new detention centres are being built throughout the country to house those the Indian state would deem 'illegal'. As of 31 January 2019, there were as many as 938 detainees locked in these centres.

Not long after he was detained, Imrul came to understand the violence of the prisons and their fixed hierarchies. The most prominent artefact from India's colonial past is how these prisoners continue to be classified. Rules established in 1894 remain in practice, and even today inmates are divided into three categories: A, B and C.

A and B inmates are persons who were deemed 'by social status, education and habits of life have been accustomed to a superior mode of living. Habitual prisoners may be included in this class by order of the Inspector General of Prisons.'[1] Category C is the 'residual category', consisting of 'prisoners who are not classified in class A and B'.[2] In effect, those with money, property or education are segregated from the poor, the uneducated and the vulnerable. Those considered 'illegal' are treated the worst, and are detained under inhuman conditions.

On his first morning in Goalpara prison, Imrul met Munir Khan, a thirty-two-year-old Pakistani national. Khan was arrested in 2010 while crossing the border from Myanmar into India's northeastern state of Tripura. He was charged under the UAPA, a law aimed at preventing actions 'directed against the integrity and sovereignty of India'. He was acquitted of all charges, including the UAPA, except illegally crossing into India. After Khan served his five-year sentence, he was told that he would be taken to the Guwahati prison for fifteen days, after which he would be sent home to Pakistan. That was six years ago.

It was through Munir Khan that Imrul learnt of others who had been held at Guwahati Central Jail indefinitely. Forty-year-old Musa, from Bangladesh, was convicted for illegally entering India. Musa, however, claimed to have left home after a fight, in anger, and have found himself on the other side of the border. While India has fenced close to 70 per cent of the border, there are parts of it that are porous and undefined.

As I had learnt on a fearful afternoon in Nagaland a few years earlier, it takes very little to find oneself on the other side of the border. In 2017, due to a thick winter's fog, three Indian border guards found themselves in Bangladesh at the northern district of Rajshahi's Paba Upazila. The BSF officers were detained and handed back to India later. If the men who guard these borders did not know where Indian ended and Bangladesh began, what chance did Musa have?

Musa was also convicted for illegally crossing the border, and had served his two-year sentence, yet he has remained in the detention centre for over five years, waiting to be sent home. During his time in the prison, Imrul got to know more of these men.

He helped them write letters and call decade-old phone numbers in the hope that their families could be reached. Almost none had been able to contact their families. In many cases, it had been far too long to hope that someone still awaited their return. Imrul also noticed that many of the men suffered from severe anxiety and depression. There was no indication of how long they would be held there—and it weighed heavily on them.

At the detention centre, there were Rohingya, Bangladeshis, Pakistanis, Nepalis, those from Hajong and Kachin tribes, and Indians who had been unilaterally declared 'foreigner'—it was like the United Nations for the underdogs.

After years of neglect, and history's deceit, these men had joined a vast underclass of undocumented people around the world locked away for misdemeanours. Rashid Ahmed, thirty-five, was the only exception. Rashid had lived in Bangladesh, right outside the Indian border town of Dauki. He claimed that he was kidnapped for a ransom and brought to India. Stories of cross-border kidnappings for ransom emerged regularly, especially along the frontier villages. Some were by petty criminals, others by local insurgent groups attempting to fund their movements through ransom.[3]

When he tried to escape from his captors, he was caught by the police, and arrested for illegally crossing the border in 2013. Rashid was the lucky one—he had made contact with this family, and now his brother had come to India, trying to secure his release.

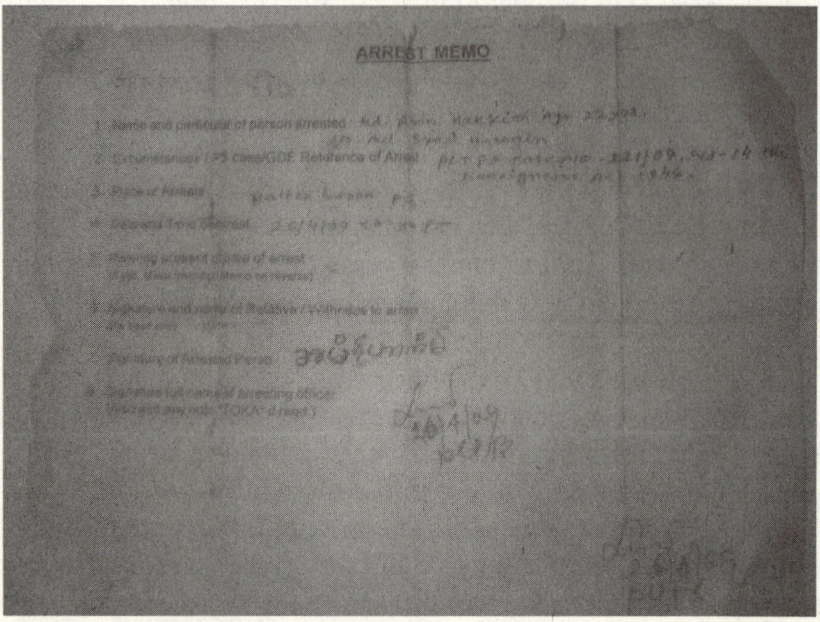
ARREST MEMO

Amir Hakim was not so lucky. Amir, now thirty, had spent most of his adult life incarcerated, and been shuffled from one prison to another in Assam. A decade ago, at twenty, Amir was convicted for illegally entering India by crossing the border under the Foreigners Act of 1946. He was arrested by the Paltan Bazaar police in downtown Guwahati and was sentenced to seven months. He had been hoping to make it safely to the small Rohingya community that had settled in Delhi.

After he had served his sentence at the Guwahati Central Jail, Amir was handed over to the Eighth Assam Police Battalion. From there he was sent back to the local police station in Guwahati for another month. When he demanded his rightful release, he got into a scuffle and was sent to the detention centre in Goalpara. He has been held at Goalpara since 16 December 2009.

Amir, like thousands of Rohingya refugees, first fled to Cox's Bazar in Bangladesh. Cox's Bazar had two government-run refugee camps—the Kutupalong camp, also called the world's largest refugee camp, and the Nayapara refugee camp, home to refugees who fled Myanmar.[4]

Amir was born in Kansama, in Buthidaung district in Myanmar's Rakhine state. In his letter, Amir writes:

Sir I had come to India from Myanmar to save my life.
As you know I am a Rohingya Muslim.
Army and Government are killing us so
when I come to India for save my life.

~

The word 'Rohingya' is used to describe Muslims of the Arakan region, along Myanmar's borderlands.

The first documented reference to Rohingya as native inhabitants of the Arakan region appears in Francis Buchanan's 'A Comparative Vocabulary of Some of the Languages Spoken in the Burma Empire' in 1799.[5] While the Rohingya trace their ancestry to initial Arab migration to the region, and archaeologists have dated eighth-century monuments that validate the long history of settlement, the state of Myanmar has claimed that they are 'illegal Muslim Bengali migrants'.

On 13 May 2016, approximately five months before the new wave of genocidal violence in Rakhine, Myanmar's military commander general, Min Aung Hlaing, stated that there were no Rohingya in Myanmar. He labelled the Rohingya as simply 'Bengalis', adding 'the term Rohingya does not exist and we will not accept it'.[6] He also stated that the Rohingya 'do not have any characteristics of culture in common with the ethnicities of Myanmar', and went on to say that the current conflict was 'fuelled because the Bengalis demanded citizenship'.[7]

Since the 1970s, under Myanmar's military dictatorship, the Rohingya have suffered various rights violations. The first wave of refugees fleeing persecution started arriving in India in 1978, and the majority of the refugees fled from the northern part of Rakhine, from the three townships of Buthidaung, Maungdaw and Rathedaung. Buthidaung, where Amir is from, has a particular history of brutality.

The Burmese Citizenship Act of 1982 laid the foundation for manufacturing the Rohingya community as a class of stateless subjects by denying them citizenship rights. The Rohingya were excluded from the 135 legally recognised ethnic groups that lived in Myanmar prior to British colonisation in 1823. The new law granted citizenship only to those who could prove that their family lived in Myanmar prior to 1823: the year of the first British military campaign on Myanmar that brought with it migrant labourers and businessmen from British India and China. For many families—with mixed ethnicities, multiple maps of belonging and varied routes of migration—the new citizenship laws arbitrarily decided who was a citizen and who was not.

It is impossibly rare to possess a hundred-year-old document that establishes one's familial claims in Myanmar. What papers can people provide to prove their belonging? What document can officially record a family history as proof of citizenship?

Prior to the 1982 citizenship law, Rohingya had access to citizenship in Myanmar, and under the leadership of Prime Minister U Nu, Myanmar's first government, following independence in 1948, recognised the Rohingya as indigenous to Myanmar.

The laws created a racialised Burmese state and introduced castes of citizenship—full citizens, associate citizens, naturalised citizens, and those isolated to be purged from Myanmar's national, political and ethnic boundaries.

Full citizens were given pink cards, with blue cards identifying associate citizens and green cards indicating naturalised citizens.

The Rohingya were not issued any ID cards. In 1995, after sustained advocacy by the UNHCR, the Burmese authorities issued them the Temporary Registration Card (TRC), or the white card.[8] The white card does not mention the person's place of birth and cannot be used as proof of citizenship.[9]

Rohingya persecution and statelessness was manufactured through these citizenship laws and the institutionalisation of hate. Once the last guarantees of citizenship were annihilated, the Rohingya had no protection left. While the UN Charter specifically stipulates that no person shall be without a state, the Rohingya are the world's largest group of stateless people.

In 2001, Rohingya were forcibly removed from their ancestral homes, and moved to Maungdaw and Buthidaung districts. Entire Muslim townships in Rakhine state were made 'Muslim-free zones'. Rohingya were not permitted to live in these townships. Mosques and graveyards were destroyed, and their lands confiscated. By 2003, violence against Muslim communities by Buddhist nationalists had increased, resulting in another wave of Rohingya displacement and forced migration.

In August 2005, the military junta that ruled created an artificial price hike of rice and other essentials. Transport of rice to the Rohingya-majority area of northern Rakhine was blocked. The Rohingya community was later prohibited from carrying, purchasing or selling rice. In the township of Buthidaung, a pound of rice was sold at four times its price. Many local and international human rights reports from this period, including from the UN Human Rights Office, confirmed this practice, and reported widespread malnutrition and starvation in Rakhine state. Amir would have been no more than fourteen when he endured this.

It was impossible to study, ply a trade or farm their land. Rape, murder and looting became the norm. Everything was taxed—from farming to fishing, collecting firewood to owning animals. There was roof tax, where Rohingya were taxed for merely having a roof over their heads.

In addition to these taxes, the military had to be given tributes and bribes to assuage their anger.

Even to get married, the Rohingya had to obtain permission from the Nasaka, the Burmese border and immigration forces in northern Rakhine. The process cost between US$ 45 and 65, which most Rohingya could not afford. And the process often took years. Buthidaung Prison, in Amir's hometown, was full of people arrested and sentenced to up to five years 'for offenses relating to marriages', and for travelling within Rakhine state without proper documents.

While military juntas had complete control over the Rohingya, the state had abandoned them. The schools were neglected and often burnt down during army raids; clean water was seldom available. If people did not die of bullet wounds or torture, they died of malaria, diarrhoea or cholera. Maternal mortality rates were abysmal, and there were just two doctors for 280,000 people in Buthidaung.

As I flipped through UN reports, and tracked down aid workers and rights activists who had worked in Buthidaung in the years and months leading up to Amir's flight, it became clear that Amir had lived in an open-air prison.

~

Amir Hakim, like many young boys of his generation, decided to leave Rakhine state. In 2009, he fled after another wave of violence swept through Buthidaung.

India was not a signatory to the 1951 UN Refugee Convention or its 1967 Protocol; it does not have a single national legal framework that lays out how refugees must be treated. Instead, over the years, India has applied varying parameters and policies to various refugee groups. About 40,000 Rohingya refugees reside in India, where they are constantly taunted and threatened with deportation. Their future remains uncertain.

In December 2019, India passed a new legislation—the CAA—which gives undocumented immigrants from Pakistan, Afghanistan and Bangladesh a path to Indian citizenship, but explicitly excludes Muslims, who make up about 15 per cent of the country's population.

The new citizenship laws will not help Amir. No matter what he and millions of his people have endured, he will always be 'illegal'.

In March of 2018, I headed to the Kalindi Kunj Rohingya camp in Delhi that sheltered over forty families. I hoped someone there would be from Buthidaung, and perhaps there would be a way to send some message back home to Amir's family. Or maybe he already had some family who had found refuge in India. With his name, age and multiple copies of his letter, I went hoping to find something—a clue, a contact or anyone from Buthidaung I might talk to.

But no one there knew or remembered Amir. I was given the numbers of a few other Rohingya refugees living in Jammu. But the calls yielded nothing. In April, just a few months after my visit, a fire gutted the camp, destroying everything, including the documents, homes and possessions of all the forty families.

II

With Imrul, I drove towards Krishnai, which is a little riverside village two hours from Guwahati. Once we left the urban early-morning traffic of Guwahati behind, the road opened onto lush picturesque landscapes. We drove into a small road that took us to a house still under construction, with two of its grey concrete walls standing without paint.

Rashminara Begum was around thirty when I met her in February 2018. She was the mother of little Nafisa, who was just over a year old. When I arrived, Nafisa was wearing a small orange frock and was being cradled by her grandmother, Jamila Begum. The walls inside the house were faded mustard yellow, with a cupboard covered with bright pink curtains. Rashminara's two other little girls, Moriom and Rupsana, ran around the house, playing. Rashminara—a mother of three who had been taken into custody as a 'foreigner' two years earlier, when she was three months pregnant with Nafisa—was currently out on bail after the Supreme Court of India intervened and asked the detention centre in Goalpara to release her.

She grew up in Kharija Manikpur, a village in Goalpara district, studying at the local primary school and later at the Habraghat Killijhar Medium English School. The Brahmaputra and Barak rivers that sustain this part of Assam also swallow large swathes of its land each monsoon. Parts of her village went underwater in 2003, and her high school closed down soon after. In 2002, while still in school, she was married to Manirul Islam, who is a tailor. Like many who have lost their material proof of citizenship to the floods and ongoing violence, Rashminara had lost her legacy documents. Like her, many I met and spoke to had lost their documents to either river or to violence.

Luckily, she was in possession of other documents, like a certificate issued by the local village secretary in 2015 that confirmed her age, place of birth, and previous and current addresses. The certificate also states that she moved to her husband's village after their marriage in 2002.

In 2016, Rashminara found out that she was listed as a doubtful voter when she went to vote in the local elections. Just a year earlier, in 2015, that classification became grounds to prosecute her under the Foreigners Act as a suspected 'foreigner', a 'Bangladeshi'. Case No. 29/K/2015 was registered against her in the Foreigners Tribunal No. 2 in Goalpara.

The family hired a lawyer, and handed over all the documents they possessed. For the next year, they saved what little they could, and Rashminara visited the tribunal at least once a month. On three occasions, her lawyer asked her to produce a witness in court to prove who she was. 'I took my mother with me three times, but each time we were there, my lawyer, Pulak Ghosh, told us that I don't need any witness for my case.'

Her mother, Jamila Begum, starts crying as Rashminara narrates the ordeal they faced: 'I went three times, but they never asked me any questions. The lawyer said the documents we had were enough to prove her nationality.' Like many who went through the gruelling process of proving their citizenship, Rashminara and her family, in hindsight, feel betrayed by their legal representation.

The Foreigners Tribunals, being quasi-judicial bodies, cannot pass judgements, they can only give 'opinions'. But acutely marginalised individuals, mostly Muslims, can be put in detention indefinitely, and declared 'foreigners', on the 'opinion' of such tribunals. Lawyers and rights activists confirm that judges often do not follow the rules of evidence, and are not bound by criminal or civil procedure codes. They act without supervision, without any challenge to their authority. The rules are often arbitrary, and they make unreasonable demands for new documents and for proof. It is not uncommon for judges to introduce new procedural requirements as the case wears on. The already poor and marginalised have been further taxed through bureaucratic corruption. A 2019 report by Amnesty International, entitled *Designed to Exclude*, found evidence that judges who declared more people foreigners received better assessments.[10] Since many of these judges were on contract, better assessments meant renewal of these contracts. Before 2015, there were only thirty-six tribunals in Assam. By 2018, a hundred tribunals were functioning, and the government plans to add 400 new tribunals. These tribunals are anti-women, anti-poor and anti-Muslim.[11]

Both Rashminara and her mother spoke about the difficulties of navigating the tribunals. 'Everyone makes money out of our misery,' Jamila Begum added. The lawyer regularly demanded more money, but kept them in the dark. In October 2016, Rashminara was declared a 'foreigner'. She was not present in court, and her lawyer never informed her. It was only when she visited the tribunal a month later to enquire about the status of her case that she learnt the outcome. She was quickly surrounded by police, detained and sent to a detention centre for foreigners in Goalpara. She later found out that the ruling in the case was based on a simple error about her date of birth: her age was recorded as thirty, thirty-two and thirty-three in various documents.

She was moved to the Kokrajhar detention camp in north Assam on 9 November 2016. 'I was three months pregnant . . . The officials knew that. I told them repeatedly that I was pregnant, I begged them . . . even then they showed no mercy.'

Her family filed a petition in the Gauhati High Court on 29 November 2016, and the court ordered the prison authorities to provide her with adequate medical facilities and move her to the district civil hospital. On 29 April 2017, still in custody but admitted to the hospital, Rashminara delivered Nafisa.

On the 22 May 2017, the Gauhati High Court upheld the judgement of the Foreigners Tribunal, declaring her a 'foreigner', but since she was a new mother, the court ordered her release on bail for three months. She filed another petition in the Supreme Court of India in June 2017. Two months later, in August 2017, the Supreme Court extended her bail. At the time of writing this chapter, the matter remains unresolved. Her bail could be revoked anytime, and she could be back in the detention centre.

In her seven months of detention, Rashminara met many women from a cross section of Assamese society. Out of the 136 detainees there, only two were Bangladeshis. Rashminara remembered the painful stories of many of these women: women who had been violently arrested, torn away from their families; women like her who had spent the last of their money fighting cases, only to find themselves in prison, and others who had furnished fifteen different documents.

She remembered a Bangladeshi family that had been detained: the woman was held with her children at Kokrajhar, while her husband, Salim, was held in the Goalpara detention centre. According to Rashminara, the longest surviving detainee in the Kokrajhar detention centre was a woman named Kalyani, who had served over nine years. 'Our jailer told us sarcastically that her husband is a Bangladeshi and that is the reason she is behind detention. But I don't know if it's true.' Rashminara told me about Marzina Begum, who was arrested in a case of mistaken identity and spent eighteen months in the prison before she was released. Marzina lived nearby, and Rashminara suggested I go see her.

As we said our goodbyes, Jamila Begum told me that the older girls, Moriom and Rupsana, have changed since Rashminara's detention. 'The girls are afraid, they don't smile as much . . . They think their mother will be taken away . . . We have lived in this country all our lives, and where do we go, where do the girls go?'

Like Myanmar, India is manufacturing foreigners out of Indian citizens.

III

After we left Rashminara's house, we tried calling Marzina Begum. When she finally picked up her phone, we asked if we could come see her. Marzina Begum lived a few miles away, near Krishnai, off the Harigaon–Balbala road in the village of Bolbolla, less than a five minutes' drive from the main road. But once the car turned right, the tar roads immediately became an unpaved dusty road made of potholes, rocks and small craters. The neglect, and silent dilapidation, was everywhere. Half a mile in, the road narrowed and the car could no longer move forward without toppling into an unbanked river running alongside. We stopped the car and started walking towards Marzina Begum's house.

Like others in most Muslim villages I had recently visited in the region, the people here had not seen an outsider in over seven years. Last time an outsider was here was when a local politician, a minister, and a cackle of bureaucrats, arrived like hyenas soon after a devastating flood that had swallowed the entire village. These were spaces where you could witness the retreat of the state.

By the time we reached Marzina Begum's house, close to twenty people were walking beside us, and another twenty or more men, women and children assembled in the small courtyard behind her house as I sat down with her.

Marzina had a round, pleasant face, and she was wearing a colourful red sari, the pallu fastened around her waist. At twenty-eight, she looked older and tired. She had married and moved here to her husband's village in 2009.

In September 2017, she was wrongly arrested and detained. The police had summons to arrest Menzina Bibi, a forty-six-year-old woman who had been declared a foreigner by the tribunal. The police arrived in the middle of the night in two vehicles. She remembers seeing sixteen or seventeen of them, and two female constables. Marzina and her husband, Kader Ali, were sleeping when they were both woken up and dragged outside by the female constables. In confusion and fear when they resisted, one of the cops put a gun to her husband's head. She was tied up, dragged and thrown into the vehicle, and taken to the local Agia police station.

India's criminal procedure code includes strict guidelines about 'arrest of persons', and more specifically the arrest of women:

> Save in exceptional circumstances, no women shall be arrested after sunset and before sunrise, and where such exceptional circumstances exist, the woman police officer shall, by making a written report, obtain the prior permission of the Judicial Magistrate of the first class within whose local jurisdiction the offence is committed or the arrest is to be made.[12]

In Marzina's case, none of these basic procedures were followed. But as I heard Marzina narrate this ordeal, it became clear that she was neither surprised nor shocked by it. Having lived through many cycles and kinds of violence, including legal, bureaucratic and police brutality, Marzina had a clear understanding, and spoke with clarity about the men and women who stood ready to commit this kind of violence. 'They don't like us, they think we don't belong here.' For many like Marzina, the cost of living was to mortgage everything—their rights, their dignity and often even their bodies.

Her family quickly gathered all the documents they could, and ran to the police station to prove her identity. They showed these documents to both the police officers in charge at the Agia station and the border police (who are tasked with restricting the free movement of a 'foreigner'), but this was not enough proof.

Marzina was then quickly taken to the detention camp in Kokrajhar. She tells me that she spent eight months and twenty days in prison.

The family hired a lawyer, who charged Rs 10,000 and did nothing. A local politician, Badruddin Ajmal, later found another lawyer, who moved the case to the high court and secured her release. Marzina was finally acquitted, but there has been no compensation. The legal cost bankrupted the family, and her husband had to leave Assam in search of work as a paid labourer. When I met her, he had been away for more than six months.

The Kokrajhar prison was a nightmare: the food was inedible, hygiene was abysmal and the detainees had poor or no medical facilities. But these were not her biggest fears. Marzina talked about being taunted by the prison guards as an 'illegal' and a 'foreigner'. One told her that she would never get out, that 'an illegal like her deserved to perish in the camp'.

According to Marzina, there were all kinds of women at the centre—Hindu Bengali women, Muslims and Rohingya refugees—some of whom had languished there for over a decade. She remembered Qaudisa Khartoum, a sixty-five-year-old woman who had been brought in when Marzina was still at the centre.

By the time we finished, it was getting dark, and the entire village had gathered. The men spoke of police excess, and night raids by the border. The NRC, which was already underway, was on everyone's mind.

Six of the villagers had started working as daily labourers at a detention camp that was being constructed.

'We are being employed to build our own prison, we are being asked to dig our graves,' said Galib Mia.

'Will they put a million of us away?' a young man in his twenties quipped.

'No,' came a voice from the crowd, 'we are cheaper dead.'

~

The next day in Howly, Barpeta district, Assam, I met close to twenty-five people who had been listed as doubtful voters, and were fighting to prove that they were citizens of India. When I arrived, the local imam at the mosque made his small office available for us to talk to people. When people knew I had arrived, more came in clutching their papers. Someone had wrongly informed them that I was a 'bureaucrat who was willing to give their papers a look over'.

Shahira Khartum doesn't know how old she is—she thinks about forty. She left school at fifteen, married when she was twenty-two. She, her grandparents and her parents were all born in Salbari in Baska district, and later moved to Barpeta.

She remembers the violence that spread to Baska in 1994, soon after the Barpeta massacre in which militant Bodos killed over a hundred Muslim refugees.

Shahira doesn't remember the month, but remembers her school being closed and that it was the beginning of the monsoon season.

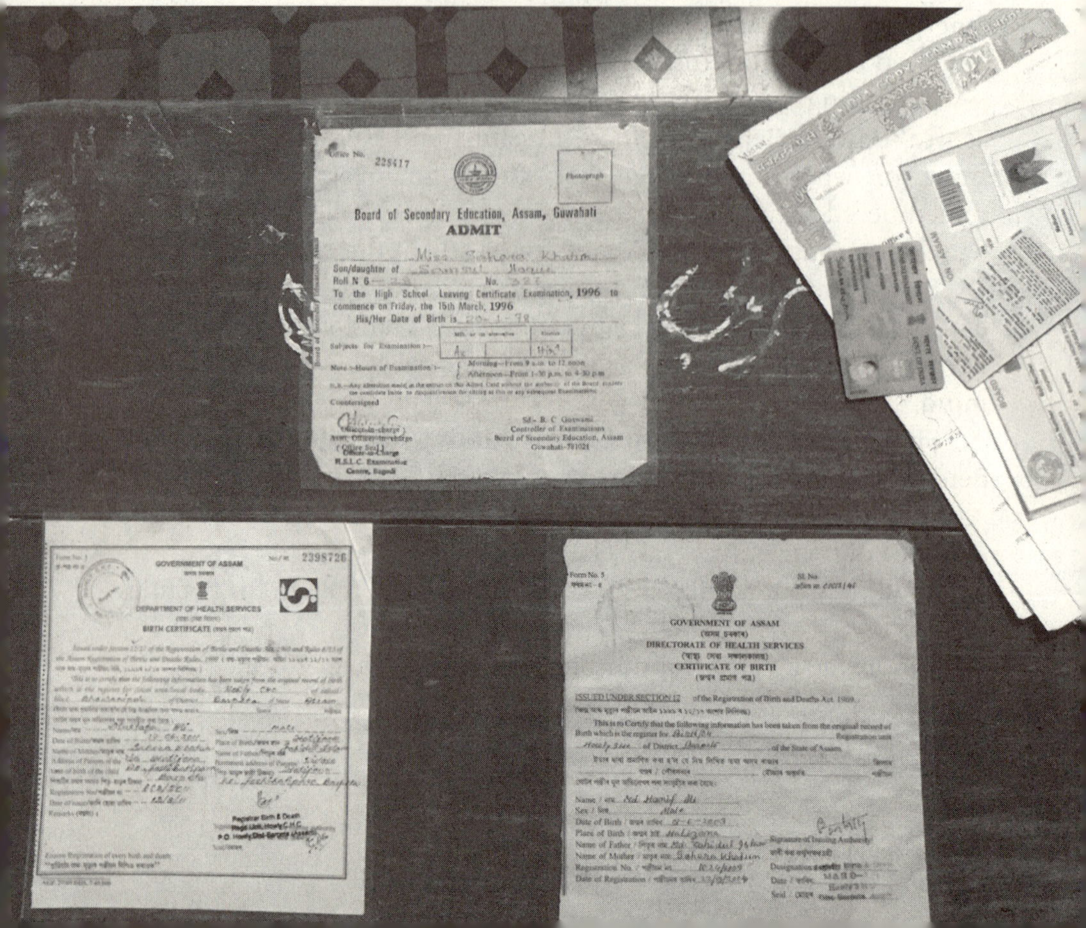

By the end of the rainy season, her house had been burnt down, and her uncle Yakoub Ali had died. Shahira was lucky; she had narrowly escaped detention.

Her family first fled to the Kayakuchi relief camp for two months, and then moved here to Howly. The family received aid in the camp, but no financial compensation. Her name was enrolled in the Howly voter's list before her marriage, but she never voted for anyone. After her marriage, she was registered as a voter at Hathijan. Around 2002 or 2003, she went to vote and found out that she was listed as a D voter. 'D' refers to 'doubtful' or 'dubious' voters, an irrational bureaucratic category introduced in Assam to disenfranchise by citing lack of citizenship documents. 'Special tribunals' under the Foreigners Act determine the D voters. Initially, a person declared a D voter was denied a voter's ID. In 2011, the Gauhati High Court passed an order that allowed D voters to be transferred to Foreigners Tribunals and be held in detention camps.

When she came to know about her 'doubtful status', Shahira's family hired a lawyer. The process was long and tedious, and the family spent close to Rs 70,000 in legal fees. In the six years it took to secure her acquittal, she appeared at the tribunal at least ten times a year. In these sixty-odd visits, the judge only questioned her once, and asked her about her parents, and how many children she had. The lawyer never told her what the process was.

During those six years, Shahira went into hiding three times. Every few years, there was panic in Howly after a group of men and women were rounded up and taken to detention camps. She moved often, from one relative's house to another, to avoid being captured. It was only after her acquittal that she finally returned home. When she went into hiding, she left her three children, aged ten, five and two, in the care of her husband's family. Since her acquittal, she has been waiting for her voter ID. She told me that there is no compensation or help from the government for those who have now proved themselves to be 'citizens'. 'What am I to say?' Shahira asked me. 'Whenever people say that I am Bangladeshi, I just go quiet. What they mean is that I am a Muslim and I don't belong here.'

Shahira was happy to have been able to prove that she is an Indian citizen; she knew of twenty other women who had already been taken away or detained.

One of those women, Rahila Khatun, sixty-two, received a summons in 2015. Like Shahira, her family found a lawyer, paid close to Rs 30,000 and received an acquittal two years later. She went to the tribunal twelve times, but was never questioned, never understood what was happening. Even from the small number of people I had met, it became clear that those with a little more money fared better. The illiterate, the working people, and those without any resources always ended up being declared 'foreigners'.

Somesh Ali, at sixty-five years of age, was made of bones, with a faded crimson red-and-white beard. As he sat down, he told me that his summons first arrived at the end of 2016. In his twenties and thirties, Somesh had farmed a small piece of land in Lakhimpur, on the north bank of the river Brahmaputra. In the 1990s, his land went underwater twice a year for three consecutive years. When the land became unfarmable, he left in search of other employment, finally settling in Howly. Somesh told me that the judge at the tribunal refused to accept his old land deeds. He didn't know whether his parents' and grandparents' names appeared in the NRC list. When I met him in 2018, the NRC exercise was still in process, and he feared he might not make the list. 'Obviously I am Indian. I would like to be called an Indian. Where else will I go, what will I do? If India says I am not theirs, why would Bangladesh take me?' Two months later, Somesh Ali was taken to a detention centre, and that was the last I heard from him.

Falu Mia was over seventy years old and lived in Howly until 1971. Then he moved to Lakhimpur, where he lived for three years, and moved back to Howly again. Born in 1945, he was older than the Indian nation state. Falu Mia never went to school, and doesn't remember where he was born. When his father left their mother, he and his brothers were constantly passed among family members who could care for them. He had no papers.

'The people here know me, they know. But that is not enough for the courts. Whom will I ask?' he wonders. 'My mother has been dead for over sixty years . . . Everyone who raised me, or could have known, is long gone.'

'It's been hard to raise 10,000 rupees to get a lawyer,' Falu Mia tells me. That is how much he makes in six months. 'I am an old man, I might die any time, I don't want to leave my children in debt over my legal fees.'

By the end of six hours of interviews, the stories of fear and anguish merged into each other. Almost all of these people had moved multiple times and for a number of reasons. The Barpeta massacre, and the flooding that made the once fertile Brahmaputra region uncultivable, displaced many of them. Almost all of them were illiterate, and the women often changed their names after marriage. Names were misspelt; documents were lost either as a result of violence or flooding, or were too old and damaged to be of use. They were all lost in the labyrinth of the state bureaucracy, subjected to corrupt lawyers and forced to endure whimsical abuse by petty officials. They feared the unfathomable legal systems and the impending knock on the door in the middle of the night.

In Assam, over sixty people have lost their lives in the process of proving that they are citizens. And due to frustration, anxiety and helplessness related to the NRC, and fearing incarceration in detention camps, others have taken their own lives. More have died under mysterious circumstances in detention camps. They are often referred to only as statistics. The lucky among them get mentioned in a news report, only to be immediately forgotten, but most are never named.

These are not stories of individual fate and ill fortune; in Assam, these stories create a mural of the far-reaching political consequences of majoritarian terror translated into law.

Their names must be remembered, listed, documented and recited.

Death by Citizenship

S. No	Name of the detainee	Name of the detention centre	Date of detention	Date of death	Cause of death
1	Naresh Koch	Goalpara Detention Camp	2017	3 Jan 2020	Koch had suffered paralysis after a stroke at a detention camp in the Goalpara district jail in lower Assam. He was taken to the Gauhati Medical College and Hospital, where he died on the night of 3 January. Koch was around fifty-five years old.
2	Dulal Chandra Paul	Tezpur Detention Camp	2017	Oct 2019	Paul had been declared a foreigner and had been incarcerated at the Tezpur Detention Camp. He reportedly suffered from diabetes and a heart condition.
3	Amrit Das	Goalpara Detention Camp	May 2017	April 2019	Das was feeling pain in his chest after he was lodged in Goalpara Detention Camp, and had complained of uneasiness on 6 April 2019, following which he was admitted to the hospital where he breathed his last.
4	Phalu Das	Goalpara Detention Camp	July 2017	Oct 2019	After his health began to deteriorate, he was admitted to a hospital on 11 October and was later referred to the Gauhati Medical College and Hospital (GMCH), where he died.
5	Subrata Dey	Goalpara Detention Camp	27 March 2018	26 May 2018	Subrata Dey was found dead under mysterious circumstances in Goalpara Detention Camp. Yet the cause of death as per the government submission is 'due to illness'.

6	Ismail Ali Tulakdar	Cachar	23 Aug 2016	30 March 2019	Due to illness
7	Sundar Moni Roy	Cachar	05 Sep 2016	04 March 2018	Due to illness
8	Tazimuddin	Tezpur	17 July 2016	30 Oct 2017	Due to illness
9	Nagen Das	Tezpur	23 Oct 2016	01 June 2018	Due to illness
10	Abu Shahid	Goalpara	28 March 2017	22 Oct 2017	Due to illness
11	Rashid Ali	Jorhat	19 Dec 2015	22 Nov 2017	Due to illness
12	Siddique Ali	Goalpara	05 May 2018	26 June 2018	Due to illness
13	Amir Ali	Goalpara	23 May 2016	24 May 2018	Due to illness
14	Dulal Miya	Goalpara	11June 2016	16 June 2016	Due to illness
15	Md Jabbar Ali	Tezpur	17 July 2017	04 Oct 2018	Due to illness
16	Khakan Mandal	Goalpara	09 March 2016	08 Oct 2018	Due to illness
17	Sashi Mohan Sarkar	Goalpara	27 July 2017	09 Dec 2018	Due to illness
18	Md Jakir Hussain	Tezpur	17 July 2016	25 Dec 2019	Due to illness
19	Sh. Amrit Das	Goalpara	20 May 2017	6 April 2019	Due to illness
20	Basudev Biswas	Tezpur	8 Aug 2015	11 May 2019	Due to illness
21	Md Suruj Ali	Tezpur	9 April 2018	06 June 2019	Due to illness
22	Sri Puna Munda	Goalpara	16 Dec 2018	10 June 2019	Due to illness
23	Hussain Ali	Tezpur	22 July 2016	28 Aug 2017	Due to illness
24	Bhulu Sadakar	Cachar	5 Oct 2015	17 March 2016	Due to illness

25	Md Abdul Kuddus Ali	Tezpur	26 July 2017	16 July 2019	Due to illness
26	Prabha Roy	Kokrajhar	20 Dec 2015	27 Sep 2016	Due to illness
27	Kabutar Basrof	Tezpur	20 Aug 2015	06 Sep 2016	Due to illness
28	Santosh Biswas	Goalpara	18 Aug 2015	02 March 2017	Due to illness
29	Nazrul Islam	Kokrajhar	26 May 2011	11 Aug 2011	Due to illness
30	Jobbar Ali	Tezpur	-	5 Oct 2018	Found dead under mysterious circumstances
31	Sona Munda	Goalpara	-	June 2019	Passed away in captivity

NRC deaths by self-harm / suicide / depression / poison consumption / emotional trauma

S. No	Name	Age (yrs)	Place	Date of death
1	Rahim Uddin	-	Assam's Hojai district	22 July 2019
2	25 - year old man	25	Dhupguri area, North Bengal	Sep 2019
3	55 - year old man	55	Jalpaiguri, North Bengal	Sep 2019
4	Shayera Begun	60	No 1 Dolabari village, 4 km from Tezpur town, Assam's Sonitpur district	31 Aug 2019
5	Noor Nehra Begum	17	Kharupetia town in Assam's Darrang district	June 2019
6	Nirod Baran Das	63	Kharupetia in Assam's Darrang district	Oct 2018
7	Sharafat Ali	68/74	Village Dhupuri, Jalpaiguri district of West Bengal (Bijni police station)	June 2019
9	Hitmat / Hikmat Ali	55	Village Kapahartari under the Kayakuchi area of Barpeta District	June 2019
10	Ashrab Ali (alleged suicide)	93	Kamrup district, Assam	May 2019
11	Deepak Debnath	49	Ghagra village of Udalguri, Assam	Oct 2018

12	Balijan Bibi	43	Kheluwapara village in Bongaigaon district of western Assam	Sep 2016
13	Gopal Das	65	Nislamari village under Tangla Police Station, Udalguri district	June 2018
14	Gauranga Roy (heart attack)	-	Assam	(Oct) 2019
15	Mujibur Rahman (heart attack)	-	Assam	2019
16	Deben Barman	70	Dhubri district	Aug 2018
17	Shahimon Bibi	45	Dhubri district	Apr 2018
18	Abola / Abala Roy	40	Dhubri district	July 2018
19	Angad Sutradhar (alleged suicide)	-	-	July 2015
20	Saibun Nesa Laskar	45	Sonai, Cachar	1 July 2015
21	Jamir Khan	75	Tinsukia	Nov 2015
22	Hanif Khan	40	Khasipur (Part-2) Silchar, Cacha	1 Jan 2018
23	Akram Uddin Barbhuyan	-	Silchar, Cachar	3 Dec 2017
24	Aklima Bewa (Daughter was a suspected foreigner by the Border Police)	62	Dankinamari, Majgaon, Bongaigaon	6/8 Sept 2016
25	Bijit Sen	60	Silchar, Cachar	19 Mar 2018
26	Sunil Baidya	58	Cachar	26 Mar 2018
27	Ratan Ray	40	Pandu, Guwahati, Kamrup	9 Apr 2018
28	Sahimoon Bibi	45	Bidyapara, Dhubri	July 2018
29	Khorgo Bahadur Gurung	57	Sadia, Tinsukia	7 July 2018
30	Deben Burman	72	Dhubri	7 Aug 2018
31	Rakesh Sharma	-	Nakhuti (part-2), Darshi Tea Estate, Majbat	8 Aug 2018

32	Nirmal Pual (alleged suicide)	60	Katirail, Katigorah, Cachar	13 Aug 2018
33	Mithun Roy	-	Palanghat, Cachar	13 Aug 2018
34	Bimal Chandra Ghose	59	Karimchowk, Mandaloi, Darrang	14 Oct 2018
35	Sanjib Das	75	Duliajan, Dhibrugarh	30 Oct 2018
36	Afjal Ali (suffered chest pain)	-	Barkajuli, Tamulpur	11 Nov 2018
37	Abdul Jalil	35	Balagudam, Abhaupuri, Bongaigaon	12 Nov 2018
38	Samsul Hoque	-	Bagariguri, Barpeta	14 Nov 2018
39	Surendra Burman	27	Srirampur Colony, Kokrajhar	19 Nov 2018
40	Monnas Ali	65	Kamarchuburi,Thelamara, Sonitpur	20 Nov 2019
41	Kailash Tanti	-	Syantaila, Dholai, Karinganj	1 Dec 2018
42	Mahibur Rehman (collapsed at the NRC sewa kendra and died)	65	Dhalachira, Nayagram, Karimganj	3 Dec 2018
43	Sandhya Chakrabarty (alleged suicide)	50	Mongoloi, Darrang	8 Feb 2019
44	Bhaben Das	48	Bholabari Bagicha, Kaliagaon, Udalgiri	4 Apr 2019
45	Brajendra Das	-	Bholabari Bagicha, Kaliagaon, Udalgiri	1989
46	Arjun Namasudra	32	Haritikar (part-1), Silchar, Cachar	8 Jun 2012
47	Dhiren Shill	53	Udaltor, Sapotgram,Dhubri	19 Jun 2015
48	Laifon Ali	-	Satagaon, Barpeta	23 Mar 2018
49	Chhatki Prajapati	-	Tinsukia	18 Aug 2018
50	Binoy Chanda	-	DImalpur, Tamulpur,Baksa	9 Sept 2018
51	Sahera Banu	-	Barpeta	1 Dec 2018

52	Shashi Sarkar	85	Tulshijhora, Chirang	7 Dec 2018
53	Abdul Qader Sheq	-	Majrabari,Bongaigaon	21 Apr 2019
54	Alfaz Uddin	-	-	7 May 2019
55	Joynal Abedin	-	Dumergiri, Abhayagiri, Bongaigaon	3 July 2019
56	Rahim Ali	37	Bantipur, Kayakuchi, Barpeta	6 July 2019
57	Kulsum Begum	-	Barkhetry, Nalbari	7 July 2019
58	Amar Majumdar	-	Silapathar, Dhemaji	8 July 2019
59	Jaynal Ali	-	Abhayapui, Bongaigaon	3 July 2019
60	Ambar Ali	59	Chunpura village under Gabaradhana police station	8 July 2019
61	Lal Chand Ali	66	Barpeta district, Assam	May 2018
62	Anwar Hussain	37	Bahmura, Goalpara	3 Dec 2017
63	Ratan Rai	40	Shatagon Village, Barpeta	9 Apr 2018
64	Subash Chandra Kalita (committed suicide due to work pressure related to NRC administration)	52	Sonapur, Assam	Feb 2018

NRC deaths due to police brutality across India

S. No	Name	Age (yrs)	Place	Date of death
1	Sam Stafford	17	Assam	12 Dec 2019
2	Dipanjal Das	19	Assam	12 Dec 2019
3	Abdul Amin	23	Assam	12 Dec 2019
4	Ishwar Nayak	25	Assam	12 Dec 2019
5	Azizul Hoque	45	Sipajhar	12 Dec 2019
6	Jaleel Kudroli	49	Mangalore	19 Dec 2019
7	Nausheen Bengre	23	Mangalore	19 Dec 2019
8	Mohammad Sageer	8(According to an article in Scroll the name of the child who died in a stampede in Varanasi is Saghir Ahmed age 11 years)	Varanasi	20 Dec 2019
9	Mohammad Vaqeel	32	Lucknow	Between 19-22 Dec 2019
10	Aftab Alam	22	Kanpur	Between 19-22 Dec 2019
11	Mohammad Saif	25	Kanpur	Between 19-22 Dec 2019
12	Anas	21	Bijnor	Between 19-22 Dec 2019
13	Mohammad Suleman	35	Bijnor	Between 19-22 Dec 2019
14	Bilal	24	Sambhal	Between 19-22 Dec 2019
15	Mohammad Shehroz	23	Sambhal	Between 19-22 Dec 2019
16	Jaheer	33	Meerut	20 Dec 2019
17	Mohsin	28	Meerut	20 Dec 2019
18	Asif	20	Meerut	20 Dec 2019
19	Areef	20	Meerut	20 Dec 2019
20	Nabi Jhaan	24	Firozabad	Between 19-22 Dec 2019
21	Faiz Khan	24	Rampur	Between 19-22 Dec 2019

22	Rashid	35	Firozabad	20 Dec 2019
23	28 year old HIV patient	28	Kanpur	20 Dec 2019
24	Alem Ansari	24	Meerut	20 Dec 2019

PART V

THE INDIA–PAKISTAN BORDER

The India–Pakistan border is heavily militarised, and both countries have thousands of troops stationed along its length, especially in the disputed Jammu and Kashmir region. This border was created in 1947 when the subcontinent was partitioned into two nations—an 1,800-mile frontier that runs through major urban areas, including Amritsar and Hussainwala, farms and inhospitable deserts. Since Partition, it has been a site of numerous conflicts between the two countries, pushing them to war in 1947, 1965 and 1999. The India–Pakistan border is often referred to as one of the most complex, violent and dangerous boundaries in the world. The entire length is fenced with 150,000 floodlights and 50,000 poles. At night, the border can be seen from space. The ongoing cycles of violence, the struggle for freedom in Kashmir, the dramatic militarisation of the region and the unresolved questions about the place of religious minorities within both countries are intimately connected to the act of Partition. Many have referred to the recent citizenship laws implemented in India as a reopening of the wounds of Partition, a revisiting of the botched amputation.

Just as the memories of Partition are multiple, and contradictory, so are the reasons leading up to it. A fraught and violent history of colonialism had fractured the population along religious lines and entrenched the idea that Hindus and Muslims were distinct political communities that cannot coexist. The last decade of that rule transformed the national political landscape and strengthened the demands for a separate Muslim homeland in the name of Pakistan. As great men negotiated a Faustian contract that butchered the continent, ordinary people lost everything—they were killed or attacked in their homes. Women were raped, assaulted and abducted in huge numbers. Entire villages were erased, and corpses lined the roadsides.

Today, nowhere is the ongoing chaos of Partition felt more acutely than in Kashmir.

Kashmir has a long history of oppression. The Mughal Army marched into the valley in 1586, followed by the Afghans, the Sikhs and finally the Dogras—all of who ruled a defiant Kashmir. Since the partition of India and Pakistan in 1947, Kashmir's sovereignty has only further eroded. Geographically caught between China, India and Pakistan, all three countries lay claim to, and currently occupy, parts of the Kashmir Valley. A Line of Control, or LoC, divides the Muslim-majority region of Kashmir between India and Pakistan. The line is a remnant of the ceasefire following the Partition, but has been contested throughout the end of the twentieth century and into the twenty-first by the global community as well as advocates for independence within the Kashmir Valley.

In the 1990s, local militants seeking independence from India staged an armed uprising against the state in Indian-occupied Kashmir. In turn, India launched a counter-insurgency operation by introducing emergency laws,[1] ushering in an era of extrajudicial killings,[2] torture chambers,[3] massacres and the suspension of civil liberties that persists today.

While armed militancy against the Indian state has declined since the 1990s, a strong people's resistance has gathered momentum in its place. In 2010, Kashmiris took to the streets in large numbers to demand freedom in one of the largest anti-India protests ever. In the summer of 2016, Kashmiris lived with intermittent curfews for over a hundred days,[4] as retribution for their protests against the Indian Army's execution of the Kashmiri militant commander Burhan Wani. When the curfews led to unrest, the Indian state responded with force, killing civilians and breaking up protests with pellet guns that left hundreds of Kashmiri youth blind.

8

KASHMIR

RECORDS OF REPRESSION

Ek Goli Ek Dushman.
One Bullet One Enemy.

– Banner at the 27 Rashtriya Rifles army camp in Aloosa

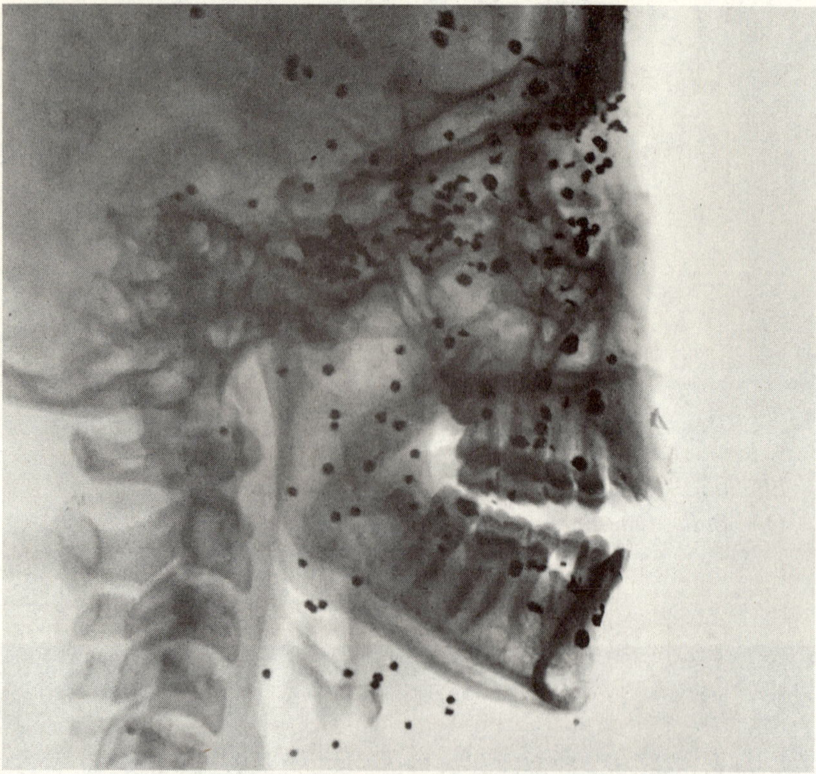

When I first started meeting families along the border villages near the town of Uri in 2014, I would often arrive with only vague outlines of stories of death and disappearances: the schoolteacher who had been lynched by the army in the 1990s in a cordon-and-search operation; the boy who was taken and who never returned home because he had been caught with a Pakistani flag after a cricket match; an emerging local politician who was tortured and killed before his body was thrown in the minefield. In the villages, these stories functioned as an address. Each house had its own scars of violence and loss. Families identified less with their door numbers, or street names, than with the names of loved ones who had disappeared, or died brutally under the Indian military presence.

After being detained at a checkpoint for over two hours, I made my way to one of the villages closest to the LoC. I had called the family I was supposed to interview two weeks earlier from Srinagar.

Their initial willingness to speak had changed in this time. The meeting lasted an hour, but the family refused to talk. They seemed anxious, afraid and apologetic. When we ended the interview, they asked me to stay a little longer for tea. As I sipped my tea, the family matriarch brought out an old notebook that had been turned into a photo album.

During the cordon-and-search operations of the 1990s insurgency, the military had raided their house and found photographs of her son with his friends. The military had accused him and his friends of being militants and dragged him away. After the incident, the family had quietly collected all their photographs and albums and burnt them. Soon after, the matriarch began collecting clippings from newspapers. When I asked what had happened to her son, she winced and said, 'He never came back.' When denied their family records, Kashmiris made albums out of photos from the newspapers. Since private lives were relentlessly surveilled, press images came to belong to the entire community, replacing memories that were systematically co-opted.

For over thirty years, Kashmiris have lived with the insidious practices of detention, torture, execution and disappearance. But extrajudicial killings, or 'encounter killings', are particularly pervasive. The term 'encounter killings' refers to the state-sanctioned tactic in which troops or the police provoke or fake an armed skirmish, resulting in the death of young men and boys suspected of being militants.[1] The murdered civilians are posthumously accused of being 'terrorists', 'Pakistani', 'insurgents', 'foreign militants' or 'separatists' killed while infiltrating Kashmir, or travelling from Kashmir into Pakistan to seek arms training. The state portrays them as legitimate targets, and in many cases, authorities have planted weapons and fake foreign ID cards on the bodies.

While the army calls these killings 'encounters', civilians call them 'fake encounters'.[2] These widespread, systematic, premeditated killings are now a feature of life in Kashmir, one that points to a broader corruption within the armed forces.[3] State-sanctioned impunity allows the military to discipline and punish the Kashmiri population through illegal use of violence and the fabrication of events leading up to these civilian deaths.[4]

Despite the atmosphere of silence I encountered at the LoC, one story did make its way to me: that of twenty-four-year-old Hilal

Ahmad Dar of Aloosa in northern Kashmir, who was killed in an 'encounter' by the Indian Army on the night of 24 July 2012, allegedly with the help of two locals. The army initially claimed that he was a militant who was killed in an armed encounter, but later retracted this story. Hilal's family believes that he was set up to be killed by local informants, then tortured and killed by army personnel.

In Kashmir, the spectacle of death, destruction and disappearance repeats endlessly. The culture of impunity has flourished in the aftermath of years of conflict, occupation and militarisation. State violence is openly exercised as the policy for governance; it is integral to how Indian sovereignty is practised in the region. Oppression is institutionalised in every aspect of life, and it is impossible to hold the state accountable. While the existence of judicial institutions holds out the promise of accountability, and a facade of redress, patterns of cover-up and denials are pervasive throughout the legal system. Families spend years fighting and waiting for answers that never arrive. Justice is extinct here. Hilal is one among thousands who were killed.

I have spent my entire adult life thinking about state violence and justice. In 1994, a gang of criminals assaulted my father outside our home, when he was about to leave for Delhi to argue his petition at the Supreme Court. It was rumoured that the ruling state politicians had planned and ordered the attack. I was ten years old. The assault was nearly fatal and left him with multiple fractures; his survival was nothing less than miraculous. He underwent major surgeries, and then a year's worth of recovery. Eighteen years later, the Madras High Court acquitted all twelve accused. Perhaps in ways I couldn't explain, I wanted to find the answers that Hilal's family never got.

To investigate what really happened to Hilal that night, I tracked down and spoke to many of the people involved in the case, including Muhammad Ramzan Lone, alias Rameez, a former militant turned army informant, and Nazir Ahmed Bhat—the two local men accused of his murder. The army's version of the story, which denies any role it had in orchestrating the fake encounter, was told through its internal investigation reports. I also obtained the state prosecutor's theory of the case and the forensic reports, both of which contradicted the army's version of events. Finally, I talked to Hilal's family, who shared the pain and trauma of losing their son to the military occupation.

These multiple different versions were full of contradictions and unanswered questions, including on the most basic facts of the case: who was Hilal Ahmad Dar, why was he brutally killed and by whom? Why was he chosen as the object of death and not someone else? What transpired in the moments leading up to his capture, torture and final death? Why did Hilal have to die? Were a few hundred rupees incentive enough to stage this encounter killing?[5] How can a premeditated murder, a fake encounter staged by the state and its collaborators, go unpunished?

The various contradictory accounts of what transpired shed light on how thirty years of increasing military occupation have transformed Kashmir into a penal colony. The story of Hilal's murder illustrates how loyalty, truth and memory mutate under occupation, how such violence turns a simple search for answers into a fight for justice, a battle against lies, a struggle to establish a record of truth.

Mohammed Kamal Rather, Hilal's Uncle

It rained incessantly on the day I met Mohammed Kamal Rather. We met at the local bus stop and walked to his house in a tiny alley in the village of Ajas in Bandipora, in northern Kashmir. Weeks before, in Srinagar, at the Jammu Kashmir Coalition of Civil Society (JKCCS) office, human rights activist Khurram Parvez had told me about Kamal, a former BSF guard who had written a book about the 'encounter killing' of his nephew, Hilal Ahmad Dar. That book, *Shaheed Hilal*, written in Urdu, tells the story of Hilal's life, death and the unrest that followed.

When we sat down to speak, Kamal brought out three thick files filled with newspaper clippings, medical examiner reports, police reports and court documents, along with a copy of his book.

Kamal spoke rapidly as I flipped through his book, which he had heavily marked and underlined. On the cover was a photograph of Hilal's funeral procession, and the back featured a close-up image of the young man's bearded face.

Inside the book, a picture of a much younger Kamal, taken shortly after he joined the BSF in 1969, graced the author's page. The younger Kamal was photographed in profile, wearing a collared shirt, his chin up and his eyes bright with a little smile. It was the kind of all-purpose photograph that most young men took in the 1980s as soon as they graduated from school or college, to attach to job applications and send to the homes of prospective brides. The young man staring back at me from the author's photo was from another world, and I was struck by how this black-and-white image of a man in his youth, from a time when death had not yet affected life, was so different from the man sitting before me. Time had been cruel to Kamal. Now, he looked exhausted and a decade older than he really was.

He spoke urgently, often repeating himself, describing the same events over and over again. He took on the voice of a seasoned preacher. It was as if, to tell the story of this loss, he had become someone else.

Around 2008, long before Hilal's death, Kamal had started meticulously cataloguing killings in the area. When his nephew died, he started the book to commemorate his life, but also to record the violence his village had experienced for years, and the destruction of his own family.

Kamal was deeply consumed by the loss of his nephew. Like many men and women I met in the valley, he was suffocating under the agony of being forgotten. He was retreating into memories of his life before this violence, while still struggling to keep the trauma alive, despite the enormous sadness it brought him.

'One day I will be gone, and I do not want his death to be forgotten. Through this book, something will remain. Some way of knowing that he had existed,' Kamal said, gazing at his nephew's photo in one the local newspapers spread out before us.

'Do you know the story of the four Hufaaz brothers who were killed?' he asked. I didn't. 'No one remembers anymore; no one knows what happened to the family. I don't want Hilal to be gone. I don't want people to forget him like we have forgotten so many of our boys.'

I tried to ask Kamal questions about his time at the BSF, and why he left. But he wanted to tell me about his nephew. Hilal was the eldest son and sole wage earner in a family of six. He worked as a security guard at Khyber Cements in another district about three hours from Aloosa. When he died, he had just come home for three days to help make arrangements for his upcoming wedding.

Kamal described his nephew as a devout Muslim affiliated with the Tablighi Jamaat, a Sunni missionary movement that focuses on returning to the fundamental tenets of Sunni Islam, particularly in matters of ritual, dress and personal behaviour. He had recently started preaching and giving sermons at the local Tablighi Jamaat-affiliated mosque. Over six feet tall, Hilal towered over others. His mother often called him a gentle giant.

'He had never picked up a gun in his life, nor was he associated with anyone or any group that would suggest it.' Kamal repeated multiple times that 'Hilal's religious ways, his beliefs, and the way he looked, [were] the reason he is dead'.

'These days if you are religious, it is easier to say that you are a militant,' he said about the government's active campaign to stamp out the perceived threat of militant Islam.

Hilal's parents watched him leave at 5.15 p.m. on 24 July 2012. That was the last time they saw their son. Early the next morning, Hilal's bullet-ridden body was found in the Ashtingoo forests. What happened between Hilal's disappearance that evening and his death remains a mystery, though rumours and conspiracy theories abound.

In the early hours of 25 July, Fayaz Ahmed, a local labourer in Ratnar, a village on the edge of the Ashtingoo forests, was collecting firewood. When Fayaz reached the woods, he saw a large contingent of the local Rashtriya Rifles (27 RR) battalion. Fayaz was detained, questioned and released. While he was being questioned, he saw a body lying lifeless face down, and described it as 'dry, with no blood'.[6] Fayaz also saw a pair of discarded gloves lying next to the body beside some empty packets of Nevla tobacco.[7] The items that Fayaz alleges he saw are not listed in the final forensic report.

Kamal said that Hilal's body was found with his hands tied behind him. His neck, ribs and spine were broken, and his face and body showed visible torture wounds. Eleven bullet marks were found in his abdomen. According to Kamal, Gujjar nomads, who use the forest as seasonal grazing fields, said that 'they heard cries and screams in the middle of the night that lasted a while, followed by firing'.

When Kamal accompanied Hilal's father, Ghulam Mohiuddin Dar, to perform the last rites and cleansing rituals, he saw torture marks all over the body. They also suspected that his neck had been broken.

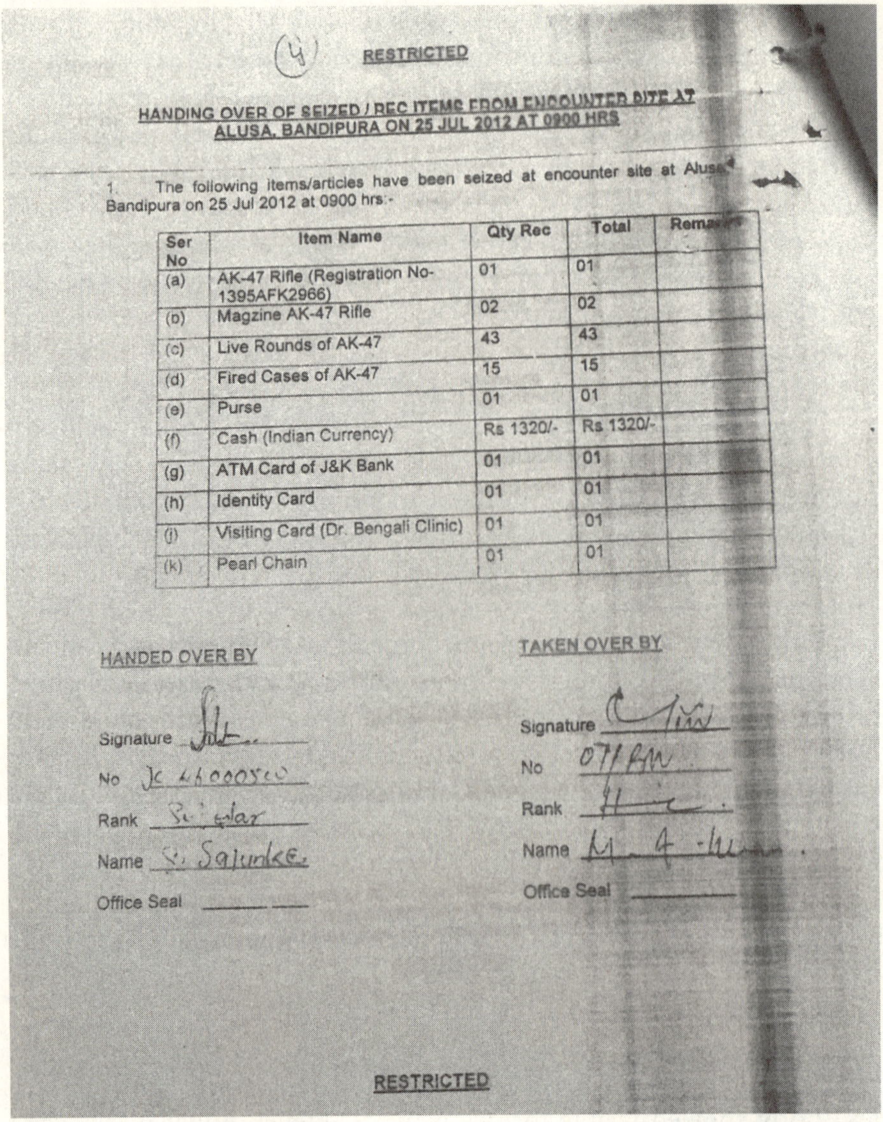

(4)

RESTRICTED

HANDING OVER OF SEIZED / REC ITEMS FROM ENCOUNTER SITE AT ALUSA, BANDIPURA ON 25 JUL 2012 AT 0900 HRS

1. The following items/articles have been seized at encounter site at Alusa Bandipura on 25 Jul 2012 at 0900 hrs:-

Ser No	Item Name	Qty Rec	Total	Remarks
(a)	AK-47 Rifle (Registration No-1395AFK2966)	01	01	
(b)	Magzine AK-47 Rifle	02	02	
(c)	Live Rounds of AK-47	43	43	
(d)	Fired Cases of AK-47	15	15	
(e)	Purse	01	01	
(f)	Cash (Indian Currency)	Rs 1320/-	Rs 1320/-	
(g)	ATM Card of J&K Bank	01	01	
(h)	Identity Card	01	01	
(j)	Visiting Card (Dr. Bengali Clinic)	01	01	
(k)	Pearl Chain	01	01	

HANDED OVER BY

Signature [illegible]

No JC [illegible]

Rank [illegible]

Name S. Salunke

Office Seal

TAKEN OVER BY

Signature [illegible]

No [illegible]

Rank [illegible]

Name [illegible]

Office Seal

RESTRICTED

In the meantime, the army issued a statement that its 27 RR battalion had killed a militant in an encounter. The army spokesperson said:

> The deceased was a militant, killed after he fired upon an ambush party. At about 23:45 hours, the ambush party noticed suspicious movement. On being challenged, the ambush party of 27 Rashtriya Rifles was fired upon. A brief firefight ensued. Later during the

> search of the site, one body and an AK-47, along with ammunition, were recovered. The body was later identified as Hilal Ahmad Dar s/o Ghulam Mohiuddin Dar r/o Village Alusa, Bandipur. The body and the recovered arms and ammunition have been handed over to the Police.[8]

Hilal's death triggered massive protests in Bandipora and other adjoining areas. When the news about the killing spread, people from the nearby villages thronged the Ashtingoo forests, shouting pro-freedom and anti-India slogans. The mourners refused to bury the body, and clashes broke out between the police and protestors. In the days that followed, local newspapers reported that at least twenty people, including police officers, were injured.[9] The police used tear gas and baton charges to disperse the protestors and, as the tensions escalated, took possession of Hilal's body during the funeral procession. The body was returned to the family later in the evening for burial, and a citywide curfew was announced.

On the evening of the funeral, Kamal said, the director general of police, along with a military commander, visited the family. 'They came to tell us it will be okay. But they never apologised.' A few days after the funeral, two men from Hilal's village were arrested and charged in connection with the killing. After six months, the police ordered the investigation closed and acquitted the army of all wrongdoing. But the two local men were charged and arrested.

Kamal said, 'We want justice.' But when I asked him what justice looked like to him, he paused and said, 'I don't know anymore. They kill us like chickens.'

'Will the army ever be held accountable?' he asked. 'The entire [Kashmiri] state—our police and our politicians—are afraid of the Indian Army. When the state is afraid of the army, then where will I find justice, how will I find justice?'

When I finished my interview with Kamal, a young woman with a blue scarf brought us tea. When she heard Hilal's name, she paused, retied her scarf and left the room. Kamal sipped his tea, but as he watched the girl leave, his eyes filled with tears. The young woman had been engaged to Hilal. 'They kill us like chickens,' he remarked again. '[The Indian Army] say I am Indian. If I am Indian, then why am I afraid?'

After a pause, he added that the two men, Rameez and Nazir, whom the police had arrested and charged with Hilal's death, had been released on bail just two days earlier.

'My sister now has to see them every day. They killed our boy, and now we have to live right next to them.'

There was a new kind of fear now: the fear of being around men who, in collaboration with the Indian military, had killed their son and nephew. The fear of running into these men on the streets and in their mosques. It was as if they lost him every day, over and over again. No one had told them that the fear felt precisely the same as pain.

Muhammad Ramzan Lone (alias Rameez), The Informant

Later that day, with the help of the local reporter, Saleem Bin Ahmed, I found the address of the first man accused in Hilal's killing—Muhammad Ramzan Lone, alias Rameez. After being released on bail, Rameez had returned home to Lahipora, Aloosa. From the guesthouse in Bandipora, we drove two hours west towards the border. When Saleem and I reached Rameez's house, Saleem went ahead and briefly spoke to an older gentleman on the porch, who called for Rameez. After consulting with the older man, Rameez agreed to talk to us.

We went inside and sat in a large west-facing room. In the evening light, Rameez's long, gaunt face looked even longer. He was a handsome man in his thirties. Like many boys of his generation, Rameez had left his home in Kashmir to fight and become a part of the anti-India militancy. He crossed the border into Pakistan from Keran around 1996, when he was fifteen, and trained in Muzaffarabad. In 2008, he was sent to Nepal with a Pakistani passport to run a handicrafts store. The details of his journey from Pakistan to Nepal and then back home are murky.

On his return to Srinagar from Nepal, the Special Task Force—the counter-insurgency division of the Jammu and Kashmir Police in Rajbagh—arrested Rameez. He was tortured by the police first, and then handed over to the military, who, he claims, detained him, first at the army camp in Aloosa and later at Watlab, for a year and a half. Rameez said he was briefly held in solitary confinement, in a room the size of a small closet. He was finally released on 15 October 2010.

Rameez said he was in touch with the men who had trained him in Muzaffarabad up until 2008. During that time, he reported back to Major Tariq in Pakistan, and his next-in-command in Ganderbal in Kashmir. He claims to have lost touch with them after his first arrest.

During our four-hour-long interview, Rameez denied ever having worked as an informant for the Indian Army. He portrayed himself as a man who had returned home and suffered the well-known consequences of being a 'surrendered militant'. When I showed him newspaper reports that referred to him as an informant, he denied being one.

A source, informer or mukhbir is someone who works for the military and the police surreptitiously by spying on his community and passing on information about the presence of 'unusual activities', movements of militants and other information the security establishment deems essential. It is not uncommon for surrendered militants to be forced to work as informants under the threat of incarceration or worse fates.

In other cases, the inducement is money. Informants are paid depending on the 'category of militants' they help identify and bring down: A++, A+, A, B and C. In an informal chat with an officer of the Territorial Army, the officer said that sometimes the informant will wait for a 'C-grade militant to grow infamous and become a B or an A' before they hunt them down.

This cash-for-kill incentive is an official policy, one that has turned the capturing and killing of 'militants' into a game of bounty hunting. The policy came under intense criticism during the notorious Machil fake-encounter case in 2010 when three men—Shezad Ahmad Khan, Riyaz Ahmad Lone and Mohammad Shafi Lone—were killed by the army in the Machil sector on the LoC in a staged 'encounter killing'.[10]

The victims were lured to the LoC by a former Special Police Officer (SPO), Bashir Ahmad, and his two associates, who promised them jobs. It was reported and later confirmed at trial that the SPO and his two accomplices received Rs 50,000 each from the army for orchestrating the killings.[11] In 2014, the military sentenced five of its personnel, including two officers, to life imprisonment for staging the murder of the three youths in Machil.[12] The verdict was later suspended, and all the men were released in July 2017.

The military spends enormous time and resources cultivating informants in every village. It has created a vast information-gathering surveillance apparatus to maintain and further its military occupation. The methods are as pervasive as they are intrusive. Men and women with compromised sociopolitical pasts or predicaments are blackmailed and recruited as individual informants. They might be surrendered militants or just families of young boys currently detained under the Jammu and Kashmir Public Safety Act, 1978, for stone pelting—almost anyone is a potential informant. Some are tortured and forced into submission. Others are bribed to turn against their community.

In Kashmir, surveillance is an equal-opportunity oppressor and, once recruited, informants act as the all-seeing, extended eye of the state. The informants have little social standing, and are often targeted by the various militant groups they've betrayed. In Palestine, some groups film and circulate executions of Israeli collaborators so that their families become outcasts as well. In Kashmir, while such videos don't exist, the act of collaborating with the army and acting as an informant carries immense social stigmatisation. In 2011, two teenage sisters from Sopore, a town in the Baramulla district northwest of Srinagar, were accused of being police informers and killed by local members of the Lashkar-e-Taiba, a militant group active throughout South Asia.[13]

When I asked about Hilal, Rameez claimed to have never met him. He said he first heard of Hilal only after his death, when the village had erupted in anger with week-long protests.

Rameez said that, after the funeral, he heard a few village elders say that Hilal was a militant who belonged to the Lakshar, and that they had seen him carrying a gun around the village. They described Hilal as a very religious boy who worked at the cement factory.

On 28 July, three days after Hilal's death, Rameez said, he received a call from a local Station House Officer (SHO), asking him to come to the police station the next day. This officer, he alleged, called him regularly for information on the locals, and often recruited other surrendered militants in the village to report to him. According to Rameez, the officers in both the army and the police had a list of surrendered and returned militants in the area. At this, Rameez again denied that he was an informant. He had never met the SHO in person, and they spoke only over the phone. He had fed this officer only local gossip about births, deaths, marriages and 'the miscellaneous'. He said he cooperated to stay out of trouble. He feared being tortured again.

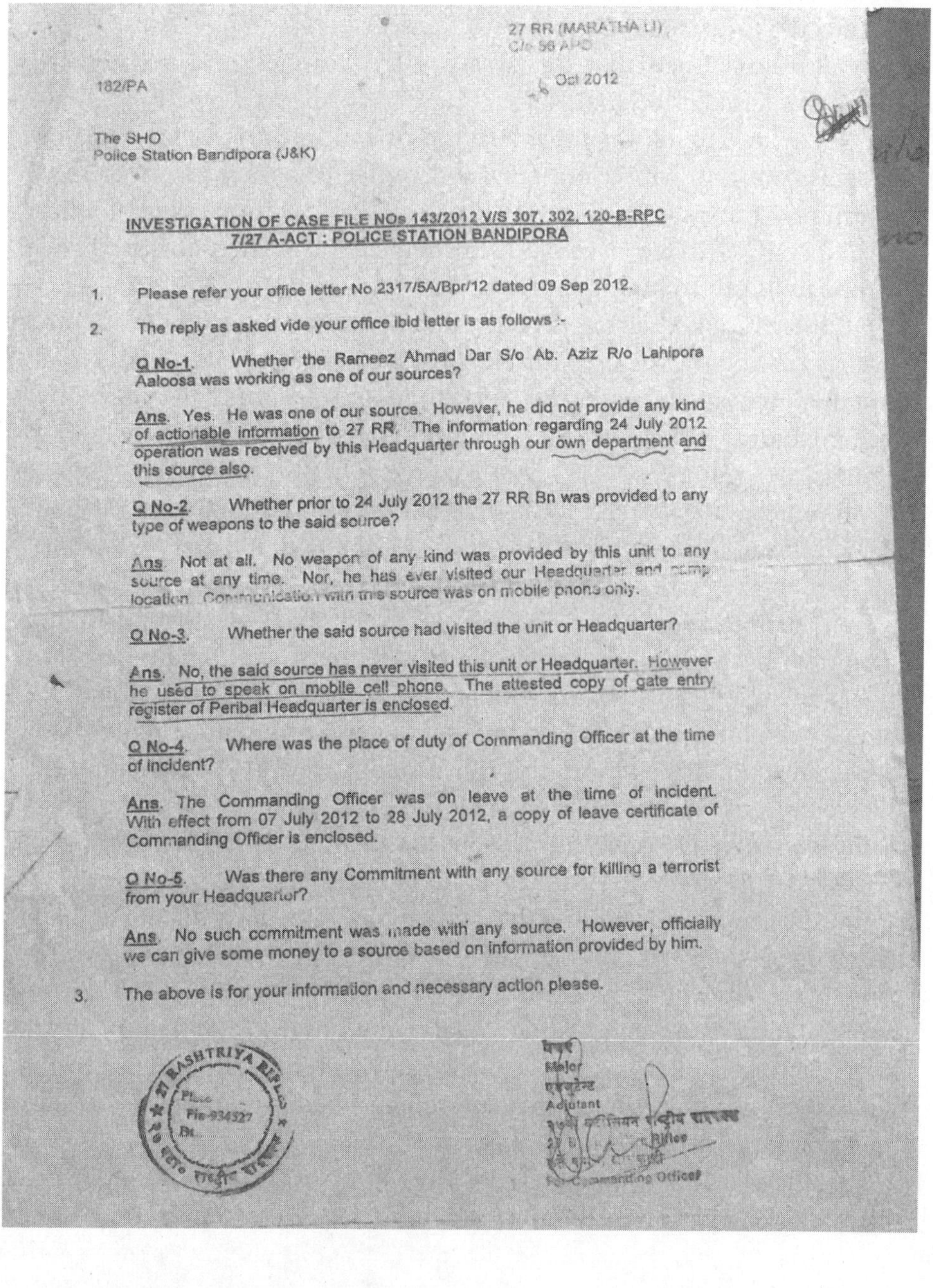

27 RR (MARATHA LI)
C/o 56 APO

182/PA

6 Oct 2012

The SHO
Police Station Bandipora (J&K)

INVESTIGATION OF CASE FILE NOs 143/2012 V/S 307, 302, 120-B-RPC 7/27 A-ACT : POLICE STATION BANDIPORA

1. Please refer your office letter No 2317/5A/Bpr/12 dated 09 Sep 2012.

2. The reply as asked vide your office ibid letter is as follows :-

Q No-1. Whether the Rameez Ahmad Dar S/o Ab. Aziz R/o Lahipora Aaloosa was working as one of our sources?

Ans. Yes. He was one of our source. However, he did not provide any kind of actionable information to 27 RR. The information regarding 24 July 2012 operation was received by this Headquarter through our own department and this source also.

Q No-2. Whether prior to 24 July 2012 the 27 RR Bn was provided to any type of weapons to the said source?

Ans. Not at all. No weapon of any kind was provided by this unit to any source at any time. Nor, he has ever visited our Headquarter and camp location. Communication with this source was on mobile phone only.

Q No-3. Whether the said source had visited the unit or Headquarter?

Ans. No, the said source has never visited this unit or Headquarter. However he used to speak on mobile cell phone. The attested copy of gate entry register of Peribal Headquarter is enclosed.

Q No-4. Where was the place of duty of Commanding Officer at the time of incident?

Ans. The Commanding Officer was on leave at the time of incident. With effect from 07 July 2012 to 28 July 2012, a copy of leave certificate of Commanding Officer is enclosed.

Q No-5. Was there any Commitment with any source for killing a terrorist from your Headquarter?

Ans. No such commitment was made with any source. However, officially we can give some money to a source based on information provided by him.

3. The above is for your information and necessary action please.

27 RASHTRIYA RIFLES
Pin-934527

Major
Adjutant
For Commanding Officer

On reaching the station, Rameez was detained, and SPO Bashir Khan at the station showed him a video of Nazir, the other accused, confessing and implicating him. When Rameez was interrogated, SPO Khan told him that subpoenaed phone records showed that Hilal had called two numbers on the night of his murder: one belonged to Nazir and the other to Rameez.

Rameez claimed that this was not his number, and insisted he had never spoken to Hilal.

The next day he was moved to the prison in Baramulla. A major general from the army came to visit him. He was then forced to sign a series of papers. Rameez stated that he had no knowledge of what he had confessed to or was made to sign. He was beaten, tortured and forced to admit to Hilal's murder.

Rameez looked at me directly, and spoke in a steady, low voice. Even as he contradicted himself, provided no proof for his claims and lied, he spoke with the perfect tenor of a man wronged by circumstance. When I pressed him for details and evidence, he talked about other things.

Rameez started talking about Nazir, and the rumours he had heard about him. Nazir, he alleged, had killed his first wife and mother-in-law with a grenade in 2002.

According to Rameez, Nazir's niece, Soni, and her friend Rafia, along with their uncle, were the real culprits who had hatched the plan to kill Hilal. Nazir, Rafia and Soni had all been detained along with him. But the girls had been released after they had paid Rs 6 lakh in bribes, and this information, he alleged, had been written out of the official police reports. Both Rafia and Soni, Rameez said, had secretly converted to Christianity, and Hilal had regularly harassed the girls to renounce their religion and become Muslims again. A few weeks before the encounter, Rameez said, Hilal had threatened the girls. If they refused to return to Islam, he would openly declare them apostates in the mosque. Rameez now became more flamboyant, saying that Hilal's mother, Fatima Begum, had testified to this in the court as a witness. (Later, I would find out from Hilal's mother that this was untrue. When I had met in her 2014, she had not even testified before the court yet.)

Rameez claimed he met Nazir for the first time when they were moved to the prison in Baramulla, where they were kept in the same holding cell. He claimed that Nazir hit him. After a pause, he smirked and added, 'Nazir might have problems, real mental problems.'

Before I concluded the interview, I asked Rameez where he was when Hilal was killed. Rameez said that he was at his in-laws' house, fifteen miles away in another village.

The things Rameez said did not add up. But I didn't know where the lies began and where the truth ended—or if there was any truth at all.

When I returned to the government guesthouse in Bandipora that night, I found a thick package waiting for me. Kamal had left a photocopy of everything he had on Hilal's death. There were police reports, Rameez's and Nazir's signed confessions, forensic and autopsy reports, the army's written response to various questions posed by the police, hand-drawn maps of the encounter site, photographs of Hilal's body at the encounter site, and the final police closure report that 'acquitted' 27 Rashtriya Rifles.

I spent the whole night looking over the files. It was impossible not to feel the immense weight of these records, which were also records of repression. The case files, police reports, army's interviews on record and confession statements, together with the evidence lists, forensic reports and interviews with the family members, all told a complicated story of former militants and local informants, and of a grieving family trying to understand the truth behind their son's death. Page after page, there was proof implicating a brutal occupying force and its symbiotic apparatus of impunity. Military occupation makes weapons out of the people they seek to control, turning them into agents of their own oppression.

Next to the signed confessions in the case file, I saw a photocopied image of Rameez and Nazir standing together. But I still did not know what had happened that night.

Nazir's Wife and Son

The next day I returned to Aloosa to speak to Nazir Ahmed Bhat, the second man accused in Hilal's killing. Nazir was not home when Saleem and I arrived. Instead, we talked to his wife and eighteen-year-old son. Nazir's house was dark, made darker by the deep-blue paint on the walls. The room we sat in looked like a shrine to Hilal, with hand-drawn posters that depicted him as a martyr, placing him next to a panoramic image of Mecca. Nazir had been accused of plotting with Rameez to bring Hilal to the site of his murder. After having met Rameez, who had denied knowing Hilal, I wasn't expecting to see a shrine.

According to his teenage son, Raees, Nazir and Hilal had become friends a few years back. Hilal's friendship transformed his father from a non-observant Muslim into a pious man who prayed and attended the mosque.

Nazir's second wife looked thin and frail. She held her six-year-old daughter, Tazeena, on her lap, and said that it was Hilal who had saved her husband from being killed, and that the family owed Hilal for his sacrifice. 'My husband is safe because Hilal sacrificed his life to save him.'

Nazir's uncle, Mansoor Ahmad Bhat, was a well-known local insurgent who was captured and killed in the 1990s. Between 1998 and 2000, the men in the family—including Nazir, his brother and Nazir's father—were regularly picked up and tortured. According to Nazir's wife, he had been tortured on at least fifteen separate occasions. Nazir had never worked; the torture had reduced him to a zombie. Throughout his life, he had drifted in and out of things. The family managed to survive by selling most of their land and through the charity of their relatives. This ongoing trial in which Nazir was the accused had already cost them more than they could afford.

In 2000, Nazir's first wife and his mother-in-law were killed in a bomb blast. Nazir's second wife claimed that no one quite knew what had happened, but a web of rumours and conspiracy theories grew around their deaths. The story's villain changed: sometimes it was Nazir, sometimes it was the army and at other times an unrequited lover. The motive ranged from money to revenge and adultery. Rameez had told us one version of this story the day before, adding grenades to the plotline.

Hilal, Raees said, had wanted to cross the border into Pakistan to train and fight for jihad. In Raees's recounting of the story, Hilal had spoken openly about these plans and Nazir wanted to join him. Raees was not sure why Rameez had chosen Hilal as a target, though it likely involved the way he dressed, his long beard and his growing reputation as someone who strictly followed the codes of Tablighi Jamaat.

According to Raees, Rameez offered to help Hilal cross the border. Rameez obtained two AK-47 guns from his contact at 27 RR and gave the weapons to Hilal to be cleaned and hidden away until the time came to cross. Hilal must have given one of these guns to Nazir, Raees thought, because after Nazir was arrested, the police searched their home and found a gun.

Rameez then asked Hilal to meet him in the forest, where he would introduce him to a militant who would help him cross over. Nazir and Hilal left together to meet Rameez that evening around four. Hilal went up the hill first, while Nazir waited behind. When Hilal realised he was going to be ambushed, he called and warned Nazir to run to safety. Hilal's call list, subpoenaed by the police, showed this last call to Nazir lasting no more than eight seconds.

About 2 a.m. on 25 July, Raees saw his father running back home petrified, bleeding from his leg. Nazir asked him to shut all the doors and windows. According to Raees, he seemed a little disoriented and anxious, and was mumbling all night. He had said that the army would come looking for him in the morning. Instead, early next morning, Rameez came for him, breaking their windows and threatening Nazir.

Later that day, Nazir was called down to the Bandipora police station, detained, and then taken to the prison in Baramulla. Then the police arrived to search his house and left with a gun.

Did Nazir have a gun in his hand when he came home that night? Raees was not sure. He didn't recollect his father bringing a gun back. Raees thought his father might have witnessed Hilal's death. He had heard stories, gathering contradictory pieces of information from his father and his stepmother when they spoke in hushed voices, and listening to the gossip he heard around the village.

On 23 July 2014, both Nazir and Rameez were released on bail.

Except for the incoherent babbling that followed when he ran back home that night from the forest, Nazir never told his son anything. Most days, his father and his stepmother behaved as though nothing had happened. Raees had lived most of his life without knowing how his grandfather and great uncle died, or learning the truth behind the strange story of the bomb blast that killed his mother and grandmother. His father's role in Hilal's murder is one more story where he did not know the truth.

When I asked Raees about his cousin Soni and her friend Rafia, their conversion to Christianity and their troubles with Hilal, Raees looked surprised and then denied the allegations. I wasn't sure how to read his reaction. Was this information new to him? Or was he surprised that I knew about the girls? Raees confirmed that Soni lived nearby and told me that she was four or five years older than him and engaged to be married. He knew that Hilal had spoken to Nazir about people secretly converting and raised concerns about people losing their faith. 'Hilal was always saying that this person or that person was a Christian. He was saying how people were converting to other religions. Even in the mosque, he said there were many Christians.'

I asked if I could get Soni's number, to talk to her. He pulled out his phone and dialled a number, but said that it was switched off. We never got Soni's number from Raees. We tried asking the neighbours about her, but Soni hadn't been seen recently and no one knew where she was.

We waited at the house until late evening for Nazir, but ultimately left without meeting him that day.

'It is hard,' Raees said, as I was leaving, 'to be called the son of a mukhbir. People think I can't be trusted, because of what my father did. But how do I tell them that he can't think right? That every time the army took him away, they only returned a fraction of him?'

Nazir Ahmed Bhat, the Co-Accused

Saleem and I returned to Nazir's house the next day to try and see him. We waited for a half an hour before leaving. Even Raees was nowhere to be found—Nazir's wife thought he might be away visiting his sister.

As we were walking toward the village mosque, I thought I recognised a man on the street. He looked like Nazir, whose picture I had seen in the case files, and Saleem walked over first to confirm his identity. Initially, Nazir refused to speak to us; he seemed nervous and hesitant. When he did agree, he didn't want to do it at his house, so instead, we sat in the front yard of a large house on the street where I found him. Nazir kept repeating that he didn't want to get into trouble.

Nazir had known Hilal for over five years. They were neighbours and became close friends in 2008. Hilal would visit him at his house all the time. Theirs was an odd friendship across generational lines. Hilal was still a teenager, and Nazir was already in his forties, yet it was the quiet and mature Hilal who played the religious mentor to Nazir, teaching him to pray and lead a disciplined life.

Nazir believed Hilal might have struggled to fit in with boys his age, many of whom were not accustomed to the new, stricter, more conservative version of Islam that Hilal practised. The lanky and long-bearded Hilal was also socially awkward around other young people, except when he preached the sermons at the mosque.

Around 2010, Nazir said, Hilal started speaking about jihad against the Indian Army as his religious duty: 'We have to sacrifice ourselves for the righteous path. We can do jihad with our bare hands,' was something Nazir remembered Hilal saying several times. In his occasional sermons at the mosque, he started preaching pro-freedom and anti-India messages, earning him a measure of popularity.

When I asked about Rafia and Soni, the girls Hilal had accused of converting to Christianity, Nazir said that Soni was his niece. Her father was also a surrendered militant. Hilal got into an argument with both girls about two weeks before he was killed. He had called Nazir, claiming that Soni had threatened him when he had asked her to convert back to Islam. Nazir tried to mediate between the parties, but his family was upset with him for still being friends with Hilal after he had harassed the girls.

When I asked about Rameez, Nazir said he knew him to be a surrendered militant. He had heard stories about Rameez crossing the border in the 1990s. A generation of boys had crossed the border or been taken away by the army to torture chambers. Nazir's uncle had also been a militant, and had been killed. Some disappeared, many died and some came back as broken men. Nearly every home in Kashmir had stories like this.

But long before Nazir became acquainted with Rameez, he heard rumours that Rameez kidnapped a girl and later married her. Nazir said he never took rumours seriously. 'People have fog between their ears,' he said and smiled. It was the only time he smiled during our entire conversation. 'We don't know what is happening anymore . . . We can't explain everything that is happening. So we make up our own stories to explain things, and after a while, everyone starts believing them. Even the person who made up the story thinks that it is the most truthful thing.'

A few days later, I met the prosecutor in Hilal's trial, who told me that while looking for Rameez's previous criminal records, he had come across a police complaint lodged against him for kidnapping a local girl, who was now his wife.

Nazir doesn't quite know how or when Hilal and Rameez met. But he knew that Rameez had started calling Hilal, promising to introduce him to people who would facilitate his crossing into Pakistan. Rameez had acted like someone who sympathised with the militancy to lure Hilal on the trip. According to Nazir, Rameez 'just set [them] up' to make money from the military or the police.

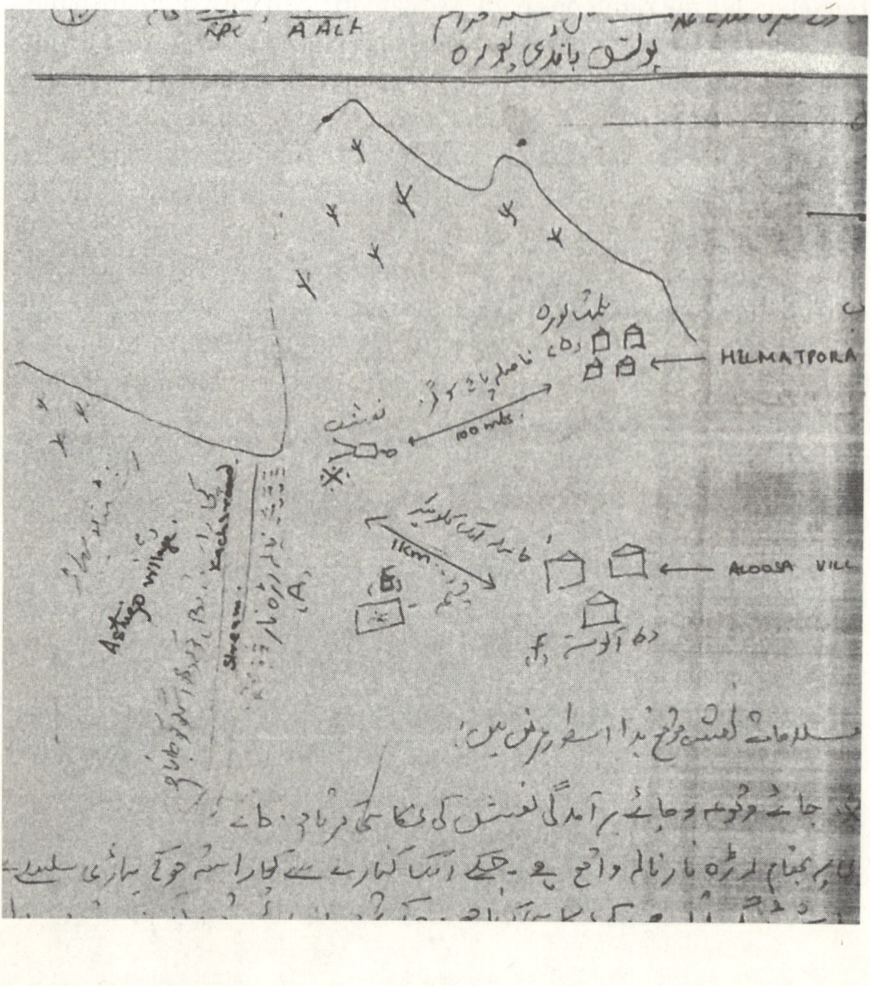

Hilal was an ideal target. He was a naive, young, religious boy who had decided that jihad was his calling. He had no local connection to insurgent groups. Grooming him into a sacrificial object was easy.

On 24 July 2012, Nazir and Hilal met multiple times. Rameez called Hilal with a time and location, and Hilal asked Nazir to come along. They left at 5.30 p.m. from the mosque, and on the way, picked up some juice to break their fast later. The plan was for all three of them to meet a guide, and that this would be the first of a series of meetings before they finally crossed the border.

Hilal and Nazir made their way up to the forest, trekking the four-mile trail, and waited for Rameez from 10.30 p.m. onwards. Rameez never came, but he called multiple times saying he was delayed, and convinced them to stay a little longer. As they waited, they heard a commotion. Hilal asked Nazir to wait and walked towards the sound of men moving. About five minutes later, Nazir got a call from Hilal.

'I am finished, you run,' were Hilal's final words to Nazir.

Nazir claimed that the rest of the night was a frenzy. He thinks he saw soldiers, but he is not sure. He ran down to the village, cutting his legs. Nazir remembered seeing his sister and daughter, but not his son, when he reached home. He pulled his kameez up to show me the scars from that night. I wasn't sure how many of the wounds were from that night and how many were from the fifteen times he had been taken in and tortured.

The next day, Nazir was summoned to the police station, where he was detained. He was then transferred to the prison in Baramulla, where an army officer interviewed him again.

I asked Nazir why he hadn't gone back with help, and he went quiet.

When I mentioned the guns, Nazir said that Rameez gave the weapons to Hilal three months prior to the ambush, but that he himself had never seen them. On the day of the encounter, Nazir claimed, he only saw the guns in the forest. The rusty weapon they found next to the body was not the gun Hilal had with him that night. The firearms Rameez had procured for Hilal were in working condition and not rusted. But when asked why no one had seen Hilal carrying a gun that day, or about the fact that he had never mentioned this before, Nazir said that Hilal had taken the guns up to the hills previously and hidden them there.

When I pressed Nazir about the guns, and told him what his son Raees had told me earlier, he said, 'The boy doesn't know what he is talking about. He was never there. I didn't have a gun with me when I ran back.' Nazir thought that the police had planted the guns when they searched his home.

Nazir became more restless when we heard the local RR platoon patrolling the village right outside the gates. He got up and started walking away. Frustrated, I ran behind him to ask if he knew what he had confessed to. Nazir said that he never did well in school—he could barely read and write. Like Rameez, Nazir said he had signed the confession without knowing what was written on it.

As we parted ways, Nazir asked me not to return, in a tone caught between desperation and pleading. He walked away quickly, disappearing into a smaller alleyway in the opposite direction from his home.

I left feeling more unsettled than before. By now, I had spoken to four men, but all of them had told me a different version of the events. It only clouded my image of who Hilal was and how he died.

Nazir left me with many unanswered questions. Was he really going to cross over with Hilal? Why would a man in his forties, with a family to take care of, agree to cross over and become a militant? Why had Nazir not come back with help? I also wanted to ask him about his life as a young man, his uncle's story as a militant, and his encounters with torture and violence. But those questions remained unanswered.

When I returned two years later, Nazir and Rameez had been rearrested, their bail revoked, and they had been taken back into custody for intimidating the witnesses.[14] They are currently held at the district jail in Baramulla. The public prosecutor, Shafeeq Ahmad Bhat, told the judge that, ever since Rameez and Nazir had been released on bail, the necessary witnesses had stopped appearing before the court. Both men lived close to these witnesses and, in various instances, intimidated them. He added that they had violated their bail conditions, including by leaving the jurisdiction and not appearing in person for every hearing during the trial.[15]

Both Rameez and Nazir had signed written confessions during their initial arrests. Their confessions, which I had read in the case file, tell a very different story from the ones they told me.

In his signed confession, Rameez said that he acquired two guns and three magazines from Commanding Officer Gill of 27 RR. He called Hilal and Nazir to the forest on the evening of 24 July: 'I asked both of them to reach Radnaar [where the encounter took place] along with weapons and informed the Army about militant movement in the area, then Major Nikal of Malangam camp informed me on Phone No 9797792410 that they [had] captured Hilal alive.'[16] Rameez's confession implicated the army as an accomplice. They gave him the gun and the motive to orchestrate killings. 27 RR confirmed that Rameez was one of their informants, but denied that they provided him with any weapons.

Still, the police did recover a gun from Nazir's house. Who gave him that gun and when? Was it Rameez on the day of their encounter, or had Hilal acquired the firearm from Rameez months earlier and then given it to Nazir? Or, if we choose to believe the version Nazir told me, when was the weapon planted and by whom?

Nazir's written confession, too, contradicted the version I heard from him. In his signed confession, Nazir claimed that Rameez was present that evening and that *he* fired at Hilal, wounding him first. The only other version that corroborates this story is the army's version, which states there were three men present. The army's interview transcript is vague and doesn't clarify who the third person is.

Over the past four years, I've struggled with these stories, often asking myself, 'Which version of truth do I believe?'

In a place like Aloosa, are there no reliable narrators left?

Hilal's Mother and Father, Fatima Begum and Ghulam Mohiuddin Dar

Having only met his uncle Kamal, I wanted to meet the rest of Hilal's family last. I tried to prepare myself as best I could, but meeting the ones left behind is never easy. Pain is for the living; the dead are immune to the consequences of death. By this point in my journey, I had spoken to hundreds of people who had lost someone violently, and those conversations were always painful and emotionally clumsy. I myself had lost friends in Kabul, Fallujah and Aleppo. In all those moments, words became impotent, even when they came from those who knew me and those I lost intimately. The night before I met

Hilal's parents, I stood in front of the rusted mirror at the government guesthouse and thought about what I would say. How would I convey my regret and tell them that I was sorry?

Ghulam Mohiuddin Dar, Hilal's father, was a tired and distracted man. But even in his exhaustion, he invited me inside and agreed to speak with me. His wife, Fatima Begum, joined him soon after, and one of their daughters left to make us tea. She looked thinner in person than in the picture, in one of the newspapers Kamal had saved, I had seen of her lamenting after Hilal's death.

'Soon after Hilal died, everyone came to see us. There would be a reporter every day. Sometimes as many as five or six would come in a day. Now it's all gone quiet. No one comes looking for us anymore. Hilal is now old news. There have been other boys, like him, many more, killed,' Fatima Begum said as she sat down.

Hilal, Ghulam said, was a good boy. He had only studied until high school, but had always been the hardworking, stable and sturdy son that a family could rely upon. He worked in the cement factory away from home and returned for a few days every month. Their home was always a pious and religious one. But it was Hilal who had introduced the teaching of Tablighi Jamaat to them.

Tablighi Jamaat, Dar went on to explain, was about being modest in dressing, and in actions—returning to how Islam once was. Hilal wanted the girls to be covered, not showing their arms, he said, as Hilal's youngest sister, a vivacious girl in her early teens, giggled and pulled her sleeves to cover her wrists. Ghulam smiled at her lovingly, and then said, 'She was too young then.'

'Is wearing his beard long [and] following the prophet a reason to be killed?' Hilal's mother asked, interrupting the silence. Every day, when she steps out of their house, she can see the path that leads to the hilltop where her son was killed. 'I heard screams that night, but I thought it was some animals. I didn't know it was my son being hunted.' After a pause, she sobbed a little and said, 'How can they declare my son a militant? My son has worked in the fields since he was nine to support our family, for his four sisters and three brothers. He was preparing for his marriage; he returned home to help with the arrangements. Why would he leave to become a militant when he knew we were dependent on him? When he was about to get married?'

The family had never heard about Rameez before the killing. Hilal had never mentioned him, and they didn't know when or where Hilal had first met him. They knew Nazir—he was Hilal's friend. Nazir, his mother recalls, visited twice that day: once at 1 p.m., and then again at 4 p.m. When Nazir came the second time, Hilal left with him for prayers and told his mother that he was going to another village to serve his Tablighi Jamaat duties. Hilal's brother ran into them on the pathway outside their house as they were heading out.

Ghulam called his son a couple of times that evening. Hilal's phone rang until 11 p.m., and then it was turned off. His parents assumed he had decided to sleep over at the mosque. When Ghulam woke up the next morning, two policemen had come to escort him to the nearby village. There he found the bullet-riddled body of his son with a rusted gun placed on his chest.

Ghulam had lost consciousness then.

'They returned his body to us, after the post-mortem.' Hilal's father, like Hilal's uncle Kamal, said that his son's body had several bruises and torture marks, along with the bullet wounds. When he washed the body before burial, Ghulam said, he saw Hilal's neck dangling like the broken neck of a toy.

After the funeral, a group of officers arrived at their home and asked him to meet 'Brigadier Dillion', who told him that 'Rameez was one of our guys. We got him from Nepal.'

Later, Commanding Officer Gill of 27 RR visited Ghulam and the rest of Hilal's family at home. Officer Gill said that if he had been there, this incident would not have happened. He offered the family Rs 6 lakh in compensation, and offered one of their other sons a job with the local government. Ghulam said he rejected that money. Other ministers and officials came to visit the family over the next week in an orchestrated spectacle: the minister of state for home affairs, accompanied by the director general of police, the principal secretary of home affairs, the inspector general of Kashmir and the deputy commissioner of Bandipora.

Six months after Hilal's death, 27 RR was acquitted of all wrongdoing. Hilal's parents continue to struggle to understand what happened that night. They have yet to find out what truly transpired, and they may never know for sure. Ghulam continues to collect newspaper reports about Hilal. They have tried to piece together the facts through these reports, but there are far too many stories about that night, and it no longer makes sense.

Rameez and Nazir—the men accused of killing Hilal—were both released on bail a few days before I visited them in 2014. Ghulam said that his wife hadn't left their home since she heard the news. She feared running into these men on the streets. But soon they must learn to live next to these men, just as they had learnt to live without their son.

Before I left, I asked Hilal's mother if they had a photograph of their family together with Hilal. She wasn't sure. But Ghulam remembered one. He told one of his girls to bring the picture they had all taken together soon after Hilal got his job at the cement factory. Ghulam held the picture in his hand and his eyes teared up. That was the last time the entire family had been together. He had forgotten that this photograph existed, and hadn't seen it since the day Hilal picked it up from the photo studio. The picture had all his children, with Hilal in the back row, towering over the others. This was the first time I had seen an image of Hilal taken when he was alive—even Kamal's book didn't include one. Ghulam said that he had nearly forgotten what his son looked like. In the past two years, he had only seen his son as a corpse in newspapers, books and human rights reports.

Saleem and I thanked the family and left. As I stepped out into the courtyard to go, I could see the Ashtingoo hills across the fields—the place where Hilal was killed. Fatima Begum and Ghulam Mohiuddin Dar saw this every day from their home. They saw the armed men in uniform that had shot their son patrol their village. And now they would have to see the men who orchestrated Hilal's killing on the streets.

This was not fear. They were living in an open-air prison that the state had built.

The Police Version

On the morning of 25 July, just a few hours after Hilal's death, the army published a press release stating that they had killed an unidentified militant during an ambush. When the police arrived at the scene, they recovered an ID card from the victim's pocket, which identified the body as Hilal's. They initially refused to move the body, stating that Hilal was not a militant who had crossed over, but a local 'who had been murdered by the army'.[17]

The local newspapers reported that 'Police filed the FIR [First Information Report] and arrested two men—Muhammad Ramzan Lone alias Rameez, an Army informant, and a local man Nazir Ahmed Bhat'[18] in connection with the killing. The initial police report stated that, on the 'night of July 24-25, 2012, Hilal Ahmad Dar of Lathipora, Aloosa was killed in a fake encounter at Ashtangoo'.[19] They suspected Hilal was tortured before he was shot dead: 'Presence of a rusted gun near the body suggested that a conspiracy was hatched to eliminate the victim.'[20] The forensic report indicated that the rusted rifle showed no trace of fingerprints.

The two medical examiner reports in the prosecution's case file differ a little: the first report verified torture marks, while the second report downplayed the visible marks on Hilal's body.

According to police investigations, the encounter was 'orchestrated' by Indian Army personnel belonging to 27 RR and one of their informants. A senior police officer from Bandipora told *The Indian Express* that 'posing as a militant sympathiser, Rameez started to entice Hilal Ahmad Dar into militancy' and that in 'March [2012], Rameez received two weapons from the Army'.[21] In his statement, the police officer said that Rameez had promised Hilal that he would arrange a meeting with foreign militants. He also asked him to find someone else who wanted to meet foreign militants. 'Hilal Dar then contacted former militant Nazir Ahmad Bhat and motivated him to meet the foreign militants,' said the officer.[22]

On the evening of 24 July, Rameez called Hilal on his cell phone and informed him that the meeting had been arranged, and that they would have to go into the forest to meet the militants.

When Hilal and Nazir reached Rameez's instructed location, they were caught in a military ambush. The soldiers opened fire on them, killing Hilal on the spot. Nazir managed to escape. The police had obtained Hilal and Rameez's call records, which suggested that 'Rameez was in constant touch with Hilal and the Army personnel'.[23]

But the police account of the story didn't explain Hilal's torture marks, and it was also the first time that Nazir was identified as a 'former militant'. No one else had referred to Nazir as a militant before. In its first reports, the police mention that 27 RR had not cooperated during the inquiry. Their final supplementary closure report states: 'Earlier, the Army unit was not cooperating, now they have replied to some vital questions, which should be treated as final evidence, hence investigation stands closed.'[24]

Despite the early accusations of wrongdoing, overwhelming evidence pointing to its complicity and a previously established pattern of impunity, the Indian Army was 'acquitted' of any wrongdoing by the police. The report also indicted Rameez and Nazir. In 2015, the human rights report *Structures of Violence* documented, through hundreds of cases, how the Indian criminal justice system—from the police to the Supreme Court—is complicit in the obfuscation of facts and evidence and how the legal regimes of impunity function to acquit the police.[25]

The Kashmir state police have investigated about fifty cases in which the army has been indicted in various killings. But the Armed Forces (Special Powers) Act (AFSPA), currently under operation in Kashmir, provides immunity to the army. AFSPA requires prior approval of the central government for civilian prosecutions of military personnel. That approval is rarely granted, as is evident from several well-known cases in Jammu and Kashmir.

Hilal's case was no different. The army can kill, maim, rape and torture with absolute impunity.

The police investigations into Hilal's death are useful for a few reasons. First, the multipage call history that the police obtained from the mobile company proves there was close contact between Rameez and 27 RR. The initial police report states that 'the accused, Muhammad Ramzan alias Rameez, had planned the fake encounter with the CO-27 RR and fired upon Hilal during the staged encounter. The army first captured Hilal, and then he was fired upon.'

Second, the telephone records subpoenaed by the police investigation tracked a total of thirty-eight calls between Rameez and Hilal over a period of six months—and twelve calls on the day Hilal died.

Third, on the day he died, Hilal spoke to both Rameez and Nazir. His last phone call was the eight-second warning he made to Nazir.

One of the army personnel interviewed in the police report stated: 'On the intervening night of July 24th and 25th we got specific information from our source Rameez, and an ambush was laid at Ashtangoo, we noticed the movement of three persons they started firing towards us and in retaliation one person got killed. He was identified as Hilal Ahmad Dar.'[26]

Who was the third person? Was it Rameez or someone else?

The local police, throughout their investigation, maintained that they had no record of Hilal's involvement in or affiliation to any militant or criminal activity; he was a civilian.

Over the course of the police investigation, *Hindustan Times* reported, the officer in charge of the inquiry—Waseem Qadiri—was demoted and transferred to the Special Operations Group in Srinagar in August 2014. The report called Qadri a 'whistleblower' and stated:

> [T]he investigation came as an embarrassment to the army, facing similar charges of staged encounter in Machil area where three civilians were allegedly killed in a fake encounter for promotions and awards in 2010. In the wake of wide media coverage of the investigation report, sources said Qadri was demoted from additional SP's post to DSP rank and transferred to the Special Operations Group in Srinagar last week. Director General of Police, Ashok Prasad, who assumed office last month, has now barred police officers up to the rank of superintendent of police from talking to the press.[27]

The final police report acquitted 27 RR of any wrongdoing. Deputy Inspector General Rajesh Kumar said: 'The investigation in the case has been closed.'[28] However, when questioned by a local journalist with the *Greater Kashmir* newspaper about the role of the army in the case, the inspector refused to comment.[29]

To many Kashmiris, the Kashmiri police is an extension of the Indian military occupation in the valley. There is a long history of distrust and a deep lack of faith in police investigations. In some of the high-profile cases of deaths, encounter killings and rapes in the last thirty years, the police have played a crucial role in protecting the army. In the Shopian case over the abduction, rape and murder of Nilofar Jan and Asiya Jan in 2009, the forensic evidence of rape was suppressed and compromised by local Kashmiri police. From the gruesome killings in March 2000 in the southern village of Pathribal to the most recent encounter killings and the rape of a young Gujjar girl in Jammu, the police have been complicit to varying degrees—'acquitting' the army of any wrongdoing, and willingly suppressing and tampering with the evidence.

The Indian Army's Version

When Hilal died, Bandipora seethed with anger. Violent protests erupted throughout the region, and thousands of people took to the streets, chanting pro-freedom, anti-India slogans. Amidst these protests, the Indian Army 'ruled out an inquiry into the matter'.[30] The general commanding officer of the 15 Corps, Lieutenant General Om Prakash, told reporters, 'For us, there is nothing to prove. It is clear . . . The army is a disciplined force and carries out operations with honesty and integrity.'[31]

No one in Bandipora believed this version of the story about how and why Hilal was killed.

As the protests grew, a curfew was enforced, and the Indian defence minister at the time, A.K. Antony, flew to Srinagar and ordered an official probe. A series of press conferences was organised, and the army issued its own press releases but refused to cooperate with the police investigation. After six months, the police acquitted the military of any wrongdoing, and only Rameez and Nazir were on the hook.

July 2020 marked the seven-year anniversary of Hilal's death.

As of September 2020, the case is still pending in Bandipora Sessions Court.

In Kashmir, state violence is openly exercised and flaunted as governance; it is integral to the way in which Indian sovereignty is practised. Hilal's trial, like many of the other cases currently pending in Kashmiri courts, presents us with an indictment of state brutality, while simultaneously inviting us to consider the complicity of those who peddle the promise of a more benign, transformed rule in Kashmir.

The soldiers responsible for Hilal's murder were incentivised to orchestrate the killings for professional advancement and money. It wasn't an accident or an anomaly, but deliberate use of unfettered power encouraged by the state. In a system operating with a cash-for-kill policy, encounter killings are not just condoned—they are encouraged.

In Kunan Poshpora, a village in Kupwara district, soldiers of the 4th Rajputana Rifles of the Sixty-Eighth Brigade allegedly raped more than fifty women in 1991. The Indian Army has consistently denied the charges as 'baseless' and called the women's struggle for justice 'mala fide'. In 1998, nineteen civilians, including eleven children and five women (one of whom was pregnant), were shot to death at point-blank range in their homes in Sailan in Poonch district. Their bodies were dismembered and disposed of. In official accounts, these heinous crimes were reported as collateral damage during an 'encounter', despite overwhelming evidence to the contrary.[32]

In a 2000 fake encounter in Pathribal, Indian military forces killed five men, and claimed the victims were 'foreign militants' responsible for the massacre of Sikhs in Chittisinghpora. During the investigation, the DNA samples of the Pathribal victims were tampered with. The Central Bureau of Investigation told the Supreme Court of India that the Pathribal killings by the army 'were cold-blooded murders and the accused officials deserve to be meted out exemplary punishment'.[33] Despite these findings, the Indian Army closed the case in January 2017, stating that 'the evidence did not establish a prima facie case against any of the accused',[34] and chose not to conduct a court martial.

Thousands of unmarked and mass graves in Jammu and Kashmir are believed to contain victims of unlawful killings, enforced disappearances, numerous fake encounters, torture, massacres and other abuses. The report *Facts Under Ground* issued by the Srinagar-based Association of the Parents of Disappeared Persons alleges that more than 8,000 people have gone missing in Jammu and Kashmir since 1989.[35] There have been innumerable army atrocities, followed by cover-ups and an endemic failure to prosecute. After years of conflict, occupation, and militarisation, a culture of impunity has flourished in the region, becoming not just a form of violence but also a structural element of everyday reality.

Judicial institutions like the Supreme Court hold out the promise of accountability and redress, but the pattern of cover-ups and denials persists. Every denial of justice extends the control of the military. In Kashmir, the few convictions we have seen have been exceptions in the service of a political end.

When Hilal's uncle, Mohammed Kamal Rather, asked, 'When the state is afraid of the army, then where will I find justice?' he was expressing a sentiment that many Kashmiris intuitively understand about the way the pillars of justice in the republic function in their borderland.

Rather than aid the system of checks and balances that impose accountability, the judiciary branch in Kashmir has become a distinctive tool of the state, penning the fiction of state accountability, while legitimising violence and counter-insurgency operations.[36]

~

We must place Hilal's death in the broader context of violence perpetrated against civilians in Kashmir and the long history of human rights violations sanctioned by the state in these borderlands. Since 1947, the Indian state has responded to the political aspirations and the social and legal demands in Kashmir through increased militarisation, repression and indiscriminate violence, including, at various times, the denial of democratic rights, the manipulation of elections, and the murder and imprisonment of Kashmir's key political leaders.

Change feels out of reach. When will we see perpetrators held accountable in a civil court under the public gaze? When will victims, survivors and their families finally have the opportunity to confront those responsible for what happened to them?

Nothing will change without an end to the military occupation—when freedom is not a rallying call but a reality.

India has emptied millions of her bullets in Kashmir, disappeared its people, and broken both homes and bodies. We have turned men against their own; we have created militants, insurgents and collaborators. We have built bunkers, golf courses, ugly dams and uglier buildings. We have purged civility and made love impossible. Yet, Kashmiris fight for their freedom every day. The writing of history in Kashmir is controlled primarily by India. Nowhere else does the state expend as much energy in shaping the narrative in its own favour. This history, which casts India as the moral heir to Kashmir, and Pakistan as the aggressor, is predicated on the silencing and erasure of the Kashmiri people and their struggle. What truths will we tell our children about Kashmir? What stories will we tell them about a republic called India and her unwilling and reluctant subjects?

In Hilal's tragic story, the border was not just a line that two nation states fought over: it was also the basis of an internment camp filled with the fear of unknown violence waiting around each corner, and sustained by deep corruption. Hilal's father said that there are days he remembers seeing his son's body and his 'heart freezes'.

'I cannot breathe. It feels like there is a noose around my neck.'

I wake up most days thinking about Hilal's family. I wonder how their worlds were made smaller by each encounter with this violence. How vast and expansive would their world be if they were not restricted by borders, ID cards, checkpoints, tear gas, violence and funerals?

9

KASHMIR TODAY

THE REVOCATION OF ARTICLE 370

The evening of 4 August 2019 was the last time I heard from my friend Nawaz Gul Qanungo, based in Indian-occupied Kashmir's largest city of Srinagar. I have called his phone and landline every day since. All I hear is the same automated voice telling me that the number is unreachable. One of his last messages to me was, 'It feels like the night before the floods,' referring to the brutal and unforgiving floods that completely submerged Kashmir in 2014.

In the early hours of 5 August, the Indian state imposed a strict curfew and an unprecedented information blockade on Kashmir. All lines of communication, including landlines, mobile phones and the Internet, were suspended. As of this writing, many Kashmiris remain cut off from their families, unable to reach them. In the days leading up to the blockade, 38,000 troops were moved into the Kashmir Valley. A recent report puts the troop count at a million.

The Indian state and many of its embedded journalists have called the situation 'normal' and under 'control'. However, there is nothing 'normal' about living in the world's most militarised region, under a violent curfew and an information blockade, while being totally cut off from the world. Since the crackdown, 4,000 people, mostly young men, have been detained. *Agence France-Presse* (*AFP*) reported that people arrested 'were flown out of Kashmir because prisons [there had] run out of capacity'.[1] Kashmir's political leaders, both pro-India and pro-independence, remain detained in unknown locations. Lawyers, journalists, local business leaders and human rights activists have also been arrested. Under what law, we don't know.

After imposing the blockade, India's ruling right-wing Bharatiya Janata Party (BJP), led by Prime Minister Narendra Modi, abrogated Article 370 and Article 35A of the Constitution—the laws that conferred special status to Kashmir—and bifurcated the state into two union territories, Jammu and Kashmir, and Ladakh. With the abolition of Article 35A, India has officially become a settler-colonial power in Kashmir. Many Kashmiris fear that India will settle non-Kashmiris there, and fundamentally change its demographic make-up.

Article 370 is a constitutional agreement that enshrined autonomous status to Kashmir and was one of the conditions of accession to India. Before the abrogation, Kashmir had a separate Constitution, its own flag and autonomy in all matters, except defence, currency and foreign affairs.

Legal expert and author of *Article 370: A Constitutional History of Jammu and Kashmir*, A.G. Noorani, has called the abrogation of Article 370 'utterly and palpably unconstitutional' and a 'deed accomplished by deceitful means'.[2] A decision that adversely affects over eight million Kashmiris was rushed through the Indian Parliament—unilaterally, without their consent—in less than two hours, without any discussion or deliberation. Kashmir is no longer Indian-administered or Indian-occupied Kashmir, it is now a land that has been forcibly annexed. More importantly, these acts should be seen as a part of the BJP government's calculated strategy of dismantling India as a constitutional republic and transforming it into an ethnonational settler-colonial state.

~

Despite the information ban, stories of horror and humiliation have begun arriving through personal messages, social media posts and ground reports from those leaving the valley. Zeba Siddiqui of *Reuters* wrote, 'I've returned after nine days under the communications blackout in Kashmir, and one word that has stuck with me is "zulm". From teenagers to the elderly, so many asked: "Kyun kar raha hai India itna zulm hum par?"/"Why is India committing such oppression on us?"'[3]

'Zulm' can mean acts that are cruel or unjust.

It has become clear that the abrogation of Article 370, and its accompanying violence, will open the bloodiest, most violent and most barbaric chapter in the long history of oppression in the valley. Since 5 August, mass detention, torture and night raids have been reported. On 7 August, day two of the siege, Kashmir witnessed its first casualty after Article 370 was abrogated. Seventeen-year-old Osaib Altaf drowned as he and his friends tried to escape armed men belonging to the CRPF, India's largest central armed police force, who harassed them for playing on a playground. The *Press Trust of India* reported that the boys were chased 'because of confusion over curfew'.[4] Speaking to *HuffPost India*, Altaf's father echoed what I have heard so many times in the valley: 'Who'll give us justice? We are under oppression. There's no justice in oppression.'[5]

Since the crackdown, protests have broken out frequently, and the Indian state has responded with more night raids by the paramilitary forces. Children have been violently arrested in their homes at night, detained without charges, beaten, wounded, hit by pellets and shot. Ali Mohammad Rah's teenage sons, aged fourteen and sixteen, were arrested in a night raid in Srinagar. According to Ali, the soldiers barged in and dragged his sons away.[6]

Unfortunately, curfews, Internet bans and indiscriminate violence are not new in Kashmir. The summer of 2016 saw over a hundred days of curfew imposed by the Indian state to quell widespread pro-independence protests. During the hundred days of curfew, the Indian forces used rubber bullets, pellet guns and assault rifles, resulting in the deaths of at least nineteen civilians, with over 8,000 civilians injured. That bloody summer also left hundreds blind, making it one of the first instances of mass blindings by a state. While the 2016 curfew was the longest imposed in the valley, it is just one of many that the valley has experienced since 1984. In Kashmir, curfew has always been a tool of repression used to crush spontaneous protest by the people.

Since Osaib Altaf drowned, there have been other casualties. Kashmiri families have claimed two other deaths—Fahmeeda Shagu and Mohammad Ayub Khan. However, the Indian state continues to deny these deaths, and has repeatedly stated that 'there is no credible proof that anyone has died in Kashmir as a result of the lockdown',[7] and that only 'eight people have been injured'.[8]

According to *AFP*, doctors have been instructed by the police not to issue death certificates.[9] It is as if proof and facts no longer matter, even if evidence exists in the form of a dead body. Similarly, the violence in Kashmir is not an aberration; instead, it has always been widespread, systematic and systemic, with the armed forces enjoying absolute impunity to kill, torture and maim. The tools of violence include extrajudicial executions, serious human rights violations, enforced disappearances, sexual violence, detention and torture, and all these acts meet the legal threshold of crimes against humanity.

~

On 25 August, the Srinagar-based journalist and my dear friend Parvaiz Bukhari sent this brief email to me: 'You perhaps know better how things are here in the blackhole than those of us inside it.' Not since the brutal years of the 1990s have civilians seen the army march into the city. The city has been divided into small units. Each unit is then physically remade into mazes connected by razor wires and steel barricades, guarded by men in riot gear. Similar to the strategies employed by the Israeli state in Palestine, entrances, exits, gates, checkpoints and diversions in the razor-wire mazes are changed multiple times throughout the day. A resident quoted in an *Associated Press* report said, 'They've changed the road map of our city, trying to make us like strangers in our own neighborhoods.'[10]

Radically remaking an occupied city is not only meant to limit protests, it is also meant to create chaos and confusion. It is as much about control as it is about disciplining and punishing Kashmiris, breaking them in every way possible. Encircling and entombing the local population with concertina wire cuts them off, quarantines communities, and makes life socially, politically and economically unbearable. Even the skies above Srinagar have changed, with drones buzzing overhead.

Many Kashmiris have now shifted their thinking to the idea that they have no option but to 'fight till the end' and resist being annihilated as a social group. In the Soura neighbourhood of Srinagar, young men from the community have built a makeshift barricade around various entry and exit points to their locality. So far they have successfully kept the Indian forces out.

The larger narrative has changed as well. While Kashmiris have endured immense violence for over thirty years, the issue has always been defined as a territorial dispute between India and Pakistan. Today, there is increasing awareness and acknowledgement of the Kashmiri demand for self-determination, and growing global solidarity with their struggle for freedom outside of the 'India versus Pakistan' construction. As a Kashmiri friend recently said, 'When they have promised to take everything from us, what is left to do but fight? So we will fight until our freedom comes. Zindabad.'

As this book goes to print, Kashmiris have lived under an unprecedented information blockade for over a year, the longest in human history. Their chants for 'azaadi', or freedom, have breached the borders of Kashmir and now echo in the streets throughout India, from Shaheen Bagh in Delhi to the street of my home in Madras.

10

RAJASTHAN

THE TYRANNY OF TERRITORY

One cold winter dusk, I stood on top of a BSF watch post along the India–Pakistan border in Rajasthan. From the watchtower, I could see the world's most extensive border fence come alive as the orange-tinged floodlights were turned on. India fenced and floodlit over 250 miles of Punjab's border with Pakistan from 1988 to 1993. By 1999, another 650 miles of the Rajasthan–Pakistan border were fenced.

The BSF officer who drove me to the watchtower, Bhim, stood next to the guard on duty. As the lights turned on, he smiled with pride.

'Nothing! No one! Absolutely no one can cross now,' he exclaimed. Pointing at the darkness on the side of the fence, he said, 'Nothing from Pakistan can come in. It's airtight!' He pronounced 'tight' as 'tit'.

Across the desert landscape, in the silence and emptiness of dusk, I could see small lights flicker on the other side of the border. When Officer Bhim repeated '*Ek dam* airtight' again, I could hear evening prayers from the mosque on the other side of the fence—not so 'air-tit' as he proclaimed.

But it is not just the azaan from the nearby mosques that the fence couldn't contain: it is also a thriving cross-border illegal heroin trade. Like on the India–Bangladesh border, farmlands caught in no man's land are double-fenced and locked up, and the farmers are given particular times to enter and exit their lands. Unlike the Bangladesh border—which is still partly porous, partly fenced, and where the international border cuts through homes, villages and shrines in a thickly populated region—India's western boundary with Pakistan is a desert landscape almost empty of people.

The sight before me was beautiful in its aesthetics and brutal in its existence. By now, I had clocked close to 10,000 miles along India's border. I had seen these same fences in Bengal, parts of the northeast and Kashmir. Every time I looked at them, I was reminded of the men in uniforms who shoot, kill and maim on order; of unthinking politicians who use fences and the fear of the other to win elections; and of a state that justifies fences in the name of freedom.

Our borders had become a spectacle, and we the cheering mob.

As the night grew dark and the last of the evening light disappeared, the floodlit border fence stretching into the horizon on both sides of the watchtower looked like molten lava running and spreading through the mountainous desert terrain. Rivalling the Great Wall of China, the fence that divides India and Pakistan can also be seen from space.

I wanted to tell Officer Bhim that, throughout human history, walls and fences had always failed. The walls of ancient Athens, the walls of Constantinople and the Great Wall of China didn't work. Even the Berlin Wall had collapsed twenty-eight years ago. This fence would also come down, like so many before it.

'We cannot let Pakistan take even an inch from us,' he said again, to break the silence.

Then I realised that the walls in people's heads, like their prejudices, were more durable than these fences made of concrete and wires.

Next to us stood the border guard, Prasad, who had started his eight-hour shift of watching this segment of the fence. I asked him if he had encountered anything since he was stationed here. 'No,' he said, 'nothing happens here.' Prasad, a pear-shaped man who was older than most BSF guards I had met along the border, said he did see a porcupine the first week he got here. He had never seen one before. Prasad placed an old military helmet on top of the porcupine and tried to take a picture, but the flash of his small cameraphone had scared the animal away.

'It took me thirty minutes to put the helmet on the porcupine,' he sighed. 'And I couldn't even get a picture.'

'Why would you do that?' I asked him.

'It gets dark, boring and lonely,' he said.

Prasad's honesty was radically different from the usual rhetoric I heard from BSF guards and officers, who portrayed themselves as heroes protecting and defending the border. What no one tells you is that a lot of soldiering is just sitting around—and occasionally trying to fit a helmet on the head of a prickly porcupine.

Prasad added that in his previous posting in Murshidabad—where Nehru once said that British rule in India had its 'unsavoury beginnings'—along the India–Bangladesh border, he 'encountered prostitutes', but here it was 'just porcupines'. The prostitutes he knew from his time there, he confided, were women that knew more about people and the world than anyone else he had ever met.

When Prasad mentioned the prostitutes, Officer Bhim stepped in to clarify that these women were 'illegals' who had crossed from Bangladesh—as if the act of crossing a border automatically rendered their bodies available for exploitation. 'They are honey pots, used to spy on our soldiers,' he told me with a serious face. Used by whom, he didn't quite clarify.

I had been to Murshidabad two years earlier. The roads leading up to the Farakka barrage—one of the many hydrodevelopmental initiatives that have dammed rivers that originate in India—were lined with shanty towns full of women who had been forced into sex work. Their numbers grew as more BSF personnel and battalions were stationed in the border region. The shanties themselves, already Muslim ghettos, had become further segregated as red-light districts. Smuggling and sex were ubiquitous, feeding off each other.

Smugglers regularly bribed the BSF with women, girls and young boys to ensure the safe passage of their goods. When a group of female smugglers crossed the border, one of them became the bribe, offering herself to the BSF or Bangladesh Border Guards (BBG). The women took turns with each crossing, so that others could carry on with the smuggling.

Prasad was irreverent in the presence of an officer, and went on to share some of the stories of love and betrayal he had witnessed while he was posted at the India–Bangladesh border. In one of these stories, a local pimp and smuggler had fallen in love with a newly arrived BSF officer from south India, who in turn fell in love with a local trans woman named Kamala, who, if the story is true, was offered to the young officer as a bribe by another pimp. Kamala then stole everything from the BSF barracks, including the officer's books, crossed the border and eloped with her young lover to Cox Bazar in Bangladesh. The love quadrangle had caused quite a sensation a few years back.

In the tone of a man who had told this story many times, Prasad took a big breath and said the real twist in the tale was that the BSF officer was a Hindu and the pimp was a Muslim.

Officer Bhim laughed aloud. 'Yes,' he said. 'These Muslim men are always plotting to steal our women. Now they won't even let our men be!'

As the kettle boiled and Prasad checked the tea for sugar, Officer Bhim repeated what I had heard many times from many officers like him: that Muslims were plotting to take over India, and their true allegiance, even those who had always lived in India, was to Pakistan.

'When the cricket match happens, all of them support Pakistan. How can you trust them after this?' he said in an annoyed tone.

He looked off into the distance. 'Air-tit,' he repeated, pointing to the fence. Just as he said it, the evening prayer from the local mosque stopped on the other side of the wall and, minutes later, the local Sikh gurdwara started its prayers. Many of the Sikhs who lived in the border areas had once lived close to the Muslim communities. The dargahs here, like mosques, recited prayers five times a day. A militarised fence and seventy years since the Partition had not changed that tradition.

~

Earlier that day, I had located the address of the Baba family. They lived about forty-three miles from the border post, and used to own a photo studio before Partition that had stayed open until the late 1960s. The young Mr Baba, smitten by the camera, had meticulously photographed the new families who arrived and settled in the region after Partition. I hoped that his family might still have the negatives, so I could recover and archive the images.

By the time I arrived at Baba's ancestral home, the last of the negatives had been thrown away or destroyed. The family found no value in holding on to the images after his death.

When I heard this, I was heartbroken. But the village held another story: Baba's younger brother, Chotu Baba, who was still alive, claimed that about twelve miles of the India–Pakistan border running through their village was drawn based on the notes and markings of a seventy-five-year-old, partially blind farmer.

When Partition was first announced, border commissions made mostly of lawyers, judges and civil servants had drawn lines on a map without giving much thought to their terrestrial counterparts. In many places, for the first few months, people did not know whether they lived in India or in Pakistan.

The actual work of demarcating the border fell to survey teams of local bureaucrats and police officers. It was not uncommon for the local farmers and village heads to accompany the survey teams as guides (and they were keen to protect their lands from being caught between the two new nations). When the survey team arrived in the Baba family's dusty village a decade after Partition, seventy-five-year-old Mota Singh, who had lost one of his eyes trying to stop a petty thief from stealing his horse, accompanied the survey team to mark the border.

With his famished horse, eye patch and a notebook made from pieces of paper his daughter had stitched together, Mota accompanied the team and wrote down every word these men said, recording where the border pillars would be placed. After a week, the surveyors left, Mota went back to his home, and the book was locked away for years.

On a hot summer morning fifteen years later, a convoy of government officials arrived to mark the border, but the survey team had lost the map. A young man who had witnessed the arrival of the survey team almost a decade earlier remembered Mota and his famished horse. A convoy was dispatched to look for Mota and his book. By then Mota was ninety, entirely blind and partly mad. But his old notebook was recovered, and the old man was taken to the site to recreate the lines and interpret his handwriting.

Mota's notes read like this: 'Ten feet from the cactus and four stones from the creek.' Which cactus plant? No one knew. And the old creek had dried up and become a part of the barren desert. The line had to be redrawn.

The village men and women who joined Chotu as he told me this story sat around him in a circle and disagreed on many of the details.

'Mota Singh had a donkey, not a horse.'

'He had no eye patch. If you stared at the hole where his eye once was, you could see his brain.'

Some said he looked like a deformed dwarf, while others said he was a handsome man with a lush moustache. Some claimed that Mota had died by the time the army arrived; others claimed that he was present and remembered everything.

In any version of the story, India and Pakistan have fought for decades over a few inches of land—a sand dune, a small island formed after a hurricane—and all the while, twelve miles of the official border might be based on the memory of a blind man.

When I finished telling Prasad and Bhim this story, Prasad nodded. 'It happens,' he said. 'India has such a long border. It is possible that some of these lines are not what they are.'

Prasad pointed to the fence and said that none of this build-up existed thirty years ago, and the idea of the border did not exist seventy years ago, and India did not exist one hundred years ago.

'Things change.' He shrugged. 'Who knows where we'll draw the next line and make another border? The way things are going, who knows,' he said. 'They lynched a poor Muslim man for singing,' he added almost as an afterthought, referring to the now infamous murder of Muslim folk singer Ahmad Khan. Soon after his murder, forty families fled Manganiyar, fearing more violence. The families were ostracised for filing a police report, and have been unable to return home. The men who killed Khan remain at large. Khan's killing happened in the aftermath of a series of gruesome lynchings across the country.

The longer I travelled, the less safe I felt. Fear was palpable, and many people I met commented on how 'something had changed'.

India was no stranger to violence. But even those who had lived through it before detected a grim turn for the worse. Violence had become respectable. The men who killed could do so not only with impunity, but were now garlanded and made into heroes. India's Harvard-educated technocrat, Jayant Sinha—an elected politician who regularly appears on the pages of *The Wall Street Journal*, *The New York Times* and CNN—praised eight men accused of lynching an unarmed Muslim man. The images of Sinha garlanding these men with marigolds were circulated widely.

'We keep looking at the border and forget the hate-filled people who are enclosed inside. Maybe we will dismantle these fixtures one day,' I said. 'All walls eventually fall.' But Officer Bhim looked at us, annoyed.

'No,' he said. 'The stories you heard were all lies. These people,' he said with contempt, 'lie all the time. Maybe they just made up stories to make you happy.'

'Perhaps,' I said. 'It is possible. But I am glad that they made up stories that I like.'

11

FAZILKA

BUNKERED TERRITORY

In 2016, Indian Army convoys were mobilised along the border with Pakistan—again. A headline read: '5 lakh people leave crops on Punjab border; Army to lay land mines.'[1]

In a 'war-like' 'exercise', over five lakh in the border districts of Amritsar, Tarn Taran, Ferozepur, Gurdaspur, Pathankot and Fazilka were asked to leave their homes.[2] Villages close to the international border—Hzareywala, Rajo Ki Ghati and Machhiwara—were evacuated to clear the ground for more land mines.[3] The army used previously outlawed weapons to create a no man's land on the border. The local gurdwaras were full of people who had fled, and others had nowhere else to go.

This was not new—fighting regularly emptied the villages, and in the seventy years since India and Pakistan won their independence, the army had returned many times to plant more land mines.[4] The people who lived here had seen multiple wars and regular cross-border shelling.

This new round of operations was an aftershock of the 13 December 2001 attack on the Indian Parliament. In response to that attack, India launched Operation Parakram, an extensive military exercise to be carried out along the western border. *The New York Times* reported in January 2002 that 'India [was] in the process of laying mines along virtually the entire length of its 1,800-mile border with Pakistan.'[5] Mines were planted in farmlands, and civilians were forced to leave the areas.[6] Also reporting in 2002, *The Guardian* called this exercise 'India's deadly defence: the 1,800 mile long minefield'.[7]

This was one of the most significant mine-laying operations in the world since 1997, when 122 nations signed the Mine Ban Treaty.[8] Anti-land-mine campaigners wrote to the then Indian prime minister, Atal Bihari Vajpayee, that they were 'gravely disturbed that Indian troops are laying new anti-personnel land mines along the border with Pakistan'. A similar letter was also sent to the leader of Pakistan, General Pervez Musharraf.

Operation Parakram lasted about a year, ending in October or November 2002. The Indian Army went back to its barracks, leaving the debris of destruction and mass displacement. People lost their homes, fields and harvests to the army occupation. While previous wars had always made this region volatile, the new military exercises ushered in a constant-war climate. Civilians and soldiers alike continue to become casualties to the land mines.

~

The bunker sat in the middle of the lush field outside of the 'war exercise' hot spot of Fazilka. It was an odd sight for me, but for the family I was staying with, empty bunkers were simply fixtures of their landscape.

'What do you expect? We are so close to Pakistan,' I was told quickly. Apparently, this was all the explanation that was needed.

That evening, I returned to the small plot of land to take pictures of the empty bunkers. When I got there, a tall older woman sat in the northern corner of the plot. Her all-white hair was tied back in a bun. Her face was long and gaunt, and her body was thin but strong. She wore a men's shirt with the sleeves rolled up over her traditional skirt.

She introduced herself as Sari Begum, owner of the small plot of land with the bunker. I asked her if I could photograph it up close. She agreed. 'The soldiers have gone. Take as many as you like,' she said, but added, 'Why would you want to photograph this ugly thing?'

I told her that, amidst this beautiful village, it seemed violent, ugly and out of place. I told her how I had been travelling along the length of the border for the past four years, trying to make sense of the country that was enclosed by these fences, and that this was the last stretch.

Sari Begum laughed. 'Why would you do such a terrible thing to yourself?' she asked and laughed again. 'You should have come here, to me, first. I would have saved you four years of your life.' People, she said, were the same everywhere. I didn't need to travel the length of this country to know India. All I needed was a bad marriage, a murderous relative or a greedy neighbour to understand this country.

Sari had lived her entire life in this village, farming her small plot of land. She had never left. But she knew what the world was like—violent, nasty and greedy. 'Sometimes you don't need to see the world to know or understand it,' she said.

'These borders [are] everywhere. Not just where our country ends. If you are a woman in this country, [they are] also inside you.'

This plot of land was all that Sari had. She was born here, she grew up here and she gave birth to her children here. All the good and evil in her life happened right here. About forty years back, a few men had come to survey her land and told her that a bunker would soon be built here to keep an eye on the border, in case the Pakistani troops marched in. She refused to allow such a structure on her land. The day they returned to build the bunker, she screamed and yelled at them, but nothing helped. The decision was made. When she continued screaming, the men asked her husband to 'take control of his wife'.

Her husband, a quiet man who was twenty years older than her, had never hit her. That day, he slapped her across the face.

The bunker was completed in a month's time. By then, her husband had decided he liked hitting her, and he continued to beat her for the next twenty years until he died of alcohol poisoning.

Every time Pakistan shelled India along the border, Sari's bunker filled with soldiers. Some were decent, and even helped her with a few chores around the farm. But most were rude. When she was younger, it was harder. They stared, lurked and sometimes harassed her.

'I have never been to the border,' said Sari. 'I have never seen the fences. Why would I walk all that way to see the desert and barriers?'

I asked her what she thought about Pakistan.

'Everything terrible that has ever happened to me happened here. All the evil people do, all the hate and greed did not come from the other side of the border. It came from this village, from the people I know. What did a Pakistani ever do to me?'

The next day, I was sitting in my guest room in the neighbouring family's house when a young man came in and informed me that Sari wanted to see me again. When I went back out to the field, Sari sat me down and showed me a necklace—the only piece of jewellery she had of her mother's. As we spoke, I learnt that Sari's story was more than the story of a bunker on her land. It was also a story of pain and violence that went back seventy years.

In the days leading up to Partition, Sari's father rounded up his friends and other men from the village to form 'hunting parties' or 'hunting gangs'. The men attacked Muslims in other villages and threatened the families to make them leave by destroying property and terrorising their communities. In the mayhem, Sari's father kidnapped a fourteen-year-old girl from a Muslim family that was fleeing and forced her into a marriage with him. Sari, the child of this kidnapping and rape, was born at the end of 1948, her exact date of birth unknown.

During the partition of India, it is estimated that close to a lakh women were raped. These assaults were deliberately planned to terrorise communities. Women's bodies became sites of great violence and trauma, and some were kidnapped and taken across the newly drawn border. The newly formed governments of India and Pakistan worked to repatriate these abducted women. Muslim women were sent to Pakistan, and Hindu and Sikh women to India. The official numbers have never been released.

Sari's mother was 'recovered', and taken back to her family in Pakistan when Sari was only a year old. Her mother's family had returned looking for her, and a deal was reached. The family paid a ransom and took Sari's mother back to Pakistan, but Sari was left behind.

When Sari was ten, her father was found murdered by the river. Only days before, a young man was spotted around the village asking about her father. A few days later, two other men who had been a part of the 'hunting gangs' were killed. Someone had returned, in Sari's words, 'to exact justice'.

The killings opened old wounds and dirty secrets in the village.

Sari was the living proof of those terrible months after Partition. She reminded people of their depravity and hate. When murderous men and women drove people from their homes and danced on their bodies. The stride towards freedom was a catastrophic march towards a holocaust that killed millions.

The Partition was genocide.

When Sari was fifteen, her paternal grandmother married her off to their farmhand, an unremarkable man who was twenty years older than her. A child of rape, 'born to a Muslim mother and murderous father', had no 'good prospects' of marriage.

On the day of her wedding, her grandmother gave her a delicate gold necklace that had belonged to her mother. Sari was also given the small plot of land her father had bought with the money he had demanded from her mother's family as ransom. The land, Sari's only other possession, was the price of her mother's freedom.

No one in the village remembered Sari's mother's real name. They only knew her by the Hindu name her father's family had given her—

Sadana. They described her as a pale, delicate girl, who spent most of her time locked up inside the house.

'I don't know who my mother is, I have never seen her. She is somewhere on the side of the border—dead or alive; I don't know.'

Whom did Sari belong to? India or Pakistan?

The women who survived the Partition, who witnessed the perils of this border, tell a different story because they live another life. A life where the violence of the border is not at the fence, or in the trenches, but at the centre of their universe.

12

SRI GANGANAGAR

THE TRACTOR BRIGADE

From the village 35BB, I made my way to the village of Nagi—a tiny border village in Sri Ganganagar. Villages in the region are named after the canal nearby. For instance, village 35BB is the thirty-fifth village on the 'BB' canal. Nagi is home to a shrine that is also a war memorial, which over the years has grown into a significant Hindu temple. As I've learnt throughout my travels, war memorials and shrines are a fixture in border regions, and often, the stories that accompany these shrines are believed like the real history of the region.

At the Nagi shrine, six large plaques were placed on the walls inside to valorise the soldiers of the Indian Army who 'sacrificed their life during the Indo-Pak War of 1971' and 'recaptured the territory occupied by Pakistan after the ceasefire'. According to the plaques, twenty-one soldiers lost their lives valiantly capturing a 'prominent dune'. Each year, the army celebrates the event through a series of spectacular light shows on the dunes.

I wondered if anyone else caught the irony. Dunes, by their nature, are transient—moving, shifting, collapsing and remaking themselves on the whims of the wind. Perhaps if the soldiers had waited, they would not have had to sacrifice twenty-one men to 'reclaim' such a thing.

In reality, very little appears to be known about the battle of Nagi. Locals old enough to remember the tumultuous years of the 1960s and '70s tell a muddled version of the events. Among the many stories I heard, one stood out, about a group of local farmers. Supposedly, the farmers spotted the Pakistani Army marching towards the border, and with no Indian Army close by, the farmers removed the silencers from their tractors and drove them towards the border. Without their silencers, the tractors roared and made noises like army tanks. The sound and commotion deterred the Pakistani troops marching into India. The valour of this event is generally agreed upon, but the dates varied: some locals claimed the event had happened around the time the dune was captured, while others said that the event had occurred much earlier.

Nobody in Nagi could, however, remember any of the men who had orchestrated this great deception. It had been over fifty years, and presumably the farmers had either left the villages over the years or died by now. Like with many of the rumours and audacious stories I had heard, I wasn't sure where the truth began and where folklore ended.

The local village sarpanch who accompanied me in Nagi was sure that the event had occurred in 1971. He was a balding man in his sixties who owned land by the border and worked closely with the army to safeguard his interests.

When I asked him why the story of the farmers and the tractor was not mentioned in the plaque inside the shrine, he said that the army eventually came to the village's aid, and military memorials were not the place to showcase civilian valour. He said, 'Sometimes we have to let them take all the credit for all the work they do to protect us.'

When I left Nagi, I was convinced that the tractor incident was a myth. But two days later, Bando paji, the patriarch of the family I was living with, took me along to meet his relatives in other villages in the area and drop off some sweets. I was staying with my friend Aneel Brar and his family. Aneel's family run a maternal and child health centre in Sri Ganganagar, providing quality, accessible healthcare to women and children in the district.

A quick visit to his family turned into a day-long affair, as he agreed to ferry many of them from one village to another. As the evening approached, we were dropping off the last of the passengers whom Paji had generously offered a ride.

He parked his car and went inside to help the women with their bags. When he returned a few minutes later, he was visibly excited. 'We found him,' he said. 'We found him!'

The woman Paji had picked up on the road turned out to be the daughter of one of the men who had driven a tractor to stop the approaching Pakistani Army.

Johinder Singh Suj was a tall, handsome nonagenarian, who looked much younger. Suj wore well-tailored trousers, a long grey raincoat and a white turban. He carried a beautifully carved walking stick. His home was flush with his children, grandchildren and great-grandchildren visiting him over the winter holidays. There was a bit of excitement, and all his grandchildren and great-grandchildren gathered around to hear him tell this story, which they had never heard before.

When we sat down to talk, I asked Suj his age, and he said, 'I am ninety-five, but write that I am eighty or younger,' and smiled.

In the fall of 1965, a local police officer called and asked men with tractors to make their way to the border. At the time, there was no army presence in the area; the nearest unit was at least a day away. The call for help came around late evening, and Suj and two neighbours mounted their tractors. About twenty farmers gathered outside a nearby village and started driving towards the border in the general direction of the Pakistani troops.

They removed the tractors' silencers, and the engines made a tremendously loud noise. They drove towards the border in the middle of the night in a U-shaped formation, hoping that shape would create the most noise and resemble a defensive position. Suj said that, without silencers, the tractors sounded like a .32-calibre, double-barrelled gun being fired in the air. The Pakistani troops eventually stood down and retreated from their position.

The whole affair lasted a day. It had been a great adventure, and the men later became local celebrities as the story of the 'tractor brigade' spread. Suj said many of the men who were part of the tractor brigade had lived through the worst of the Partition only a few years before the incident.

'Everyone had been both the victim and the perpetrator. We had our families killed and, when we saw a Muslim being murdered, we turned a blind eye. Back then we thought one of you, one of us, was some kind of justice. If they captured our village, the soldiers who had lost their own families could have retaliated on us as revenge.'

Suj said that the idea had worked. 'It was a simple idea, an audacious one.' The day after the tractor brigade, army reinforcements arrived. 'This country is made of people who have nothing—no power, no rights, no money. Every day, to survive, we think up great ideas and make grand plans. Yes, we fail often, but when we succeed it is marvellous.'

Over the years, the tractor brigade's little coup became a part of regional folklore, mixed and remixed with other events. Most of the men from that day are now dead, and of the others, only Suj still lives in the area. But like many people who are a part of this book, Suj's real story begins outside of that tenuous space we now call India.

Suj was born in Hyderabad, in the Sindh province, now one of Pakistan's four provinces and the historical home of the Sindhi people. He told me the name of the district, the county and the village he was from: Tharparkar (district), Digdi tehsil (county), Village 202. As I wrote these down, Suj bent over and corrected how I spelt Digdi. When I rewrote it, he smiled.

'I want to make sure you have the details of my home right,' he added. Almost seventy years later, he still calls the place he left his home. He told me about his high school—Mir Mohammad Haji Baksh Tanda Jan Mohammad—and the beautiful Sindhi girl he had loved. He couldn't remember her name anymore, but he could still remember her face.

Suj left his home when the killings started, at just twenty years of age. His family left everything behind, hoping to return one day, hoping that their country wouldn't be divided, that eventually the violence would stop and that men would return to their senses. He had rarely spoken about this history. It was not something most people who lived it talked about. Everyone was busy trying to rebuild their lives and mourn their dead.

'We buried or burnt everything—even memories. Now it's been too long, and no one cares. And, sometimes, after all this time, my memory fails.'

The only things Suj brought with him were two textbooks from his middle school: a geography textbook and a science textbook, both in Sindhi.

He lovingly brought out his books and showed me a 1936 map of undivided British India from his geography textbook. In it, he had taken a pencil and drawn a line dividing India and Pakistan, and later

added another line dividing India and East Pakistan when it became Bangladesh.

Suj spent the next hour remembering all the details of this home—the streets, the smells and the landscape. He still knew the names of the railway stops that connected the undivided continent before Partition: Mirpur Khas, Mirwais, Khushela, Digi, Tanda Jan Mohammad, Juda Ghadham, Roshna Bhag, Nuwakot, Doranara and Shadi Pelli.

'I don't think there is another place on this earth as beautiful as Digdi. I would like to return,' he said, 'but my knees are bad and who will take me there? It is too late now.'

By the time we finished, his grandchildren and others who sat around him had left. 'These stories are not interesting or important to them. They are young, and they only know an India with cafes, movies and Bollywood music.'

When I left, Suj walked out with me. 'We lost something else too,' he said. 'I spoke Punjabi, Sindhi, Urdu and Farsi. These languages did not belong to one person back then, [they] belonged to all of us. The food my mother made that I remember was not Punjabi. Instead, our Sindhi Muslim neighbours, who had lived next to us for generations, influenced it. Today, you can live in a city of a million people, and still not meet people unlike you. We have become small-minded people; where you are born, your religion and the language you speak define everything. Urdu is now a Muslim language. Like its people, the language is also exiled in ghettos. Farsi is no longer the language of the educated. No one learns it. The borders have made our minds smaller, our languages to die without care and our people petty.'

India is not yet a nation, she's a puzzle rearranging herself.

13

AMRITSAR AND NEW YORK

HISTORIES PARTITIONED

How many stories have we lost to your history?

My seven-year-long journey across the land borders of India ends at Jallianwala Bagh, the site of a 1919 colonial massacre in the city of Amritsar, in Punjab. Amritsar lies fifteen miles east of today's border with Pakistan, and was culturally and demographically transformed in the aftermath of Partition. Today, a narrow lane still opens onto the site of the now well-memorialised slaughter of unarmed civilians.

Reginald Dyer, a brigadier general of the British Army, had brought guns and troops through this small, constricted passage to attack men, women and children who had gathered at the Bagh on 13 April 1919—the day of Baisakhi, a harvest festival celebrated throughout Punjab. The only exits to the park were blocked, and General Dyer fired at unarmed civilians without any warning. In the chaos that followed, thousands were massacred that evening.

I know this history by heart. It is taught in schools, re-enacted in plays and widely written about. But in the long history of massacres that India has witnessed, not all are remembered, recorded or taught.

The site is now a landscaped garden filled with tourists, young lovers, crying babies and children running around with plastic guns, with many stopping at various spots to take selfies. At the centre of the garden is a memorial plaque, and to its right is the 'martyrs' well', where many jumped to their death, thinking they could save themselves. The well is now enclosed in a glass structure.

Further into the park is the decaying Martyrs' Gallery and a museum where portraits of 'freedom fighters' are hung—faded, cracked, mouldy and uncared for, just like the nation's memory.

A bullet-ridden wall has been preserved, and the plaque at the site reads:

> The wall has its own historic significance as it has thirty-six bullet marks which can be easily seen at present and these were fired into the crowd by the order of General Dyer. Moreover, no warning was given to disperse before Dyer opened fire which [sic] was gathered here against the Rowlatt Act. One Thousand Six Hundred and Fifty Rounds were fired.

I leave the site feeling unsettled, almost disappointed. I wonder if the museum's portraits, the garden and the memorial plaque do the opposite of their intended goal: rather than teach us to remember, they teach us to forget. I wonder about the descendants of those massacred, and what they had inherited. What aspects of the past have we preserved, how does this inform our present, and what will we leave behind for the future?

~

A year after I visited the Bagh, Natasha Javed, a Pakistani friend of mine now living in New York, tweeted that she had just found out that her great-great-grandfather had been killed in the 1919 massacre. She was struggling to come to terms with this information—not just the violence of the massacre but also the pain that this erasure had caused her family.

On a chilly November night in 2019, I went over to Natasha's home, which was not far away from my own. Natasha's husband put their beautiful son Kabir to sleep, and we began speaking about my upcoming visit to India to see my parents, and if it was still safe to go.

Narendra Modi, India's current prime minister, known widely as 'the divider-in-chief' and a 'purveyor of hate', had returned to power in May 2019. In a few short months, a series of unconstitutional legislations were passed—like the revocation of Article 370 in Kashmir, and changes to the UAPA, a law that gave the government unprecedented power to designate individuals unilaterally as terrorists.

Over 10,000 people were charged with sedition in the district of Khunti in Jharkhand for raising stone slabs with provisions of the Indian Constitution on it. The NRC was in full swing in Assam, and eight large internment camps that would house the many men and women who would be designated as 'illegals' were already close to completion. By the time I sat down to write this in 2019, twenty-nine people held in a detention centre in Assam had already died.

The year 2019 marked the hundred-year anniversary of the Jallianwala Bagh massacre. As I sifted through old newspaper reports in the archives, and personal accounts in the form of diaries and letters about the massacre, it became clear that, from the distance of a century, it was impossible to ignore the parallels to present-day India.

Natasha and her mother have had many conversations over the years about their family history. Yet, this revelation about her great-great-grandfather's death had come to her in an unexpected way.

When talking to her mother, Natasha had always struggled to understand how the four preceding generations of women in her family had acted, and tried to make sense of the choices they had made. What made them so willing to give up what was theirs, to concede so much space even when they didn't have to? Her grandmother and her three sisters, Natasha's grandaunts, had married into affluent families, had children and lived comfortable lives. Yet, Natasha sensed a darkness, a certain sadness and submissiveness they carried, that she couldn't understand the roots of.

She often used to question her mother: why did Nano (Natasha's maternal grandma) make a particular decision or act in a specific way? Her husband (Natasha's grandfather) belonged to a progressive family; Nano had so many opportunities, yet she faded into the background.

When Natasha told me about these conversations with her mother, I understood her words, angst and frustration. Perhaps all daughters ask these questions, trying to make sense of their family histories and realities. We are constantly assembling these puzzles in our minds, and are always a few pieces short of piecing together the prologue to our own memory. We are perpetually in search of some lost anecdote or some ghost of a character, some knowledge that would serve as the missing piece.

Natasha's mother, Mano, explained that, to understand the lives of her grandaunts and great-grandaunts, they must be seen in the context of their lived realities—loss, chaos and crisis. They were not just doting elder relatives; they were the products of a turbulent history.

During one of these intense conversations Natasha's mother said, 'You know, it all started with my grandmother and her sister losing their father in their adolescence . . . he was shot dead in Jallianwala Bagh.' Natasha was shocked; how could she not have known this detail?

In 1919, Mir Abdul Rahim—Natasha's great-great-grandfather—was a twenty-three-year-old hakim with a young family. He had just become interested in the nascent struggle for freedom in the subcontinent. Punjab at this time was brewing with dissent.

During World War I, the British government of India had enacted a series of repressive emergency powers that were intended to curb dissent. At the end of the war, 'Indians' assumed that these measures would be repealed, and they expected to be given more political autonomy. But the 1918 Montagu-Chelmsford Report—a set of strategies for constitutional reform in colonial India presented to the British Parliament—instead recommended limited local self-government and extended the repressive wartime measures.

On 10 March 1919, the Anarchical and Revolutionary Crimes Act, known as the Rowlatt Act for the English lawyer who chaired the committee, was passed, 'indefinitely extending the emergency measures of preventive indefinite detention, incarceration without trial and judicial review'.[1] The Act suspended the rule of law and enabled the British administration to effectively combat what they perceived as the 'major threat of revolutionary nationalism, the spread of Bolshevism, and to deal with the potential radicalization of demobilized Indian troops'.[2]

Calls for revolution were ripe, anti-British protests were blooming everywhere, and local nationalist leaders like Drs S. Kitchlew and Satyapal travelled through Punjab making speeches against the Crown and denouncing the repressive Rowlatt Act.

At the height of the agitation in Lahore, over 20,000 people took to the street to protest. In Amritsar, local leaders were arrested and banished from the city. Anger and discontent sparked violent protests on 10 April 1919. Civilians were killed, buildings were burnt, and angry mobs looted and killed several foreign nationals, including Christian missionaries. General Dyer was tasked with restoring order, and among the measures he implemented was a ban on all public gatherings.

Melicent Wathen, the wife of Gerard Wathen, head of Khalsa College in Amritsar, wrote in her diary that, on 11 April, 'planes hovered round' Amritsar, 'but no bomb was dropped'.[3] The threat of bombing Amritsar from the air was not mentioned in the official records, but the British airplanes did drop bombs and fire machine guns on Indian crowds elsewhere in Punjab during the unrest. The Disorders Inquiry Committee was appointed soon after the massacre to investigate disturbances in Punjab, Delhi and Bombay that took place between 1919 and 1920, and their report mentioned the aerial bombing of Gujranwala in undivided Punjab during the protests.[4]

Young Mir Abdul Rahim was caught in the middle of this frenzy, and like hundreds and thousands of men from his generation, he started feeling strongly against the British colonial occupation of India.

On the afternoon of 13 April, men, women and children gathered in Jallianwala Bagh. Many came to celebrate Baisakhi, and others came to protest and listen to the public speeches.

Dyer and his regiment comprising Gurkha and Baloch soldiers arrived, sealed the Bagh's only exit, and, without warning, opened fire on the crowds. After they ceased firing, the troops immediately withdrew from the place, leaving behind the dead and wounded.

On that fateful day, Rahim went to Jallianwala Bagh, and was shot twice in his thigh. He succumbed to the wounds some days later.

When Rahim was gunned down that day at the age of twenty-three, he left behind a twenty-year-old wife and two children, aged three and one. From that moment on, this becomes a story about four generations of women, and how the rapidly transforming subcontinent and its various borders—physical, political and gendered—would affect them over and over again.

After much struggle, the family patriarchs finally gave Rahim's young wife a small place to live in Amritsar. The young widow's entire being then centred around raising her daughters, protecting them and finding them suitable husbands. Over the years, she withered away. Widowed at twenty-one, she never married again, and one day, without warning, she died.

Natasha called Rahim's oldest daughter, her great-grandmother, 'Badi Ammi'. When Badi Ammi was no older than sixteen, she was married to a suave young businessman, Mian Abdul Aziz. A bit of an Anglophile, he worked as an authorised supplier for the British. Growing up without a father, Badi Ammi, along with her mother and sister, must have lived a precarious life at the heart of brutal patriarchy, with a tumultuous political life unfolding in the background as the subcontinent's struggle for freedom heightened. Nothing was safe, and nothing was guaranteed.

Natasha thought that Badi Ammi's relationship with her young husband was not an equal one by any measure. She remembered her as a woman who feared words and spoke very little. Badi Ammi had four daughters and a son; her eldest daughter was Natasha's grandmother, Nuzhat Khawja. While Badi Ammi married and raised a family, her orphaned sister Khalaji's life plunged into another kind of hell. Natasha believed that someone very close to the family was sexually abusing her.

Khalaji was engaged a few times, but people in the family always broke off her engagements. Unmarried, she lived with Badi Ammi's family all her life. She was a young girl without a father, who had nothing to her name, and someone much older than her was sexually abusing her. According to Natasha, whoever the abuser was must have been an influential member of the family, because no one talked about what happened to her.

Khalaji died in her sixties.

'She just died . . . you know . . . Her story is just there. There is nobody who is ever going to bear witness to it now,' Natasha said, adding, 'No one would dare say anything because . . . it was like this dark secret, a skeleton in your closet, and nobody wants to open it.'

Natasha's mother and her sisters remembered Khalaji through the constant retelling of stories. There are little vignettes about her living with them, being very loving to the children in the family and cooking for them. But the broken engagements and multiple instances of sexual violence that Khalaji endured were never talked about. The abuse was permitted, but talking about it was forbidden.

Despite the silence, the women—Natasha's grandmother, her mother and her aunts—always knew. As children, they grew up in the same house, with an unspeakable secret lurking just beneath the shadows. They saw glimpses, perhaps heard whispers, even cries of anguish. It is as if the women had discovered these elaborate ways to keep silent, be quiet and never utter a word. They knew something terrible was happening to someone they loved, and yet they had to be quiet about this, pretend that everything was fine. It was only when Natasha's own grandmother died that her mother and her sisters started speaking about what had happened to Khalaji.

Like a puzzle piece falling into place, the difficult and often incomprehensible choices of the women in her family came to make sense to Natasha when seen in this new light. In one violent moment, two little girls lost their right to a protected life, and from that moment on, it became about survival.

This one act of state terror, Rahim's death, devastated not only the three women in his life, but the loss, fear and insecurity were inherited and became part of their social fabric. 'Inherited losses are the worst to encounter as they are mistaken as fate,' said Natasha.

As I heard Natasha speak, I thought of another Pakistani friend, who told me her family's history when I first started writing this book. The women in her family always lived like there were packed suitcases in the living room, always ready to leave, never brave enough to put down roots. 'Once we packed our bags, we could never unpack [them],' she told me. It didn't matter how many homes you moved through, how many borders you crossed, how many times you remade your life; the suitcase was always there. Like an invisible prison, a circular border was drawn around you.

'We crossed [from India to Pakistan] to be a part of a new nation, and then came the dictators. We packed the suitcase and left again . . . You have no idea what it is to live under a military dictatorship, Suchitra. No country should ever suffer what we went through.'

After the Jallianwala Bagh massacre, the city of Amritsar was in constant upheaval. Soon after the massacre, General Dyer passed the 'crawling order', whereby British soldiers manned the main street, and Indians who passed through had to do so on their bellies. A refusal to follow this order resulted in public flogging. The massive outrage and anger fuelled the non-cooperation movement of 1920. Led by M.K. Gandhi, the movement organised a boycott of the legislative councils, courts and schools, and mobilised mass support against India's British rule.

Twenty-eight years after the Jallianwala Bagh massacre, Natasha's family moved from Amritsar to Lahore in the season of rioting that would lead to Partition in August 1947. Natasha's grandmother, Nuzhat, then just a child, had heard stories of women committing suicide, fearing rape and capture amidst this widespread violence. If the mobs arrived at their doors, they would 'have to do something about it as well'.

Nuzhat, then no more than eleven, was told that they had just a few hours to pack everything. She ran to her room and grabbed her radio, the only possession she took with her when fleeing Amritsar. The women, now three generations of them, made their way to a new home, a new country and a new nationality. They lost everything they'd ever owned all over again.

When you are forced to leave, you not only lose the land your ancestors lived in, you lose a part of them as well. With every act of migration, you lose a little bit of your history, you leave your dead behind, their graves, the streets they walked on and the ground beneath their feet. You are made a little hollow by the act of departure, and the home you abandon remakes itself in your absence.

The immediate violence of Partition ebbed and flowed, but the sexual abuse Khalaji experienced didn't stop. Did Rahim's wife know that her daughter was being abused? Did she try to put an end to this nightmare? How did these women, all three generations of them, live with the knowledge of this violence under the same roof? The women, and their descendants, were not only victims of the upheaval caused by the Partition, but were also colonised by patriarchy. Patriarchy did not crumble in the face of Partition, the latter only consolidated its hold.

Natasha told me that her grandmother and her siblings had perhaps inherited the fear of men. Yet, their story of fear, loss and trauma is universal. The other women I spoke to, many of those who appear in this book, carried this with them too. They participated in history as actors, and as bards who are keepers and retellers of stories within homes, whether in India, Pakistan, Bangladesh or Burma.

'They have seen all sorts of things that men and patriarchy can do financially, emotionally and sexually to women . . . If you have a mother who was so scared, and if she inherited that fear, obviously, you pass some of that to your own daughter. You pass that indirectly to your daughters.'

~

April 2019 marked the centenary of the Jallianwala Bagh massacre. A hundred years later, does the body keep score of all our trauma, does it also pass on some of it? Are we bound to history by the tears and fears of our ancestors? When does this cycle of fear and pain end? As the children of Partition, are we condemned to forever carry history within us, but never fully possess it?

Natasha and I wondered if we were better off than our grandmothers, our great-grandmothers and our aunts. 'If I were born into violence, witnessed it and lived with it as a part of my everyday existence, how would I separate myself from this?' Natasha paused. 'But on some level, why did my mother take so long to talk about Jallianwala Bagh with me?'

After learning about how her great-great-grandfather Rahim had died, Natasha told me that she was angry at history and what it did to her ancestors. 'They were not treated as humans anymore. They just became products of violence and patriarchy. I don't think they had any rights. I don't think they knew what their rights were and being someone who is now looking back . . . I see how my mother could have seen stuff in her mother and she had to constantly resist . . . but whose fault is this?'

Natasha's mother, Mano Javed, resisted and questioned patriarchy within her household while growing up. This often placed her in conflict with her own mother, Nuzhat. When subservience and dutifulness was perpetually demanded only from the women, her mother's resistance was seen as 'disobedient thinking'. While this resistance was essential and liberating to her mother, it was frightening to her grandmother.

Despite the family's long history and connection to the city of Amritsar, where they lived before the Partition, they cannot go back. 'What is Lahore from Amritsar? It is no more than fifty kilometres apart. My Nani could never go back to her house. They have all died.' Natasha and her mother, Mano, who is almost sixty, cannot return to Amritsar, either. 'My mother can never be there, and that is violence on its own.'

Cyril Radcliffe, chairman of the Boundary Commission, in an interview to journalist Kuldip Nayar said that he had initially given Lahore to India.[5] He had already 'earmarked Calcutta for India', and when he 'realized that Pakistan would not have any large city', he then reversed his decision in favour of Pakistan.[6]

For a long time, Natasha's mother could not find people she could connect with, who had gone through the same tragic loss as her family. There was no way to remember. There was no way to heal. Conversations about the past were private acts, which occurred in isolated spaces.

Natasha's grandmother never spoke much about the Partition, and 'when she did, she felt guilty talking about it. She felt like it was no longer hers . . . she shouldn't be talking about it . . .' To remember Amritsar as her home after all the bloodshed, and so much lost, felt like a betrayal. If you gave up so much for this new home, was it fair to still long for the one you left behind?

Natasha's grandmother embraced Indian cinema, songs and art to fill the spaces vacated by silence. She watched every Indian movie that made its way to Pakistan in the theatre, and when Indian films were banned, she watched pirated versions at home. She memorised songs from Indian films, sung them and danced to them at weddings, 'until all her children believed [them] to be equally theirs'. Nuzhat spent hours analysing and discussing Indian films and art. Natasha always thought of these long conversations as entertainment.

With hindsight, Natasha believes that cinema was a telescope. It brought her grandmother closer to the life that was abruptly taken away from her on the eve of the Partition. 'She prayed for Amitabh', a famous Bollywood actor, when he was near-fatally wounded during the shooting of a film in the 1980s, and she always referred to the young actor Aamir Khan affectionately as 'mera [my] Amir Khan'.

Today, Natasha wonders how upsetting the recent turn of events in India would have been for her grandmother. She knew that Pakistan did not turn out to be the Promised Land, but India's descent into a similar abyss would have stolen from her the memory of a place she once knew as home.

'If my mother starts today identifying this history with India, what will she become? A traitor? What will she be labelled as? A traitor to Pakistan?

'It is inhuman, I think, [that] our own history is just separated by these borders. My truth lies on the other side of the border, but I am not able to say that openly because I [was] also born with a Pakistani passport. I realised much later in life that this entire identity is created out of so much hatred and so much violence. I don't know what to do with it, to be honest, because once you read my history, you realise that my entire being was on the other side.'

This was the final layer of violence: to be separated from one's history, to be forcefully emptied of it. It was not just India that was denied to Natasha and her family, it was also the shared history that has been denied to all of us. Seventy years later, we are no closer to writing a true people's history of the Partition. There are grand narratives, politics and palace intrigues that happened in high places, but the human history, like the memory's puzzle, remains incomplete.

~

We still don't know the exact number of people who died in Jallianwala Bagh, and many who died that day remain unnamed. Soon after the massacre, martial law was imposed, and people were afraid to come out to claim the bodies of their dead. An unofficial inquiry committee headed by the National Congress Party followed the massacre, and the British government set up its own Disorders Inquiry Committee, also known as the Hunter Committee, to investigate the massacre. The British official figure of the dead was 379, but the actual numbers were much higher. Gerard Wathen, the then principal of Khalsa College, in a letter written five days after the shooting, claimed that 1,042 people had died. In 1964, the prime minister's office conducted another survey and came up with a count of 388 names, including names of seven people whose families now live in Pakistan.

A 2018 investigation by the Partition Museum in Amritsar identified more names and raised the number to 547. Many names are still missing from this list, including Mir Abdul Rahim.

On the bodies of the nameless dead, islands of resistance transformed into a national struggle that ended in the violent birth of two nations—India and Pakistan. Partition affected over twenty million people. So, here we are, an entire subcontinent of people who have inherited violence and trauma. 'And we are not allowed to heal,' Natasha told me.

Four of Natasha's grandparents were from Kashmir. One set of grandparents moved from Kashmir to Sialkot in Pakistan, and her great-grandfather Rahim's family moved to Amritsar. He was a Kashmiri who died for India's freedom struggle.

As Natasha laid out her family tree, she told me, 'This is all so complicated. There are complicated layers to it, and for me to acknowledge them and dig them is very hurtful, because it completely starts giving me another identity which I don't have, you know?' If we peel back these layers and acknowledge history's mess of multiple migrations, we become someone else, something wholly different, someone with a very different identity.

Where do men like Rahim, who died at night in Jallianwala Bagh, figure in this history?

When did Jallianwala Bagh become *Indian* history?

'If I bring up Jallianwala Bagh now,' Natasha said, 'a lot of people will say it's not my struggle, they will tell me that I'm a traitor. My family is not supposed to be talking about this. And they will tell me this on both sides of the border today.'

Natasha told me that, in Pakistan, whatever happened before 1947 is not Pakistani history, it's Indian. When they partitioned the soil, they partitioned history along with it.

Through the 1970s and '80s, Pakistan embarked on a process of Islamisation, and introduced a series of legislation aimed at religious minorities. The systematic process of rewriting history in Pakistan started in 1981 under General Zia-ul-Haq's military dictatorship to 'induce pride for the nation's past, enthusiasm for the present, and unshakeable faith in the stability and longevity of Pakistan'. The Constitution was abandoned, textbooks were rewritten, the pork-eating, port-wine-drinking Muhammad Ali Jinnah was transformed into Pakistan's first governor-general, and a 'man of orthodox religious views who sought the creation of a theocratic state'.[7] The shared history of the subcontinent's struggle for freedom from the British was erased, and the new 'heroes of the Pakistan Movement' were created.

Almost forty years later, India is now on the same path, rewriting history and remaking its citizens. The portrait of the man who plotted the assassination of Mahatma Gandhi now hangs in the Indian Parliament.

When I started reading about Zia's reign in Pakistan, I also discovered that the audio recordings of Jinnah's speech on 11 August 1947, three days before the creation of the country, where he calls for a secular Pakistan, had mysteriously disappeared. *BBC News* reported, 'Successive military governments in Pakistan were accused of attempting to downplay, even remove, the speech from official records.'[8] Murtaza Solangi, the former director general of Radio Pakistan, called it 'a case of criminal, wilful destruction of our history'.[9]

In his quest to find those audio recordings, Solangi contacted the BBC archives and AIR in Delhi. Indian officials initially told him that they had the tapes, but later denied having them.

Indian officials, however, have confirmed the existence of two other speeches, now called the Jinnah tapes, but not the speech from 11 August. It's not just Jinnah whose work has been obscured. The work of writer Saadat Hasan Manto, one of the foremost chroniclers of Partition, is theoretically held in the AIR archive. *Outlook*, a news magazine, reported that 'when historian Ayesha Jalal, Manto's grandniece, sought the recordings as part of ongoing research, she was told by officials that the recordings did not exist. Yet, persistent queries have revealed that All India Radio does have a recording of a Manto play.'[10]

Similarly, recordings of Indian actors Dilip Kumar and Prithviraj Kapoor are with Pakistan's broadcasting authority. Kumar, born Muhammad Yusuf Khan, and Kapoor are both legendary Indian actors from Peshawar in undivided India, who later migrated to Bombay.

Natasha was right when she told me, 'My history lies on the other side of the border.'

India and Pakistan took very different paths seventy years ago, but a defining divergence between them was that India produced a Constitution. Pakistan didn't.

Following Pakistan's independence, it took nine years to produce the first Constitution in 1956. On the day of its adoption, two main parties rejected the Constitution, ultimately leading to its abrogation and the imposition of the country's first martial law on 7 October 1958. General Ayub Khan, the military dictator who assumed power, enacted the 1962 Constitution through an executive order.

The current Pakistani Constitution—a third version enacted by the constituent assembly in 1973—has been suspended twice: first by General Zia-ul-Haq between 1977 and 1985, and later by General Musharraf between 1999 and 2002.

As Natasha put it, 'From day one, our political struggle was a struggle to establish a democracy. Unlike Indians, we did not have a democracy. We are a nation who has just been fighting for democracy! We have had this struggle since forever.' When Zia assumed power, he passed new legislation that discriminated against women. The 1984 'law of evidence' stated that a woman's legal testimony was only half as valuable as a man's. In response, the women in Pakistan took to the streets and burnt their dupattas. They marched towards the Lahore High Court to challenge the new laws of evidence. During those tumultuous times, these women were lathi-charged, assaulted and arrested. In the absence of a Constitution and a civil society, and in the face of systematic purges of dissenting voices, 'there was nothing but our bodies to throw against the state'.

'Indians didn't have that struggle. You had it very easy. You had a Constitution. You had a civil society. You had institutions, systems and a Constitution that was upheld as supreme. We never had that. We didn't have the judiciary that we would rely on, we didn't have the institutions we could rely on and we didn't have any safety. You have students' unions, there are no students' unions in Pakistan. That is the first thing what Zia did. He dismantled everything. All we had was ourselves, and we put our bodies on the line, threw ourselves in the fire, you know? . . . We always knew that the cost of speaking up is your life and your family.'

To this day, students and activists who are critical of the establishment in Pakistan are rounded up, and no one knows if or when they will come back. Years later, some families are still waiting outside the courts. The number of people who have disappeared in Pakistan is incalculable.

And it isn't just Pakistan. Najeeb Ahmed, a student at Jawaharlal Nehru University in New Delhi, India, went missing under suspicious circumstances on 15 October 2016 after a scuffle with alleged members of Akhil Bharatiya Vidyarthi Parishad (ABVP), a right-wing Indian student organisation affiliated with the Hindu nationalist paramilitary group Rashtriya Swayamsevak Sangh (RSS).

Fours years since his disappearance, Najeeb's mother, Fatima Nafis, continues to wait.

The Indian professor G.N. Saibaba, a paraplegic, is languishing in prison for allegedly having Maoist links. The evidence mounted by the state against Saibaba and others was letters, newspapers, umbrellas, pamphlets, books on Marxism and videos seized during searches the legality of which the defence has repeatedly challenged in the courts. The scholar and rationalist M.M. Kalburgi was shot dead by two assailants on bikes outside his house in Dharwad on 30 August 2015, while the journalist Gauri Lankesh was killed on 5 September 2017. They were both killed for resisting the RSS, the BJP and the Sangh Parivar, a collection of right-wing Hindu nationalist organisations created and supported under the umbrella of the RSS.

When Natasha meets Indians in the United States who praise Modi, she wants to tell them that once the genie is out of the bottle it can't be contained. Pakistani people know this intimately; they know what it means to have a country without a solid Constitution, built on hate and contempt for communities that make up its own people.

'A point comes where the fire reaches your home. And I just don't know how to get this message across to Indians. I just don't know how to tell them that what you have—your Constitution and institutions—are important. You are drowning them in the drain. You don't know it cannot be reversed. Once it goes down the drain, it is just endless trauma and endless fighting and there is no vision.'

The India that Natasha once thought of as a fantasyland is gone. On the eve of the 2019 elections, *The Telegraph* newspaper's editorial board wrote that institutional demise and erosion 'is an early symptom of the implosion of democracy—and elections'.[11] A slew of recent verdicts and silence over the incarceration of rights defenders, scholars and activists have led many to believe that there is a 'crisis of legitimacy plaguing the Supreme Court of India'.[12] The BJP, the world's richest political party, armed with a private militia,[13] now controls a largely pliable news media.[14] Kashmir remains violently silenced.[15] The 'world's largest democracy' is now a Hindu Rashtra:[16] the recent CAA, the NRC and the National Population Register (NPR) have already enabled this transformation.

~

There are moments of hope as an organic student-led protest movement blooms throughout India, and 'Azaadi, azaadi' reverberates at every protest I have been to. I want to hold on to the hope that new beginnings are possible.

When I leave Natasha's home that night, I leave with an immense sense of loss and of love. Love that Natasha has shown me, by telling me her story, sitting with me to make sense of ourselves, our lives, and how to reconcile our present with the murkiness of the past. I also leave with an overwhelming sense of loss of our shared histories, of how we could not have this conversation in Lahore or Madras, sitting in our homes.

My visa to Pakistan was never granted, and this book will always be incomplete without that journey. Natasha's family has never returned to Amritsar, or seen Kashmir. How many places in the world can a Kashmiri who became Punjabi, and a Tamilian who doesn't know where she belongs, have a conversation about the borders that alienate us? Not many.

But we have the duty to break these borders, to reclaim what was denied to us, so as to not pass this loss on to our children.

I get home after 11 p.m. that night. I go over and kiss my three-year-old daughter, Meera.

I think about Natasha's little one, Kabir, sleeping across town.

If not for us, we owe it to our children, to purge this hate that has separated families and histories over seventy years. We owe it to Meera and Kabir.

ACKNOWLEDGEMENTS

Ram: I am convinced that no writer, living or dead, has had a spouse like you. You travelled to four continents and various cities for me. When distance became inevitable, you made sure that I always had a home to return to, no matter how long I was gone. You read my many drafts, lied lovingly and told me that it was brilliant, even as I stumbled with the early chapters. You made space for a book that took eight years of my life. You let me be. You let me grow.

Amma: This world is a cruel place without a mother. I am blessed to have you in my corner, always fighting for me and loving me. You taught me to be persistent, uncompromising and disciplined. Everything good in me is yours.

Appa: When I was fourteen, you pointed out a line in an essay, 'It is the givers and not the takers, who inherit this world,' which I copied into a book I reserved for quotes. 'To inherit this world', what grand ambition to be sown in a child whose sense of the world was still the four corners of her home? You read the final manuscript and texted me late at night, 'I am proud of you.' No accolade, no achievement will ever come close to those five words.

Sruthi: How do I quantify, describe or even make sense of everything you do for us. For being kind, selfless and generous. For taking care of Amma and Appa, and always going above and beyond for everyone. Being the centre of our little universe and keeping us all together.

Lucy: This book is here because of you. You made all this possible. Thanks for taking on an unknown writer who brought you a messy idea with wild roots and unruly branches. You nurtured my ideas, challenged me and made me an infinitely better writer. *Lucy: il miglior fabbro.*

Ajitha and Ryan: For the kindness, love and generosity you brought to this text. For commissioning and championing this book.

Carl: For your guidance and wisdom throughout the publication and beyond.

Bhakti: Thanks for being a friend, my first editor, my Yoda and much more.

Nachiappan: My oldest and dearest friend, you read every draft of this book and nudged me forward.

To my friends, old and new, who helped make this book possible, I am lucky to have all of you in my life: Dave Besseling, my editor at *GQ*, and for that phone call. Rasha Chatta, we will always have Cairo. Michael Bronner, Michael Busch and Asim Rafiqui. Gaiutra Bahadur, for being the author I aspire to be, and for introducing me to Lucy. Parvaiz Bukhari, for so much that I can never quantify. Nawaz Gul Qanungo, for your great reserves of kindness. Danish Husain, for your poetry. Francesca Recchia, my comrade in trenches. Mona Bhan, for the close reading of the chapter, your scholarship and chutzpah. Ather Zia, for your poetry and love.

Ritesh Uttamchandani, Sukhman Dhami and Sarfaraz. Natasha Javed, for being a bard and sharing your story with me.

Without you, the many journeys and encounters would not be possible: Uday Tripathi, JKCCS, Khurram Parvez, Saleem Bin Ahmad, Anil Brar, Imrul Islam, Jamshed, Asim Bhai, Lefty, Sari Begum, Mr N and the many who don't appear in these pages.

Finally, Mariyam Raza, for compiling the list of deaths caused by the NRC.

GLOSSARY OF INHUMAN WORDS

detention camps: The Indian government stripped two million people, mostly Muslims, of their citizenship. Now it wants to put them in camps. The first camp, currently under construction, is the size of seven football fields. The workers who helped build India's first detention camp for illegal migrants may end up there.

doubtful voter (or **D voter**): A group of voters disenfranchised by the Election Commission of India in 1997.

foreigner: A person who is not a citizen of India.

illegal immigration: Refers to the migration of people into a country in violation of the immigration laws of that country, or the continued residence of people without the legal right to live in that country.

'illegal immigrants': This term is neither 'accurate' nor 'neutral'. Not having documents makes you undocumented, not illegal. No human being is illegal.

Miya: In Assam, the term 'Miya' is used as a slur to brand Assamese Muslims of Bengali heritage as migrants from West Bengal or, worse, illegal immigrants from Bangladesh—a grave accusation, given that the National Register of Citizens proposes to rob such persons of their Indian citizenship.

The National Register of Citizens (NRC): The NRC is an official record of those who are legal Indian citizens. It includes demographic information about all those individuals who qualify as citizens of India as per the Citizenship Act, 1955. The register was first prepared after the 1951 census of India, and since then, it has not been updated until recently. So far, such a database has only been maintained for the state of Assam. However, in November 2019, Minister of Home Affairs Amit Shah declared during a parliamentary session that the register would be extended to the entire country. In Assam, almost two million people who long to belong to India have found their names missing from the list, and are at the risk of being declared stateless. The Indian government has announced its intention of extending the NRC to the rest of India. The legislation was passed. This could create the world's largest underclass of statelessness, on a scale previously unknown. When the final draft of Assam's NRC was published, there was much speculation on the citizenship of over forty lakh people who were left out. The register, meant to be a definitive list of genuine Indian citizens in Assam, is being updated for the first time since the chaotic post-Partition days of 1951. One of the stated aims of the exercise is to identify those the state defines as 'illegal immigrants'. This includes anyone who cannot prove that they or their ancestors entered the country before midnight of 24 March 1971. The office of the NRC in Assam has pointed out that the current list is just a draft, and that those left out have not been declared foreigners.

Opposite Party (OP): A person who appears before the Foreigners Tribunal claiming to be an Indian citizen.

termites: 'Illegal immigrants are termites', according to Amit Shah, minister of home affairs, who was president of the Bharatiya Janata Party from 2014 to 2020. Calling humans vermin is a prelude to violence. In 1994, broadcasts from Radio Rwanda labelled Tutsis as 'inyenzi', or cockroaches, and 'ibinhindugemb', or heinous monsters, who consumed the organs of Hutus. Similarly, during the Armenian genocide, the Armenians were called an 'invasive infection in Muslim Turkish society' and 'parasites outside the confines of their homeland, sucking off the marrow of the people of the host country, before moving on to another host country'.

NOTES

PROLOGUE: (My) Ishmael

1. Elie Wiesel, 'Con l'incubo che tutto sia accaduto invano,' *La Stampa*, Turin, 14 April 1987, p. 3.

INTRODUCTION

1. Amartya Sen, 'Imperial Illusions,' *New Republic*, 31 December 2007, https://newrepublic.com/article/61784/imperial-illusions.
2. Ian Copland, 'Princely States and the Raj,' *Economic and Political Weekly*, 39, no. 8, 2004, pp. 807–809, www.jstor.org/stable/4414671.
3. Ian J. Barrow, *Making History, Drawing Territory: British Mapping in India, c. 1756–1905*, Oxford University Press, New York, 2003, pp. 83–84; 'James Rennell: The Father of the Indian Survey,' University of Michigan Online Exhibits, https://www.lib.umich.edu/online-exhibits/exhibits/show/india-maps/rennell: 'Aside from the precisionist aspect of the Great Trigonometrical Survey it should be noted that there was always a strong element of control in the mapping of South Asia. As Ian Barrow states: "there was a sense among surveyors and the [East India Company]'s high bureaucracy that trigonometrical mapping would enhance the reputation of the Company as an enlightened patron because of its rigorous and scientific nature . . . This rhetoric of scientific progress and improvement was a significant factor contributing to the character of colonial rule in India during the nineteenth century. The Survey not only helped the state gather information and knowledge, it also—and this was its greatest advantage over route surveys—added legitimacy to colonial rule by making it seem that this form of science in India would not only result in India's progress but would also improve geodesy."'
4. Cynthia Keppley Mahmood, 'Rethinking Indian Communalism: Culture and Counter-Culture,' *Asian Survey*, 33, no. 7, July 1993, pp. 722–737, https://www.jstor.org/stable/2645359.

5. *Encyclopaedia Britannica*, 11th ed. (1910–11), vol. 14, s.v. 'India', p. 386.
6. Prashant Bharadwaj, Asim Ijaz Khwaja and Atif R. Mian, 'The Big March: Migratory Flows after the Partition of India', HKS Working Paper No. RWP08-029, Harvard University, John F. Kennedy School of Government, Cambridge, MA, 2008, https://papers.ssrn.com/sol3/papers.cfm?abstract_id=1124093.
7. Prashant Bharadwaj, Asim Khwaja and Atif Mian, 'The big march: migratory flows after the partition of India', *Economic and Political Weekly*, 2008, p. 39.
8. Joya Chatterji, 'The Fashioning of a Frontier: The Radcliffe Line and Bengal's Border Landscape, 1947–52', *Modern Asian Studies*, 33, no. 1, 1999, p. 186, www.jstor.org/stable/313155.
9. Kuldip Nayar, *Scoop!: Inside Stories from the Partition to the Present*, HarperCollins Publishers, Noida, 2006, p. 34.
10. Prashant Bharadwaj, Asim Ijaz Khwaja and Atif R. Mian, 'The Big March: Migratory Flows after the Partition of India', HKS Working Paper No. RWP08-029, Harvard University, John F. Kennedy School of Government, Cambridge, MA, 2008, https://papers.ssrn.com/sol3/papers.cfm?abstract_id=1124093; Prashant Bharadwaj, Asim I. Khwaja and Atif R. Mian, 'Population Exchange and its Impact on Literacy, Occupation and Gender: Evidence from the Partition of India', *International Migration*, 53, vol. 4, 2014, pp. 90–106, https://doi.org/10.1111/imig.12039.
11. Margaret Bourke-White, *Portrait of Myself*, Simon and Schuster, New York, 1963, p. 187.
12. Harsha Kumari Singh, 'Muslim Folk Singer Killed Over Performance; 200 Muslims Flee Village', *NDTV*, 11 October 2017, https://www.ndtv.com/india-news/200-muslims-leave-village-after-a-folk-singer-killed-allegedly-by-priest-1761507.
13. 'Violent Cow Protection in India: Vigilante Groups Attack Minorities', Human Rights Watch, 18 February 2019, https://www.hrw.org/report/2019/02/18/violent-cow-protection-india/vigilante-groups-attack-minorities.
14. Sugam Pokharel and Catherine E. Shoichet, 'This 6-year-old from India died in the Arizona desert. She loved dancing and dreamed of meeting her dad', *CNN*, 12 July 2019.
15. Devjyot Ghoshal, 'Amit Shah Vows to Throw Illegal Immigrants into Bay of Bengal,' *Reuters*, 12 April 2019, https://www.reuters.com/article/india-election-speech/amit-shah-vows-to-throw-illegal-immigrants-into-bay-of-bengal-idUSKCN1RO1YD.

16. Faizan Mustafa and Aymen Mohammed, 'Ayodhya judgement is a setback to evidence law', *The Indian Express*, 10 November 2019, https://indianexpress.com/article/opinion/columns/supreme-court-ayodhya-verdict-ram-mandir-muslims-hindu-babri-mosque-demolition-6112170/; Ipsita Chakravarty, 'What explains the silence among Muslim communities on the Ayodhya judgment?', *Scroll*, 14 November 2019, https://scroll.in/article/943510/what-explains-the-silence-among-muslim-communities-on-the-ayodhya-judgment; Soutik Biswas, 'Babri mosque: India's Muslims feel more abandoned than ever', *BBC*, 30 September 2020, https://www.bbc.com/news/world-asia-india-54356713.
17. Founded in 1996 by Gregory Stanton, Genocide Watch is an American watchdog organisation that exists to predict, prevent, stop and punish genocide and other forms of mass murder. Gregory H. Stanton, 'Genocide Alert for Kashmir, India', Genocide Watch, 15 August 2019, https://www.genocidewatch.com/single-post/2019/08/15/Genocide-Alert-for-Kashmir-India; Gregory H. Stanton, 'Genocide Watch for Assam, India – Renewed', Genocide Watch, renewed 18 August 2019, https://www.genocidewatch.com/single-post/2019/08/18/Genocide-Watch-for-Assam-India---renewed.
18. 'CAA Has Made 6 Lakh Refugees Stateless, Says Rights Group', *The Hindu*, 19 March 2020, https://www.thehindu.com/news/national/other-states/caa-has-made-6-lakh-refugees-forever-stateless-says-rights-group/article31103492.ece.
19. Christophe Jaffrelot, 'Communal Riots in Gujarat: The State at Risk?', Working Paper no. 17, Heidelberg Papers in South Asian and Comparative Politics, University of Heidelberg, Germany, July 2003, https://doi.org/10.11588/heidok.00004127.
20. Suchitra Vijayan, 'Heckling Asaduddin Owaisi in Parliament with Chants of Jai Shri Ram Smacks of an Age-Old Idea of Muscular, Divisive Hindutva', *Firstpost*, 20 June 2019, https://www.firstpost.com/india/heckling-asaduddin-owaisi-in-parliament-with-chants-of-jai-shri-ram-smacks-of-an-age-old-idea-of-muscular-divisive-hindutva-6850771.html.
21. Edward W. Said, *Culture and Imperialism*, Vintage Books, New York, 1994, p. 3.
22. 'Borders only become borders when cartographies come into existence': Professor Romila Thapar. Notes from the open-house organised by 'History for Peace' on 24 December 2017 in Kolkata, https://archive.indianculturalforum.in/2017/12/28/borders-only-become-borders-when-cartographies-come-into-existence-professor-romila-thapar-somok-roy/.

PART I: THE AFGHANISTAN-PAKISTAN BORDER

1. Christian Tripodi, 'Grand Strategy and the Graveyard of Assumptions: Britain and Afghanistan, 1839–1919', *Journal of Strategic Studies*, 33.5, 2010, pp. 701–725.
2. Ibid.
3. Alexander Morrison, 'Introduction: Killing the Cotton Canard and getting rid of the Great Game: rewriting the Russian conquest of Central Asia, 1814–1895', *Central Asian Survey*, 33, no. 2, 2014, p. 131.
4. Gerald Morgan, *Anglo-Russian Rivalry in Central Asia: 1810-1895*, Epilogue by Lt. Col. (retd) Geoffrey Wheeler, Routledge, London, 1981, p. 231.
5. Mridu Rai, 'The Consolidation of Dogra Legitimacy in Kashmir: Hindu Rulers and a Hindu State' in *Hindu Rulers, Muslim Subjects: Islam, Rights, and the History of Kashmir*, Princeton University Press, Princeton, 2004, pp. 80–127.
6. Maj. Agha Humayun Amin, 'The War of Lost Opportunities (Part I)', *Defence Journal*, April 2000, http://www.defencejournal.com/2000/apr/war-lost.htm.
7. Thomas Barfield, *Afghanistan: A Cultural and Political History*, Princeton University Press, Princeton, 2010, p. 1 and 13.

1. SAR HAWZA: Trapped in the Coloniser's Map

1. Bijan Omrani, 'The Durand Line: History and Problems of the Afghan-Pakistan Border', *Asian Affairs*, 40, vol. 2, 2009, pp. 177–195, https://doi.org/10.1080/03068370902871508.
2. Ibid.
3. Ibid.
4. Ibid.

PART II: THE INDIA-BANGLADESH BORDER

1. Smruti S. Pattanaik, 'India-Bangladesh Land Border: A Flawed Inheritance and a Problematic Future', *Strategic Analysis*, 35, vol. 5, 2011, p. 745 , https://doi.org/10.1080/09700161.2011.591763.
2. N.S. Jamwal, 'Border Management: Dilemma of Guarding the India-Bangladesh Border', *Strategic Analysis*, 28, no. 1, Jan–Mar 2004, pp. 5–36, DOI: 10.1080/09700160408450116.
3. Press Trust of India, 'Difficult to watch Indo-Bangla border', *Rediff*, 6 October 2006, https://www.rediff.com/news/2006/oct/06bangla.htm.
4. Willem van Schendel, 'Spaces of Engagement: How Borderlands, Illegal Flows, and Territorial States Interlock', in *Illicit Flows and Criminal*

Things: States, Borders, and the Other Side of Globalization, Willem van Schendel and Itty Abraham (eds), Indiana University Press, Bloomington, 2005, pp. 38–68.

5. Willem van Schendel, *The Bengal Borderland: Beyond State and Nation in South Asia*, Anthem Press, London, 2005, p. 40.
6. Joya Chatterji, 'The Fashioning of a Frontier: The Radcliffe Line and Bengal's Border Landscape, 1947–52', *Modern Asian Studies*, 33, no. 1, 1999, p. 193, www.jstor.org/stable/313155.
7. Smruti S. Pattanaik, 'India–Bangladesh Land Border: A Flawed Inheritance and a Problematic Future', *Strategic Analysis*, 35, vol. 5, 2011, https://doi.org/10.1080/09700161.2011.591763.
8. Jawaharlal Nehru, *Indian Foreign Policy: Selected Speeches, September 1946–April 1961*, Publications Division, Government of India, 1961, p. 49. Cited in Smruti S. Pattanaik, 'India–Bangladesh Land Border'.
9. Shahzeb Jillani, 'Scars of Bangladesh Independence War 40 Years On,' *BBC News*, 13 December 2011, https://www.bbc.com/news/world-asia-16111843.

2. PANITAR: Playing Cricket in No Man's Land

1. Ministry of External Affairs, 'Frequently Asked Questions on Protected Area Permit (PAP) / Restricted Area Permit (RAP) Regime', https://www.mea.gov.in/Images/pdf/ForeigD-FAQs-onPAPandRAP.pdf.
2. 'Disputed Bay of Bengal Island Disappears into Sea,' *Telegraph*, 24 March 2010, https://www.telegraph.co.uk./news/worldnews/asia/india/7513350/Disputed-Bay-of-Bengal-island-disappears-into-sea.html.
3. 'Disputed Bay of Bengal Island "Vanishes", Say Scientists', *BBC News*, 24 March 2010, http://news.bbc.co.uk/1/hi/8584665.stm.
4. Willem van Schendel, *The Bengal Borderland: Beyond State and Nation in South Asia*, Anthem Press, London, 2005.
5. Human Rights Watch, 'India/Bangladesh: Indiscriminate Killings, Abuse by Border Officers', 9 December 2010, https://www.hrw.org/news/2010/12/09/india/bangladesh-indiscriminate-killings-abuse-border-officers; Human Rights Watch, 'Trigger Happy: Excessive Use of Force by Indian Troops at the Bangladesh Border', 9 December 2010, https://www.hrw.org/report/2010/12/09/trigger-happy/excessive-use-force-indian-troops-bangladesh-border.
6. Special Correspondent, 'CBI arrests BSF commandant in cattle-smuggling case', *The Hindu*, 18 November 2020, https://www.thehindu.com/news/national/cbi-arrests-bsf-commandant-in-cattle-smuggling-

case/article33121161.ece; Sandhya Ravishankar, 'Why cattle continue to be smuggled from West Bengal's border areas to Bangladesh', *The Economic Times*, 29 March 2015, https://economictimes.indiatimes.com/news/politics-and-nation/why-cattle-continue-to-be-smuggled-from-west-bengals-border-areas-to-bangladesh/articleshow/46729538.cms.

7. 'India Acquits Felani Killer', *Dhaka Tribune*, 6 September 2013, https://www.dhakatribune.com/uncategorized/2013/09/06/india-acquits-felani-killer.
8. Suchitra Vijayan, 'Border Crossings', *The Hindu*, 3 May 2014, https://www.thehindu.com/features/magazine/border-crossings/article5973146.ece.
9. *Stories My Country Told Me: Eqbal Ahmad and the Partitioning of India*, directed by H.O. Nazareth, 1996, https://www.youtube.com/watch?v=9opz5b-C4Do.
10. *Encyclopaedia Britannica*, 9th ed., vol. 11, 113, s.v. 'Gaur'; D.C. Sircar, *Studies in the Geography of Ancient and Medieval India*, Motilal Banarsidass, Delhi, 1971, pp. 118–30.
11. Richard M. Eaton, *The Rise of Islam and the Bengal Frontier, 1204–1760*, University of California Press, Berkeley and Los Angeles, 1993.
12. E. Vesey Westmacott, 'Gaur; its Ruins and Inscriptions', *Calcutta Review*, 69, no. 137, July 1879, pp. 68–83, https://search.proquest.com/openview/18fe879da1192879/1?pq-origsite=gscholar&cbl=54072.
13. Odhikar, *Teenage Girl, Felani, Killed by the BSF Firing at Anantapur Border under Kurigram District: Fact-Finding Report*, 7 January 2011, http://odhikar.org/wp-content/uploads/2011/03/Felani-killed-BSF-Fact-finding-report-2011-eng.pdf.

3. NEAR JALPAIGURI: 'They Stole My Dreams'

1. Hosna Jahan Shewly, 'Life, the Law and the Politics of Abandonment: Everyday Geographies of the Enclaves in India and Bangladesh', Durham theses, Durham University, 2012, https://core.ac.uk/download/pdf/9641035.pdf; David N. Gellner (ed.), *Borderland Lives in Northern South Asia*, Duke University Press, Durham and London, 2013, https://library.oapen.org/bitstream/handle/20.500.12657/31797/625238.pdf: 'As Van Schendel (2005a: ch. 3) argues, very little of the border actually separated majority Muslim and Hindu districts, and in practice the border more frequently ran through areas where there was a majority of the same religious group on both sides. Further, "the clear lines that appeared on the maps used by colonial officials, including the Bengal Boundary (or Radcliffe) did not correspond with anything visible 'out

there.' There was no way unequivocally to recognize the new border on the ground" (55–56) (see figure 9.2). In practice, the border was worked out through lengthy and often contentious legal and political negotiations between India and Pakistan. Many of the ambiguities resulting from this process, including the enclaves themselves, continue to plague border residents and are the source of ongoing conflicts.'

2. Agreement between Governments of India and Pakistan Regarding Procedures to End Disputes and Incidents Along the Indo-East Pakistan Border Areas, New Delhi, 23 October 1959, referred to as the Ground Rules of 1959, https://peacemaker.un.org/sites/peacemaker.un.org/files/IN%20PK_591023_Agreement%20to%20End%20Disputes%20and%20Incidents%20along%20the%20Indo-East%20Pakistan%20Border%20Areas.pdf.
3. Subir Bhaumik, 'Photo ID Cards for Indian Cattle', *BBC News*, 30 August 2007, http://news.bbc.co.uk/2/hi/south_asia/6970305.stm.
4. Louise Moon, 'India Plans to Give 88 Million Cows "Identity Cards" Which Can Be Tracked Online', *The Telegraph*, 4 January 2017, https://www.telegraph.co.uk/news/2017/01/04/india-plans-give-88-million-cows-identity-cards-can-tracked/.
5. Reese Jones, 'Geopolitical Boundary Narratives, the Global War on Terror and Border Fencing in India', Transactions of the Institute of British Geographers, 34, no. 3, July 2009, p. 293.
6. Ibid.
7. Ibid.

PART III: THE INDIA–CHINA BORDER

1. Ibid.
2. Ibid.
3. A.G. Noorani, 'Facts of history', *Frontline*, 12 September 2003, https://frontline.thehindu.com/world-affairs/article30218740.ece.
4. Mihir Bhonsale, 'Understanding Sino-Indian Border Issues: An Analysis of Incidents Reported in the Indian Media', Occasional Paper of the Observer Research Foundation, 12 February 2018, https://www.orfonline.org/research/understanding-sino-indian-border-issues-an-analysis-of-incidents-reported-in-the-indian-media/.
5. Ibid.
6. Ibid.
7. John W. Garver, *Protracted Contest: Sino-Indian Rivalry in the Twentieth Century*, University of Seattle Press, Seattle, 2001, p. 79.

4. TAWANG: Cartographic Confusion

1. See for instance, Rajat Pandit, 'Defence minister to probe BRO scam', 21 April 2011; https://timesofindia.indiatimes.com/india/Defence-minister-to-probe-BRO-scam/articleshow/8042115.cms; PTI, 'Disproportionate assets case: Defence Ministry asks CBI to probe complaints against two Major Generals', 13 July 2018, https://economictimes.indiatimes.com/news/defence/disproportionate-assets-case-defence-ministry-asks-cbi-to-probe-complaints-against-two-major-generals/articleshow/50759706.cms.
2. D.K. Palit, *War in the High Himalayas,* Palgrave Macmillan, India, 1992, pp. 38.
3. Dibyesh Anand, 'Remembering 1962 Sino-Indian Border War: Politics of Memory', *Journal of Defence Studies*, 6, no. 4, 2012, p. 229, http://www.idsa.in/jds/6_4_2012_Remembering1962SinoIndianBorderWar_DibyeshAnand.
4. Ibid., p. 230.
5. Ibid.
6. Steven A. Hoffmann, 'Rethinking the Linkage between Tibet and the China-India Border Conflict: A Realist Approach', *Journal of Cold War Studies*, 8, no. 3, 2006, pp. 165–194, doi:10.2307/26925946. Also see: Phunchok Stobdan, *The Great Game in the Buddhist Himalayas: India and China's Quest for Strategic Dominance*, Penguin, Delhi, 2019.
7. Urmi Bhattacharjee, 'Seat of Ancient Buddhism Threatened by Fifteen Proposed Dams', International Rivers, 15 January 2013, https://www.internationalrivers.org/blogs/259/seat-of-ancient-buddhism-threatened-by-fifteen-proposed-dams.
8. Ibid.
9. Bérénice Guyot-Réchard, *Shadow States: India, China and the Himalayas, 1910–1962*, Cambridge University Press, Cambridge, 2017, p. 179.
10. Sonia Shukla, 'Forging New Frontiers: Integrating Tawang with India, 1951', *China Report*, 48, no. 4, November 2012, pp. 407–426, doi:10.1177/0009445512471174.
11. Ibid.
12. Bérénice Guyot-Réchard, 'Tour Diaries and Itinerant Governance in the Eastern Himalayas, 1909–1962', *The Historical Journal*, 60, no. 4, 2017, p. 1,023.
13. Guyot-Réchard, Bérénice, *Shadow States*, p. 124.
14. Ibid.
15. Nari Rustomji, *Enchanted Frontiers: Sikkim, Bhutan, and India's Northeastern Borderlands*, Oxford University Press, Bombay, 1971, p. 114.

16. S.M. Krishnatry, *Border Tagins of Arunachal Pradesh: Unarmed Expedition, 1956*, National Book Trust, New Delhi, 2005, p. 33, quoted in Bérénice Guyot-Réchard, *Shadow States: India, China and the Himalayas, 1910–1962*, Cambridge University Press, Cambridge, 2017, p. 124.
17. Matthew H. Edney, *Mapping an Empire: The Geographical Construction of British India, 1765-1843*, Oxford University Press, Delhi, 1999, p. 1.
18. Neville Maxwell, 'China's "Aggression in 1962" and the "Hindu Bomb"', *World Policy Journal*, 16, no. 2, Summer 1999, p. 111, https://www.jstor.org/stable/40209630.
19. A.G. Noorani, 'Facts of history', *Frontline*, 12 September 2003, https://frontline.thehindu.com/world-affairs/article30218740.ece.
20. Brig. J.P. Dalvi, *Himalayan Blunder: The Curtain-Raiser to the Sino-Indian War of 1962*, Natraj Publishers, Dehra Dun, 1997, p. xiii.
21. Ibid., p. xvii.
22. Ibid., p. xiv.
23. C.U. Aitchison, *A Collection of Treaties, Engagements, and Sanads Relating to India and Neighbouring Countries*, Government of India Central Publication Branch, Calcutta, 1929–33.
24. Karunakar Gupta, 'Hidden History of the Sino-Indian Frontier: II: 1954-1959', *Economic and Political Weekly*, 1974, pp. 765–772; Karunakar Gupta, 'Distortions in the History of Sino-Indian Frontiers', *Economic and Political Weekly*, 1980, pp. 1,265–1,270.
25. Karunakar Gupta, 'Hidden History of the Sino-Indian Frontier', p. 765.
26. Alastair Lamb, 'The Hidden History of the Sino-Indian Frontier: By Karunakar Gupta [Calcutta: Minerva, 1974. 176 Pp. Rs. 30.00.]', *The China Quarterly*, 66, 1976, pp. 386–388, doi:10.1017/S0305741000033841.

5. NAGALAND: Unimagined by My Nation's Cartography

1. Radhika Singha, 'The Short Career of the Indian Labour Corps in France, 1917–1919', *International Labor and Working-Class History*, 87, 2015, p. 27, doi:10.1017/S014754791500006X.
2. Inner Line Permit or ILP. It is possible to apply online for a Nagaland ILP, https://ilp.nagaland.gov.in/, https://www.nagaland.gov.in/portal/portal/StatePortal/OnlineService/IssueILPService.
3. Sanghamitra Misra, 'The Nature of Colonial Intervention in the Naga Hills, 1840–80', *Economic & Political Weekly*, 33, no. 51, December 1998, p. 3,274.
4. Ibid., p. 3,275.

5. Subir Bhaumik, 'Will the Famous Indian WWII Stilwell Road Reopen?' *BBC News*, 8 February 2011, https://www.bbc.com/news/world-south-asia-12269095.
6. B.B. Dutta, 'Insurgency and Economic Development in India's North-East' in *India's North-East: The Process of Change and Development*, R.K. Samanta (ed.), B.R. Publishing Corporation, Delhi, 1994, p. 4.
7. Sajal Nag, 'Disciplining Villages and Restoring Peace in the Countryside' in *Government of Peace: Social Governance, Security and the Problematic of Peace*, Ranabir Samaddar (ed.), Routledge, London, 2016, p. 66.
8. Nandini Sundar, 'Interning insurgent populations: The buried histories of Indian democracy', *Economic and Political Weekly*, 46, no. 6, February 2011, p. 48.
9. Khrukulu Khusoh, 'Fifty Years of Armed Forces (Special Powers) Act in India: A Critical Review', *International Journal of Technical Research and Application*, Special Issue, 18, June 2015, p. 5.
10. Ibid.
11. Ibid.
12. Ibid, p. 51.

6. NELLIE: Stuck Between Remembering and Forgetting

1. 'Assam Foreigners Tribunal,' Amnesty International India, 7 February 2020, https://amnesty.org.in/assam-foreigners-tribunal/.
2. Rajeev Mantri and Harsh Gupta, 'Nellie and Delhi: "Secular" riots versus "communal" riots', *Firstpost*, 12 February 2014, https://www.firstpost.com/india/nellie-and-delhi-secular-riots-versus-communal-riots-1384231.html.
3. Gayatri Korgaonkar, '36 Years On, Survivors of Nellie Massacre Suffer in Perpetuity, 40% Out of NRC: CJP's Assam State Co-ordinator, Zamser Ali Reports from Nellie', Citizens for Justice and Peace, 9 November 2019, https://cjp.org.in/36-years-on-survivors-of-nellie-massacre-suffer-in-perpetuity-40-out-of-nrc/.
4. Gregory H. Stanton, 'Genocide Watch for Assam, India – Renewed', Genocide Watch, 18 August 2019, https://www.genocidewatch.com/single-post/2019/08/18/Genocide-Watch-for-Assam-India---renewed.
5. Sigal Samuel, 'India's Massive, Scary New Detention Camps, Explained', *Vox*, 17 September 2019, https://www.vox.com/future-perfect/2019/9/17/20861427/india-assam-citizenship-muslim-detention-camps.

7. GUWAHATI: Tales of Three Detentions

1. Human Rights Watch, *Prison Conditions in India*, New York, 1991, p. 29.
2. Ibid.
3. Willem van Schendel, *The Bengal Borderland: Beyond State and Nation in South Asia*, Anthem Press, London, 2005, p. 341.
4. 'The 2010–2020 UN News Decade in Review, Part Three', *UN News*, 27 December 2019, https://news.un.org/en/story/2019/12/1053761.
5. See, Francis Buchanan, 'A Comparative Vocabulary of Some of the Languages Spoken in the Burma Empire', *Asiatic Researches*, 5, 1799, pp. 219–240.
6. 'There Are No Rohingyas in Myanmar: Military Chief', *Nation Thailand*, 15 May 2016, https://www.nationthailand.com/news/30285997.
7. 'U.N. Chief "Shocked" by Top Myanmar General's Comments on Rohingya,' *Reuters*, 27 March 2018, https://in.reuters.com/article/idINKBN1H31VM.
8. Chris Lewa, 'North Arakan: An Open Prison for the Rohingya in Burma', *Forced Migration Review*, 32, 2009, p. 11, https://www.fmreview.org/sites/fmr/files/FMRdownloads/en/statelessness/lewa.pdf.
9. Ibid.
10. Amnesty International India, *Designed To Exclude: How India's Courts Are Allowing Foreigners Tribunals to Render People Stateless in Assam*, Indians for Amnesty International Trust, Bangalore, 2019, p. 5, https://amnesty.org.in/wp-content/uploads/2019/11/Assam-Foreigners-Tribunals-Report-1.pdf.
11. Human Rights Watch, 'Shoot the Traitors: Discrimination Against Muslims under India's New Citizenship Policy', 9 April 2020, https://www.hrw.org/report/2020/04/09/shoot-traitors/discrimination-against-muslims-under-indias-new-citizenship-policy.
12. Section 46(4) of the Criminal Procedure Code, 1973, which governs the arrest of women.

PART V: THE INDIA–PAKISTAN BORDER

1. The Armed Forces (Jammu and Kashmir) Special Powers Act, 1990, Indian Ministry of Law and Justice, http://legislative.gov.in/actsofparliamentfromtheyear/armed-forces-jammu-and-kashmir-special-powers-act-1990; Human Rights Watch, *Human Rights Watch World Report 1993—India*, Human Rights Watch, 1 January 1993, https://www.refworld.org/docid/467fca6917.html.

2. Amnesty International, 'India: Sopore: A Case Study of Extrajudicial Killings in Jammu and Kashmir', April 1993, https://www.amnesty.org/download/Documents/188000/asa200171993en.pdf; Haley Duschinski, 'Reproducing Regimes of Impunity', *Cultural Studies* 24, no. 1, pp. 110–132, https://doi.org/10.1080/09502380903221117.
3. Jason Burke, 'WikiLeaks Cables: India Accused of Systematic Use of Torture in Kashmir', *The Guardian*, 16 December 2010, https://www.theguardian.com/world/2010/dec/16/wikileaks-cables-indian-torture-kashmir.
4. Press Trust of India, 'Wani's Killing: Curfew Lifted Across Kashmir after 99 Days of Unrest', *India Today*, 15 October 2016, https://www.indiatoday.in/india/jammu-and-kashmir/story/kashmir-unrest-curfew-across-kashmir-lifted-burhan-wani-346696-2016-10-15.

8. KASHMIR: Records of Repression

1. Haley Duschinski, 'Reproducing Regimes of Impunity', *Cultural Studies*, 24, no. 1, p. 111, https://doi.org/10.1080/09502380903221117.
2. Ibid.
3. Ather Zia, 'The Killable Kashmiri and Weaponised Democracy', in *Resisting Disappearance: Military Occupation and Women's Activism in Kashmir*, Decolonizing Feminisms, Washington University Press, Seattle, pp. 50–61; Patricia Gossman, Human Rights Watch and Human Rights Watch Asia, *India's secret army in Kashmir: New patterns of abuse emerge in the conflict*, New York, 1996.
4. *Structures of Violence: The Indian State in Jammu and Kashmir*, The International Peoples' Tribunal on Human Rights and Justice in Indian-Administered Kashmir [IPTK] and The Association of Parents of Disappeared Persons [APDP], Srinagar, September 2015, https://jkccs.files.wordpress.com/2017/05/structures-of-violence-e28093-main-report.pdf; 'Everyone Lives in Fear: Patterns of Impunity in Jammu and Kashmir', 18, no.11(C), Human Rights Watch, https://www.hrw.org/report/2006/09/11/everyone-lives-fear/patterns-impunity-jammu-and-kashmir.
5. Naseer Ganai, 'J&K government issues award money of Rs 12.5 lakh for killing militant', 11 February 2016, https://www.indiatoday.in/mail-today/story/jandk-government-issues-award-money-of-rs-12-5-lakh-for-killing-militant-308175-2016-02-11; Angana P. Chatterji, International People's Tribunal on Human Rights and Justice in Indian-administered Kashmir & Association of Parents of Disappeared Persons, *Buried Evidence: Unknown, Unmarked, and Mass Graves in Indian-*

administered Kashmir: A Preliminary Report, 2009; Pankaj Mishra, 'Death in Kashmir', *The New York Review*, 21 September 2000, https://www.nybooks.com/articles/2000/09/21/death-in-kashmir/.

6. Suhail Ajmal, 'Bandipora Seethes in Anger', *Greater Kashmir*, 14 March 2015, https://www.greaterkashmir.com/news/more/news/bandipora-seethes-in-anger/.
7. Ibid.
8. Ahmed Ali Fayyaz, 'Corps Commander, DGP Face First Killing in Bandipore', *Early Times*, 25 July 2012, http://www.earlytimes.in/newsdet.aspx?q=96807.
9. 'Protest in Valley after Youth Killed in Army Firing', *India TV News*, 25 July 2012, https://www.indiatvnews.com/news/india/protest-valley-youth-killed-army-firing-17126.html; Suhail Ajmal, 'Day 3: Bandipora on Boil; 30 Injured In Fresh Clashes', *Greater Kashmir*, 27 July 2012, https://kashmirglobal.com/2012/07/27/day-3-bandipora-on-boil-30-injured-in-fresh-clashes-greater-kashmir.html.
10. Human Rights Watch, *'Everyone Lives in Fear: Patterns of Impunity in Jammu and Kashmir'*, 11 September 2006, https://www.hrw.org/report/2006/09/11/everyone-lives-fear/patterns-impunity-jammu-and-kashmir; Tariq Ali, Hilal Bhatt, Angana P. Chatterji, Pankaj Mishra and Arundhati Roy, *Kashmir: The Case for Freedom*, Verso, London, 2011.
11. Naseer Ganai, 'J&K Government Issues Award Money of Rs 12.5 Lakh for Killing Militant', *India Today*, 11 February 2016, https://www.indiatoday.in/mail-today/story/jandk-government-issues-award-money-of-rs-12-5-lakh-for-killing-militant-308175-2016-02-11.
12. Human Rights Watch, *World Report 2016: Events of 2015*, 2016, p. 298, https://www.hrw.org/sites/default/files/world_report_download/wr2016_web.pdf.
13. Press Trust of India, 'Two Sisters Shot Dead by LeT Militants in Kashmir', *The Hindu*, 1 February 2011; Firdous Syed, 'Caught Between Militants and Forces in Kashmir', *DNA*, 9 February 2011, https://www.dnaindia.com/india/comment-caught-between-militants-and-forces-in-kashmir-1505203.
14. Sheikh Saleem, 'Aloosa Fake Encounter: Court Cancels Bail of Two Army Informers, Sent to Jail', *Rising Kashmir*, 11 March 2016, http://risingkashmir.com/news/aloosa-fake-encounter-court-cancels-bail-of-two-army-informers-sent-to-jail.
15. Ibid.
16. 'Bandipora Fake Encounter Police Close Case, Indicts Army Informer', Monthly Newsletter of the Public Commission of Human Rights, 186, September 2012, p. 5.

17. Peerzada Ashiq, 'Army Orders Probe in Youth's Death as Police Hint at Troops' Involvement', *Hindustan Times*, 31 July 2012, https://www.hindustantimes.com/chandigarh/army-orders-probe-in-youth-s-death-as-police-hint-at-troops-involvement/story-u2zT37KW4dLGYIVf4hVbaK.html.
18. Suhail Ajmal, 'Informer Hatched Conspiracy to Stage Encounter', *Greater Kashmir*, 14 March 2015, https://www.greaterkashmir.com/news/more/news/informer-hatched-conspiracy-to-stage-encounter/.
19. Case files, police report, October 2012.
20. 'Bandipora Fake Encounter Police Close Case, Indicts Army Informer', Monthly Newsletter of the Public Commission of Human Rights, 186, September 2012, p. 5.
21. Bashaarat Masood, 'Bandipore Encounter Staged, Informer Lured Youth: Police,' *The Indian Express*, 30 July 2012, http://archive.indianexpress.com/news/bandipore-encounter-staged-informer-lured-youth-police/981221/.
22. Ibid.
23. Ibid.
24. Police final supplementary report, No.2776/5A/012/PSB, 23 November 2012, cited in Suhail Ajmal, 'Police Close Bandipora Fake Encounter Case,' *Greater Kashmir*, 14 March 2015, https://www.greaterkashmir.com/news/more/news/police-close-bandipora-fake-encounter-case/.
25. *Structures of Violence: The Indian State in Jammu and Kashmir*, The International Peoples' Tribunal on Human Rights and Justice in Indian-Administered Kashmir [IPTK] and The Association of Parents of Disappeared Persons [APDP], Srinagar, September 2015, https://jkccs.files.wordpress.com/2017/05/structures-of-violence-e28093-main-report.pdf.
26. Suhail Ajmal, 'Informer Hatched Conspiracy to Stage Encounter', *Greater Kashmir*, 14 March 2015, https://www.greaterkashmir.com/news/more/news/informer-hatched-conspiracy-to-stage-encounter/.
27. Peerzada Ashiq, 'Kashmir: Whistleblower Cop in "Staged" Encounter Transferred, Demoted', *Hindustan Times*, 14 August 2012, https://www.hindustantimes.com/india/kashmir-whistleblower-cop-in-staged-encounter-transferred-demoted/story-quOoqXQGOdSzWriGUKbkLM.html.
28. Suhail Ajmal, 'Police Close Bandipora Fake Encounter Case', *Greater Kashmir*, 14 March 2015, https://www.greaterkashmir.com/news/more/news/police-close-bandipora-fake-encounter-case/.
29. Ibid.

30. Press Trust of India, 'J&K: Army Rules out Inquiry into Youth's Killing', Zee News, 26 July 2012, https://zeenews.india.com/news/jammu-and-kashmir/jandk-army-rules-out-inquiry-into-youths-killing_789817.html.
31. Firdous Syed, 'Forget Balm, Army Must Stop Inflicting Fresh Wounds', *DNA*, 2 August 2012, https://www.dnaindia.com/analysis/column-forget-balm-army-must-stop-inflicting-fresh-wounds-1722940.
32. S. Ghosh, *The Anatomy of a Massacre: The Mass Killings at Sailan, August 3-4, 1998*, Jammu Kashmir Coalition of Civil Society, Srinagar, 2014, https://www.scribd.com/document/235731215/The-Anatomy-of-a-Massacre-The-Mass-Killings-at-Sailan.
33. Suchitra Vijayan, 'Military Justice in a Political Season', *The Hindu*, 11 November 2016, https://www.thehindu.com/opinion/op-ed/Military-justice-in-a-political-season/article11013671.ece.
34. Despite these findings, the Indian Army closed the case in January 2017, stating that 'the evidence did not establish a prima facie case against any of the accused'.
35. Association of Parents of Disappeared Persons (APDP), 'Facts Underground', JKCCS, Srinagar, 2008, https://jkccs.files.wordpress.com/2017/05/facts-under-ground-first-report-on-mass-graves-in-kashmir.pdf.
36. Haley Duschinski and Shrimoyee Nandini Ghosh, 'Constituting the occupation: preventive detention and permanent emergency in Kashmir', *The Journal of Legal Pluralism and Unofficial Law*, 49, no. 3, 2017, pp. 314–337. DOI: 10.1080/07329113.2017.1347850.

9. KASHMIR TODAY: The Revocation of Article 370

1. '4,000 Detained in Kashmir Since Autonomy Stripped: Govt Sources', *Agence France-Presse*, 18 August 2019, https://www.france24.com/en/20190818-4-000-detained-in-kashmir-since-autonomy-stripped-govt-sources.
2. Indian American Muslim Council, 'Indian Americans Condemn Unconstitutional Revocation of Article 370, Massive Repression in Kashmir', 7 August 2019, https://www.iamc.com/indian-americans-condemn-unconstitutional-revocation-of-article-370-massive-repression-in-kashmir/.
3. Zeba Siddiqui, Twitter, 21 August 2019, https://twitter.com/zebatweets/status/1164105359516024832.
4. Press Trust of India, 'J&K Crisis: Over 500 Political Workers and Leaders in Detention in Kashmir', *Business Standard*, 7 August

2019, https://www.business-standard.com/article/current-affairs/j-k-crisis-over-500-political-workers-and-leaders-in-detention-in-kashmir-119080701825_1.html.

5. Safwat Zargar, 'Kashmir's First Casualty After Article 370: 17-Year-Old Drowns Fleeing CRPF', *HuffPost India*, 8 July 2019, https://www.huffingtonpost.in/entry/kashmir-first-civilian-casualty-after-article-370-revoked_in_5d4ab624e4b0066eb70aaca3.
6. Parvaiz Bukhari, 'Teens Swept up in Night Raids in Kashmir Clampdown', Yahoo! News, 20 August 2019, https://news.yahoo.com/teens-swept-night-raids-kashmir-clampdown-135554337.html.
7. Jalees Andrabi (*AFP*), 'Kashmir families demand answers for "unaccounted for" deaths', *Yahoo! News*, 21 August 2019, https://news.yahoo.com/kashmir-families-demand-answers-unaccounted-deaths-071208840.html.
8. Ibid.
9. *AFP*, 'Kashmir families demand answers for "unaccounted for" deaths, France 24, 21 August 2019, https://www.france24.com/en/20190821-kashmir-families-demand-answers-for-unaccounted-for-deaths.
10. Aijaz Hussain, 'Kashmir's Main City a Maze of Razor Wire and Steel Barriers', *AP*, 13 August 2019, https://apnews.com/aa7048cf325646298fb773d7cb12d3b6.

11. FAZILKA: Bunkered Territory

1. Vinay Sharma, '5 Lakh People Leave Crops on Punjab Border; Army to Lay Land Mines', *The Economic Times*, 1 October 2016, https://economictimes.indiatimes.com/news/politics-and-nation/5-lakpeople-leave-crops-on-punjab-border-army-to-lay-land-mines/articleshow/54617461.cms.
2. Ibid.
3. Ibid.
4. Human Rights Watch Backgrounder, 'Recent Landmine Use by India and Pakistan', May 2002, https://www.hrw.org/legacy/backgrounder/arms/ind-pak-landmines.pdf.
5. Somini Sengupta, 'India's Landmines Mean Bitter Harvest for Farmers', *The New York Times*, 4 January 2002, https://www.nytimes.com/2002/01/04/world/india-s-minefields-mean-bitter-harvest-for-farmers.html.
6. Ibid.
7. Simon Tisdall and Ewen MacAskill, 'India's Deadly Defence: The 1,800 Mile Long Minefield', *The Guardian*, 9 January 2002, https://www.theguardian.com/world/2002/jan/10/india.kashmir.

8. Human Rights Watch Backgrounder, 'Recent Landmine Use by India and Pakistan', May 2002, https://www.hrw.org/legacy/backgrounder/arms/ind-pak-landmines.pdf.

13. AMRITSAR AND NEW YORK: Histories Partitioned

1. The Anarchical and Revolutionary Crimes Act of 1919, Imperial Legislative Council, 18 March 1919.
2. Kim A. Wagner, 'Fear and Loathing in Amritsar: An Intimate Account of Colonial Crisis', *itinerario*, 42, Special Issue 1, April 2018, no. 15, https://www.cambridge.org/core/journals/itinerario/article/fear-and-loathing-in-amritsar-an-intimate-account-of-colonial-crisis/3E9032CFEE54F3B2ED7A062216EE5EB6/core-reader.
3. Ibid., p. 7.
4. Committee on Disturbances in Bombay, Delhi, and the Punjab, *Report: Disorders Inquiry Committee 1919-1920*, Superintendent Government Printing, Calcutta, 1920.
5. Kuldip Nayar, *Scoop!: Inside Stories from the Partition to the Present*, HarperCollins Publishers, Noida, 2006, p. 34.
6. Ibid.
7. Nadeem Paracha, 'Smokers' corner: the "religious card"', *Dawn*, 13 October 2019, https://www.dawn.com/news/1510546.
8. Shahzeb Jillani, 'The Search for Jinnah's Vision of Pakistan', *BBC News*, 11 September 2013, https://www.bbc.com/news/world-asia-24034873.
9. Ibid.
10. Anuradha Raman, 'Clipped Speech', *Outlook*, 9 September 2013, https://magazine.outlookindia.com/story/clipped-speech/287634.
11. The Editorial Board, 'Institutional erosion is an early symptom of the implosion of democracy—and elections', *The Telegraph*, 11 April 2019, https://www.telegraphindia.com/opinion/institutional-erosion-is-an-early-symptom-of-the-implosion-of-democracy-and-elections/cid/1688523.
12. Anuj Bhuwania, 'The crisis of legitimacy plaguing the Supreme Court in Modi era is now hidden in plain sight', *Scroll*, 1 December 2020, https://scroll.in/article/979818/the-crisis-of-legitimacy-plaguing-the-supreme-court-in-modi-era-is-now-hidden-in-plain-sight.
13. Shoaib Daniyal, 'RSS boast that it could mobilise a militia is a sign of how violent India has become', *Scroll*, 13 February 2018, https://scroll.in/article/868493/the-daily-fix-rss-boast-that-it-could-mobilise-a-militia-is-a-sign-of-how-violent-india-has-become.

14. Reporters Without Borders, 'Media Ownership Monitor: Who owns the media in India?', 29 May 2019, https://rsf.org/en/news/media-ownership-monitor-who-owns-media-india; Archis Mohan, 'BJP richest political party with Rs 10.03 billion income in FY17: ADR', *Business Standard*, 11 April 2018, https://www.business-standard.com/article/politics/bjp-richest-political-party-with-rs-10-03-billion-income-in-fy17-adr-118041001008_1.html.
15. Jammu Kashmir Coalition of Civil Society, 'Kashmir's Internet Siege', August 2020, https://jkccs.net/report-kashmirs-internet-siege/.
16. Parvathi Benu, 'India is already a Hindu Rashtra: What Subramanian Swamy had to say about the Indian politics and the Constitution', Edex Live, 9 January 2020, https://www.edexlive.com/news/2020/jan/09/india-is-already-a-hindu-rashtra-what-subramanian-swamy-had-to-say-about-the-indian-politics-and-th-9848.html.

A NOTE ON THE MAPS

p. 10: Memoir of a Map of Hindoostan; or, The Mogul empire: with an introduction, illustrative of the geography and present division of that country: and a map of the countries situated between the heads of the Indian rivers, and the Caspian Sea, 1792.

This map originally appears in Matthew H. Edney, *Mapping an Empire : The Geographical Construction of British India, 1765-1843*, University of Chicago Press, Chicago, 1997. It was reproduced in 'Maps and Map-making in India'. The map was an exhibit in 'India in the World' at the Clark Library, created in conjunction with the Winter 2014 LSA Theme Semester, on display from 16 January–22 April 2014.

p. 12: AP Wirephoto Map, The process of Partition, 1947, appears on the Columbia partition archives maps. Link to the original title: http://www.columbia.edu/itc/mealac/pritchett/00maplinks/modern/maps1947/map060447b.jpg.

p. 112: Map speculating on a possible division of India from the *Daily Herald* newspaper, 4 June 1947, The National Archives, UK, (CAB 21/2038).

INDEX

Achingmori (village), Upper Subansiri district, Arunachal Pradesh 80
Achingmori incident (1953) 83
Afghan Local Police (ALP) 29
Afghanistan 5, 6, 7, 14, 15, 21, 24, 25, 26, 27, 28, 31, 32, 33, 34, 37, 51, 105, 133, 234
Afghanistan–Pakistan border 7, 24, 25, 26, 27, 234
Agence France-Presse (AFP) 188
Ahmad Bashir 165
Ahmad Eqbal 54, 236
Ahmadi people 21
Ahmed Fayaz 161
Ahmed Najeeb 225
Ahmed Rashid 128
Aitchison's Treaties (1929–33) 89
Ajas (village), Bandipora, northern Kashmir 159
Ajmal Badruddin 139
Akbar 9, 23, 27
Akhil Bharatiya Vidyarthi Parishad (ABVP) 225
Aksai Chin 15, 77, 78
Alauddin Khilji 9, 56
Ali Ashraf 58
Ali Kader 138
Ali Mohammad Amjad 58
Ali Somesh 142, 143
Ali Yakoub 141
Aligharh Muslim University 22
All Assam Students' Union (AASU) 113
All India Radio (AIR) 62
Almadhoun Ghayath 110
Aloosa, northern Kashmir 158
Altaf Osaib 190
Alwar, Rajasthan 19
Ambedkar B.R. 22
Ammi Badi 217
Amnesty International 135, 240, 241, 242
Amritsar, Punjab 212
Amudia border outpost, India–Bangladesh border 53
Anantapur, India–Bangladesh border 49, 52, 236
Anarchical and Revolutionary Crimes Act (Rowlatt Act) (1919) 215, 247
Andhra Pradesh 51
Andhra–Odisha border 51
Anglo-Afghan War 26
Anglo-Burmese War (1885) 91
Anglo-Sikh Wars 26
Antony A.K. 184
Arab Spring 6, 83
Arakan region (India–Myanmar border) 129
Archaeological Survey of India 56
Armed Forces (Special Powers) Act (AFSPA) in Kashmir 182
Armenian genocide 230
Article 35A of the Indian Constitution 189

Article 370: A Constitutional History of Jammu and Kashmir (Noorani) 189
Article 370 of the Indian Constitution 189
Arunachal Pradesh 15, 16, 41, 78, 79, 80, 85, 94, 239
Arusha, Tanzania 6
Ashoka 9
Ashtingoo forests, Kashmir 161, 163
Assam 18, 21, 47, 58, 79, 82, 94, 96, 102, 104, 106, 110, 111, 112, 113, 114, 116, 118, 122, 123, 125, 126, 129, 134, 135, 136, 139, 140, 141, 143, 144, 146, 147, 149, 150, 214, 229, 230, 233, 240, 241
Assam Rifles 82, 106
Associated Press 191
Association of Parents of Disappeared Persons (APDP) 245
Athens, Greece 194
Aurangzeb 9
Ayodhya, Uttar Pradesh 20, 21, 23, 232, 233
'Azad Kashmir' (Pakistan-administered Kashmir) 27
Aziz Mian Abdul 217

Baba Chotu 197
Baba Jaswant \(Jaswant Singh Rawat) shrine of 80
Babri Masjid 20, 23
Baisakhi 212, 216
Balochistan 15
Bandipora, northern Kashmir 159
Bangladesh 1, 10, 14, 15, 16, 21, 39, 40, 41, 42, 43, 44, 45, 46, 47, 49, 50, 52, 53, 54, 55, 57, 58, 59, 61, 62, 63, 65, 67, 68, 69, 70, 71, 72, 73, 75, 79, 92, 111, 112, 127, 128, 129, 133, 134, 136, 137, 141, 143, 193, 195, 196, 210, 219, 229, 234, 235, 236
Bangladesh Border Guards (BBG) 195
Bangladesh Liberation War (1971) 68
Barak river 111, 134
Barak valley 68
Baramulla 166, 168, 171, 175, 176
Barpeta massacre (1994) 140, 143
Barrow Ian J. 231
Basirhat, India–Bangladesh border 50, 54, 59
Baska district, Assam 140
Battle of Imphal (1944) 100
Battle of Kohima (1944) 100
Battle of Nagi (1971) 206
Battuta Ibn 2
Bay of Bengal 41, 42, 232, 235
BB (village), Sri Ganganagar 206
BBC 71, 102, 224, 233, 235, 237, 240, 247
Beglar Joseph 55
Begum Fatima 168, 177, 178, 181
Begum Jamila 133, 134, 136, 137
Begum Marzina 137, 138
Begum Rashminara 133
Begum Sari 202
Bengal Eastern Frontier Regulations (1873) 94
Bengal Sultanate 55
Bergdahl Bowe 28
Berlin Wall 194
Bhai Asim 54, 55, 56, 57, 58
Bharatiya Janata Party (BJP) 189
Bhat Mansoor Ahmad 170
Bhat Nazir Ahmed 158, 169, 172, 181
Bhat Shafeeq Ahmad 176
Bhola cylone (1974) 42
Bhomra–Ghojadanga border crossing, India–Bangladesh border 59
Bhutan 15, 83, 111, 238
Bibi Menzina 138

Bin Ahmed Saleem 164
Bodo people 104
Bolbolla (village), Assam 137
Bollywood 61, 210, 221
Bomdila-Tawang highway, West Kameng district, Arunachal Pradesh 84
Borbori (village), Assam 113
Border Roads Organisation (BRO) 79
Border Security Force (BSF) 41
Borguri (village), Assam 122
Bosnia 7, 24, 113
Boundary Commission 12, 40, 221
Bourke-White Margaret 14, 232
Brahmaputra river 111, 134, 142
Brahmaputra valley 94
Brar Aneel 207
British East India Company 26
British India. *See also* Partition of India (1947) 15, 25, 26, 31, 32, 37, 47, 78, 83, 88, 89, 91, 103, 130, 209, 239
British Library 55, 56, 93
British Parliament 10, 215
Buchanan Francis 129, 241
Buddhists 21
Bukhari Parvaiz 191, 246
Bumla Pass 85
Burma. *See also* Myanmar (formerly Burma) 15, 62, 91, 92, 98, 106, 111, 125, 129, 148, 219, 241
Burmese Army 104
Burmese Citizenship Act of 1982 130
Burnes Alexander 31
Buthidaung district, Rakhine state, Myanmar 129, 131

Cachar detention centre, Assam 144, 145, 146
Cairo, Egypt 4, 6, 7
Calcutta, India 14, 16, 41, 42, 44, 54, 61, 62, 63, 94, 95, 101, 102, 108, 121, 221, 236, 239, 247
Caroe Olaf 89
Cavafy Constantine P. 64
Cavagnari Louis 31
Central America 20
Central Bureau of Investigation 185
Central Intelligence Agency (CIA) (US) 27
Central Legislative Assembly 10
Central Reserve Police Force (CRPF) 116, 190
Chandragupta 9
Chandrapupta Maurya 9
Chennai. *See also* Madras, India 5, 14, 16, 17, 158, 192, 227
Chin people 15, 22, 34, 62, 77, 78, 79, 80, 81, 82, 84, 85, 86, 88, 89, 111, 130, 154, 194, 238, 239
China 15, 62, 77, 78, 79, 81, 82, 84, 85, 86, 88, 89, 111, 130, 154, 194, 237, 238, 239
Chittisinghpora massacre in Kashmir (2000) 185
Christians 21, 172
Citizens for Justice and Peace (Assam-based rights organisation) 122, 240
Citizenship Act of 1955 122
Citizenship Amendment Act (CAA) 21
CNN 5, 198, 232
'A Comparative Vocabulary of Some of the Languages Spoken in the Burma Empire' (Buchanan) 129, 241
Constantinople 194
Constitution Drafting Committee 13
Cox's Bazar, Bangladesh 129
Currie William Mackinion 101

Dalai Lama sixth 79
Dalvi John 86

Dantal (village), Jaisalmer, Rajasthan 19
Dar Ghulam Mohiuddin 161, 163, 177, 178, 181
Dar Hilal Ahmad 159, 163, 181, 183
Dauki, Meghalaya 128
Delhi 19, 20, 22, 55, 56, 57, 63, 81, 120, 129, 133, 158, 192, 216, 224, 225, 236, 237, 238, 239, 240, 247
Delhi Sultanate 57
Designed to Exclude (2019 Amnesty International report) 135, 241
Dhaka 58, 72, 73, 236
Dibrugarh detention center in Assam 126
Dirang (village), Arunachal Pradesh 84
Disorders Inquiry Committee (Hunter Committee) 216, 222, 247
Dogra rule in Kashmir 26
Dohotia Habi (Nellie mass grave) 114
D'Souza Henry 101
Dubai 5
Durand Henry Mortimer 31
Durand Line 15, 25, 26, 31, 32, 33, 37, 234
Dyer Reginald 212

East Pakistan. *See also* Bangladesh 40, 44, 47, 68, 111, 210, 237
Edney Matthew 83
Egypt British-occupied 25
Eid 2, 19, 233
823rd Aviation Engineer Battalion 102
Eighth Assam Police Battalion 129
Election Commission of India 122, 229
Eleyasar Sepoy 101
'The Emergency' (1975–77) 60, 215
Enchanted Frontiers: Sikkim Bhutan and India's Northeastern Borderlands (Rustomji) 83, 238

Facts Under Ground (Association of Parents of Disappeared Persons) 186
Farakka barrage, Murshidabad, West Bengal 195
Farsi language 210, 211
Fazilka, Punjab 200, 201, 202, 203, 205, 246
Ferozepur, Punjab 201
First World War 215
Foreigners Act of 1946 129
Foreigners (Tribunals) Order of 1964 122
Foreigners Tribunals (Assam) 122, 123, 126, 135, 141, 241
Fourth Rajputana Rifles of the Sixty-Eighth Brigade 185
France 97, 105, 188, 239, 245, 246

Gandhi Indira 60, 120, 121
Gandhi Mahatma 223
Garrison Hill's War Cemetery (Nagaland) 99, 100
Gauda (Gaur), India–Bangladesh border 50, 54, 55, 57
Gauhati High Court (Assam) 126, 136, 141
Genocide Watch 21, 122, 233, 240
Ghosh Amiya 53, 59
Ghosh Pulak 134
Goalpara detention centre (District Jail) in Assam 137
Gosaba (village), Sundarbans 42
Gramsci Antonio 121
Great Wall of China 194
Greater Kashmir newspaper 184
Ground Rules (1959) 68, 69, 237
The Guardian 201, 242, 247

Gujarat (state in western India) 20, 57, 69, 233
Gujjar nomads 161
Gul Hassan 101
Gunamanta Masjid 57
Gupta Empire 9, 55
Gupta Karunakar 88, 239
Gurdaspur, Punjab 201
Guwahati 111, 119, 120, 124, 125, 126, 127, 129, 131, 133, 135, 137, 139, 141, 143, 145, 147, 148, 149, 151, 241
Guwahati Central Jail 127, 129
Gwizantsu Mowu 98

Habraghat Killijhar Medium English School in the Goalpara district Assam 134
The Hague 4, 6
Hajong tribe 128
Hakim Amir 125, 126, 129, 132
Hamilton Daniel 42
Haryana 19, 69
Hazara people 21
Hazra Sugata 42
Hezb-e-Islami 28
The Hidden History of the Sino-Indian Frontier (Gupta) 89, 239
Himalayan Blunder (Dalvi) 86, 87, 239
Hindu Bengalis 116
Hindu nationalists 20, 225, 226
Hindu Rashtra 23, 226, 248
Hindustan Times 183, 244
Hlaing Min Aung 130
Hossain Mosharaf 58
Howly, Barpeta district, Assam 140, 147, 149
HuffPost India 190, 246
Hunter Alberta 102
Hussain Nobin 113, 114, 122, 123
Hyderabad, Sindh province, Pakistan 209
Hzareywala, Punjab 201

Ichamati river 44
In the Graveyard of Empires (Jones) 37
India Office Records (IOR) 93
India Today 9, 96, 120, 242, 243
India–Bangladesh border 1, 15, 39, 50, 53, 65, 75, 79, 193, 195, 234
India–China border 1, 77, 78, 79, 88, 237
India–Myanmar border 1, 91, 92
Indian Army 40, 80, 81, 82, 83, 84, 85, 86, 97, 101, 104, 105, 106, 154, 158, 163, 165, 173, 181, 182, 184, 185, 201, 206, 207, 245
Indian Express 181, 233, 244
Indian Ministry of Defence 73, 241
Indian Ministry of Home Affairs 20
Indian Ministry of Tourism 73
Indian Parliament 40, 189, 201, 223
Indian Reserve Battalion 104
Indian Seventh Brigade 86
Indian Supreme Court 21
India–China–Afghanistan trijunction 77
India–China–Nepal trijunction 77
India–Pakistan border 1, 15, 153, 193, 197, 241
Indo-Pakistani War of 1971 206
Inner Line Permit (ILP) 41
'Inquilab zindabad' (slogan) 22
Inspector General of Prisons 127
Institute of Archaeology (India) 54
International Criminal Tribunal for Rwanda 6
International Security Assistance Forces (ISAF) 37
Iraq 6, 7, 102

Isak-Muivah faction of The National Socialist Council of Nagaland (NSCN-IM) 103
Islam Imrul 125
Islam Manirul 134
Islam Nurul 52, 58, 59
Itanagar, Arunachal Pradesh 79

Jackson Andrew 102
'Jai Shri Ram' (rallying cry) 22, 23, 233
Jaisalmer, Rajasthan 19
Jalal Ayesha 224
Jallianwala Bagh massacre in Amritsar (1919) 214, 218, 219, 220
Jalpaiguri, West Bengal 64, 65, 67, 69, 71, 73, 77, 146, 147, 236
Jamia Millia Islamia University 22
Jammu and Kashmir. *See also* Kashmir 21, 26, 77, 153, 164, 166, 182, 186, 189, 241, 242, 243, 244
Jammu and Kashmir Police 164
Jammu and Kashmir Public Safety Act (1978) 166
Jammu Kashmir Coalition of Civil Society (JKCCS) 159
Jammu massacre (October 1947) 26
Jan Nilofar and Asiya 184
JanaSakthi (Communist Tamil newspaper) 14
Japan 91, 97, 99, 100, 101, 103, 106
Javed Mano 220
Javed Natasha 213
Jawaharlal Nehru University, New Delhi 225
Jenkins Francis 96
Jharkhand 214
Jinnah Muhammad Ali 223
Johnson Line 77
Jones Reese 73, 237
Jorhat detention centre in Assam 126, 145

Kabul, Afghanistan 4, 5, 27, 31, 177
Kachin tribe 128
Kalburgi M.M. 226
Kalimpong, West Bengal 95
Kalindi Kunj Rohingya camp in Delhi 133
Kalyanasundaram J.M. 14
Kameng Frontier Division 80
Kanyakumari, Tamil Nadu 16, 51
Kapoor Prithviraj 224
Kardar Abdul Hafeez 63
Kargil War (1999) 27
Kashmir. *See also* Jammu and Kashmir 1, 4, 15, 16, 17, 18, 21, 24, 26, 27, 77, 105, 113, 153, 154, 155, 157, 158, 159, 161, 163, 164, 165, 166, 167, 169, 171, 173, 175, 177, 179, 181, 182, 183, 184, 185, 186, 187, 188, 189, 190, 191, 192, 194, 213, 223, 226, 227, 233, 234, 241, 242, 243, 244, 245, 246, 247, 248
Kashmir state police 182
Kashmiri shawl-weavers' massacre (1865) 26
Kaul Brij Mohan 86
Kaur Balwinder 11
Kayakuchi relief camp in Assam 141
Kerala 61
Keran, Kashmir 17, 164
Khalsa College, Amritsar 216, 222
Khan Aamir 221
Khan Ahmad 19, 165, 198
Khan Akbar 27
Khan Ayub 190, 224
Khan Bashir 168
Khan Darwar 100
Khan Mohammad Ayub 190
Khan Munir 127

Khan Pehlu 19
Khan Shezad Ahmad 165
Kharija Manikpur (village), Goalpara district, Assam 134
Khartoum Qaudisa 139
Khartum Shahira 140
Khathing Ralengnao (Bob) 82
Khatum Jamila 117
Khatun Felani 52, 58
Khatun Rahila 142
Khawja Nuhzat 217
Khiamniungan region (India–Myanmar border) 98
Khunti district, Jharkhand 214
Kinoshita Mikio 103
Kitchlew Saifuddin 215
Kohima, Nagaland 97, 99, 100, 101, 102, 103
Kokrajhar detention centre in Assam 137
Kolkata. *See also* Calcutta India 61, 233
Kotwali Darwaza (Kotwali Gate) 55, 56, 57
Krishnai (village), Assam 133, 137
Krishnatry S.M. 83, 239
Kuki Jamkishei 101
Kumar Dilip 224
Kumar Rajesh 184
Kunan Poshpora (village), Kupwara district, Kashmir 185
Kupwara, Kashmir 18, 105, 185
Kutch (village), India–Pakistan border 69
Kutupalong refugee camp, Cox's Bazar, Bangladesh 129
Kyaw Htin 92

Ladakh 78, 189
Lahore 215, 219, 220, 221, 225, 227
Lakhimpur, Assam 142, 143
Lamb Alastair 89, 239
Land Boundary Agreement (1974) between India and Bangladesh 68
Lankesh Gauri 226
Lashkar-e-Taiba (militant group) 166
Ledo Road 102
Leone Amulya 23
Levi Primo 2
Line of Actual Control (LAC) (India-China border) 77
Line of Control (LoC) (Kashmir) 15, 154
Lone Mohammad Shafi 165
Lone Muhammad Ramzan (alias Rameez) 158, 164, 181
Lone Riyaz Ahmad 165
Longkhum (village), Nagaland 105
Longwa (village), Nagaland 94

Machhiwara, Punjab 201
Machil fake-encounter case (2010) 165
Madras 5, 14, 16, 17, 158, 192, 227
Madras High Court 158
Mahananda river 65
Malda, India–Bangladesh border 46, 50, 54, 55, 58
Mamtong (village), Nagaland 105
Manganiyar community of Muslims 19
Mangmetong (village), Nagaland 105
Manipur 94, 96, 103, 108
Manto Saadat Hasan 224
Maungdaw district, Rakhine state, Myanmar 130, 131
Maurya Empire 9
McMahon Line 14, 15, 77, 78, 88, 89, 92
Meerut, Uttar Pradesh 19, 150, 151
Meghalaya 94, 96
Mexico 20
Mia Falu 143

Mia Galib 139
Mine Ban Treaty (1997) 201
'Miya' (term) 112, 145, 229
Mizo people 92
Mizoram 94
Modi Narendra 20, 71, 189, 213
Mogamma (Cairo building) 6, 7
Mohammed Jan 30
Mohani Maulana Hasrat 22
Mokokchung district, Nagaland 105
Monpa community 83
Montagu-Chelmsford Report (1918) 215
Morgan Gerald 25, 234
Mughal Army 154
Mughal Empire 9
mujahideen 27, 34
Mukhabarat (Egyptian intelligence services) 6
Mundiyan, Kashmir 17
Murikhawa (village and border outpost), India–Bangladesh border 65
Murshidabad, West Bengal 195
Musharraf Pervez 201
Muslim Bengalis 54
Muslim League 55
Muttalib Abdul 117
Muzaffarabad, 'Azad Kashmir' 164, 165
Myanmar (formerly Burma). *See also* India–Myanmar border 21, 22, 86, 91, 92, 94, 102, 104, 106, 108, 125, 127, 129, 130, 137, 241

Naga Army 98, 103
Naga Club 97
Naga Hills 94, 101, 105, 239
Naga Labour Corps 97
Naga National Council (NNC) 98
Naga Regiment (Indian Army) 85
Nagaland 16, 41, 86, 93, 94, 95, 96, 97, 98, 99, 100, 101, 103, 104, 105, 109, 127, 239
Nagaland House (Calcutta) 94
Nagaland Peace Accord (3 August 2015) 100
Nagaon district, Assam 110
Nagi (village), Sri Ganganagar, Rajasthan 206
Nasaka (Burmese border security and immigration force) 108, 132
National Campaign Against Torture (NCAT) 22
National Congress Party 222
National League for Democracy (Burma) 91
National Population Register (NPR) 226
National Register of Citizens (NRC) 21, 144, 229
National Socialist Council of Nagaland (NSCN) 103
Naxalite–Maoist insurgency 51
Nayapara refugee camp, Cox's Bazar, Bangladesh 129
Nayar Kuldip 12, 232, 247
Nehru Jawaharlal 13, 225, 235
Nellie massacre (1983) in Assam's Nagaon district 113, 120, 121, 240
Nepal 15, 62, 77, 101, 128, 164, 179
New Moore Island (South Talpatti) 42, 43
New York Times 198, 201, 246
Ngangom Robin 108
9/11 attacks 5
Noakhali, Bangladesh 61, 63
Nongkynrih Kynpham Sing 96
Noorani A.G. 77, 189, 237, 239
North East Frontier Agency (NEFA) 77
North-West Frontier Provinces 89

Nu U 92, 130
Nuremberg Laws 14, 21

Odhikar (human rights organisation) 59, 236
Omrani Bijan 32, 234
Operation Enduring Freedom (US) 5
Operation Parakram 201
Orgun, Paktika province, Afghanistan vii, 28, 29, 33
Outlook (news magazine) 224, 247

Paji Bando 207
Pakistan. *See also* Afghanistan-Pakistan border; India-Pakistan border 7, 10, 11, 12, 13, 14, 15, 17, 19, 21, 23, 24, 25, 26, 27, 28, 30, 31, 32, 33, 34, 35, 37, 39, 40, 44, 47, 54, 55, 62, 63, 68, 69, 77, 101, 111, 127, 128, 133, 153, 154, 156, 157, 164, 165, 170, 174, 187, 192, 193, 194, 196, 197, 198, 201, 202, 203, 204, 205, 206, 207, 208, 209, 210, 212, 213, 218, 219, 221, 222, 223, 224, 225, 226, 227, 234, 237, 241, 246, 247
Paktika province, Afghanistan vii, 28, 29, 33
Pala Empire 55
Palestine 6, 24, 113, 166, 191
Paltan Bazaar police 129
Panitar (village), India–Bangladesh border 41, 43, 44, 45, 46, 47, 49, 51, 53, 55, 57, 59, 61, 64, 235
Partition Museum in Amritsar 222
Partition of India (1947) 15, 32, 154, 204, 232
Parvez Khurram 159
Pashtun tribes 32, 33
Patel Vallabhbhai 77
Pathan, Kashmir 201
'Pathan invasion' 26, 27
Pathankot, Punjab 201
Pathribal, Kashmir 184, 185
Pemberton R.B. 96
People's Liberation Army (PLA) of China 85
Peshawar, Pakistan 34, 100, 224
Petrapole checkpoint, India–Bangladesh border 50
Phizo Angami Zapu 98
Phulbari (village), India–Bangladesh border 52, 58
Prakash Om 184
Prasad Ashok 183
Press Trust of India 190, 234, 242, 243, 245, 246
Punjab 67, 193, 201, 210, 211, 212, 215, 216, 227, 246, 247

Qadiri Waseem 183
Qanungo Nawaz Gul 188

Radcliffe Cyril 12, 39, 68, 221
Radcliffe Line 15, 40, 68, 232, 235
Radio Pakistan 224
Radio Rwanda 230
Rah Ali Mohammad 190
Rahim Mir Abdul 215, 216, 222
Rahman Khan Emir Abdur 15, 31
Rajasthan. *See also* Sri Ganganagar 19, 193, 195, 197, 199
Rajo Ki Ghati, Punjab 201
Rajshahi, Bangladesh 127
Rakhine state, Myanmar 129, 131, 132
Ram Rajya 11
Rashid Abdul 117
Rashtriya Swayamsevak Sangh (RSS) 225
Rathedaung district, Rakhine state, Myanmar 129, 131, 132
Rather Mohammed Kamal 159, 186
Ratnar, Kashmir 161

Ravenshaw John Henry 56
Red Corridor, Andhra–Odisha border 51
Redden Rupert Bennett 101
Resettlement Legal Aid Project 6
Reuters 189, 232, 241
Right to Information Act 21
Rohingya people 108, 125, 129, 133, 139
Route Jeep 28, 37
Rowlatt Act (1919) 213, 215
Russian Empire 15, 31
Rustomji Nari 83, 238
Rwanda 6, 7, 24, 113, 230

Saibaba G.N. 226
Said Edward W. 233
Sailan, Poonch district, Kashmir 185
Sangh Parivar 226
Sangti valley, Arunachal Pradesh 84
Sar Hawza district, Paktika province, Afghanistan 28, 29, 33
Sato J. 103
Satyapal 215
School of Oceanographic Studies at Jadavpur University in Calcutta 42
'Scramble for Africa' 25
Second World War 91, 97, 99, 100, 102, 106
Sela Pass 80
Sen Amartya 9, 231
Seyie Khrisanisa 98
Shagu Fahmeeda 190
Shah Amit 20, 229, 230, 232
Shaheen Bagh protest 22, 192
Sher Jung Thapa shrine of 80
Shillong Accord of 1975 104
Sialkot, Pakistan 223
Siang Frontier Division 82
Siddiqui Zeba 189, 246
Sikh Empire 26
Sikhs 11, 20, 21, 154, 185, 196
Sikkim 16, 79, 83, 94, 111, 238
Silchar detention centre in Assam 126, 147, 149
Simla Agreement (3 July 1972) 15, 92
Simla Convention (1913–14) 78, 81, 89
Sindhi people 209
Singh Bhawan 120, 121
Singh Hari 26, 27
Singh Mota 197, 198
Singh Virender 120
Sinha Jayant 198
Sino-Indian Border War of 1962 238
Sino-Pakistan agreement 77
Solangi Murtaza 224
Soviet-occupied Afghanistan 27
Special Operations Group in Srinagar, Kashmir 183
Special Police Officer (SPO) 165
Special Task Force (Jammu and Kashmir Police) 164
Sri Ganganagar, Rajasthan 206, 207, 209, 211
Srinagar, Kashmir 17, 26, 27, 156, 159, 164, 166, 183, 184, 186, 188, 190, 191, 242, 243, 244, 245
Station House Officer (SHO) 166
Stilwell Park 102
Structures of Violence: The Indian State in Jammu and Kashmir (2015 report) 242, 244
Sudan 6, 7
Suj Johinder Singh 208
Sulaiman Mountains 28
Sundarbans 16, 41, 42, 43
Sunni Islam 161
Supreme Court of India 134, 136, 185, 226
Suthar Ramesh 19
Suu Kyi Aung San 91

Tablighi Jamaat (Sunni missionary movement) 161, 170, 178, 179
Tagin tribe 82, 83, 165, 239
Tahrir Square, Cairo, Egypt 6
Taki, India–Bangladesh border 54, 59
Talaat Harb Street, Cairo, Egypt 7
Taliban 27, 28, 29, 30, 33, 34
Talyarkhan Bobby 62
Tamil language 14, 22, 51, 91, 95, 227
Tamil Nadu 51
Tamils Burmese 91
Tamils Sri Lankan 22
Tarn Taran, Punjab 201
Tawang (Buddhist monastery town), India–China border 79, 81, 82, 83, 84, 85, 238
Teetwal (village), Kupwara, Kashmir 18
The Telegraph (Calcutta) 121, 237, 247
Telugu language 51, 52
Temporary Registration Card (TRC) (white card) 131
Tetulia, India–Bangladesh border 65
Tezpur detention centre in Assam 144
Thapar Romila 24, 233
Tharparkar, Digdi tehsil, Pakistan 209
Tibet 15, 22, 62, 77, 78, 79, 80, 81, 82, 83, 84, 85, 86, 88, 92, 105, 111, 238
Tripura 94, 127
Tuensang, Nagaland 104, 105, 106
Twenty-Seven Rashtriya Rifles (27 RR) battalion 155, 161, 162, 169

UK Independence Party (UKIP) 101
United Nations Charter 128
United Nations High Commissioner for Refugees (UNHCR) 131
United Nations Human Rights Office 132
United Nations Refugee Convention and 1967 Protocol 133
Unlawful Activities (Prevention) Act (UAPA) 21, 213
The Untold Story (Kaul) 86
Urdu language 159, 210, 211
Uri, Kashmir 17, 156
US Border Patrol 20
US military base in Sar Hawza, Afghanistan 28, 29, 33, 34
US–Mexico border 20
Uttamchandani Ritesh 119
Uttar Pradesh (state in northern India) 22, 69, 101

Vajpayee Atal Bihari 201
Vemula Rohith 22
Vishva Hindu Parishad 20

Wakhan Corridor in Afghanistan 27
Wani Burhan 154
War Crimes Tribunal for Yugoslavia 3, 6
Wathen Gerard 216, 222
Wathen Melicent 216
West Bengal 41, 65, 71, 112, 147, 229, 236
Wiesel Elie 2, 231

Xinjiang province, China 77, 78

Yahya khel, Paktika province, Afghanistan 28

Zar Kabal 101
Zhou Enlai 77
Zia-ul-Haq 223, 225

'By the end of my travels, I found myself not with one map of India, but many maps that looked far different from the one I thought I knew.'

India is a land of borders, its peripheries nestling against seven countries. Over seven years, across 9,000 miles, Suchitra Vijayan travelled these borderlands. The more she travelled, the clearer it became to her that local history and memory bear no resemblance to the political history of the nation that claims these lands and peoples.

From the densely populated border that India shares with Bangladesh to the highly disputed one with Pakistan, the stories in this book engage with how people live, struggle, fight and survive. A man escapes the floodlights that invade his home by blocking out all light, children use a border pillar as a handy cricket stump, and a family live out their lives beside the men who orchestrated their son's death. These are stories that question our ideas of what freedom means and what it means to be a citizen. At a time when millions in India face loss of citizenship—the largest crisis of manufactured statelessness in human history—Vijayan's clear-eyed, empathetic reportage provides a re-examination of the idea of territorial sovereignty.

Midnight's Borders, featuring over forty original photographs, is a compelling narrative of a country in crisis, turning against its own people even as it copes with the legacy of colonialism and Partition. As the margins close in on the mainland, this necessary account forces a reckoning with the brutality that informs India's relationship with its borderlands.